P9-DCP-775

Miraculous Living

A GUIDED JOURNEY
IN KABBALAH
THROUGH THE TEN GATES
OF THE TREE OF LIFE

RABBI SHONI LABOWITZ

A FIRESIDE BOOK
Published by Simon & Schuster

FIRESIDE
Rockefeller Center
1230 Avenue of the Americas
New York, NY 10020

First Fireside Edition 1998

FIRESIDE and colophon are registered trademarks of
Simon & Schuster Inc.

Designed by Jeanette Olender

Manufactured in the United States of America

3   5   7   9   10   8   6   4   2

The Library of Congress has cataloged the Simon & Schuster edition
as follows:
Labowitz, Shoni.
Miraculous living: a guided journey in kabbalah through
the ten gates of the tree of life/Shoni Labowitz.
p. cm.
1. Spiritual life—Judaism.
2. Self-actualization (Psychology)—Religious aspects—Judaism.
3. Jewish way of life.
I. Title.
BM723.L23   1996   296.7′4—dc20
96-19269   CIP
ISBN 0-684-81444-7
0-684-83556-8 (Pbk)

Acknowledgments

A miracle happens, and then you look back and notice all the people and events in your life that pushed and prompted you to the place where you were ready to empty, open, and receive it. This book is a miracle. It happened when I met my agents, John Brockman and Katinka Matson, in a cemetery in South Florida. John looked at me and said, "Rabbi, I know there is a book in you." At that moment my life was changed, an exciting relationship with two dynamic literary agents began, and *Miraculous Living* was conceived.

As I look back to those who helped prepare me for the miracle of this book, I begin with my family. I am grateful to my parents, Rabbi Herschel and Nechama Leibowitz, for having embued me with a love for learning and an appreciation for spirituality. I am grateful to my children, Marc, Arik, Pierre, Christina, and Marina, for visiting, playing, and praying with me during the pauses between chapters. My deepest gratitude goes to Phillip, my soul mate, playmate, partner, and friend, for staying in synch with me physically, emotionally, and spiritually during the months of writing. My love of God is most often mirrored in the love, trust, compassion, and humility I experience when our souls embrace. As my life changed during the course of writing this book, so too did his.

I am grateful to those who paved the path that I now walk: my mentor, Rabbi Zalman Schachter-Shalomi, for inspiring me to explore kabbalistic texts and interface with God, and for showing me how to interface with God; my teachers and friends the authors Dr. Joan Kaye, for guiding me into the mythical magic of Jean Houston and the spiritual realms of Buddhism, and Dr. Joan Borysenko and Dr. Carl Hammerschlag, for taking me under their wings and guiding me into new spiritual arenas; Nola and George Firestone, Dr. Harvey Frank, Dr. Aaron Boorstein, Deborah Fuller, Ellen Safran, Cheyenne Chernov, Caryn Farrell, the TAO Women's Spirituality Group, David Rubenstein, Ricki Tannen, Carol Chess, Heidi List, and Tanya Russo, for their timely advice, feedback, and emotional support; Rebbetzin Ruth Leibowitz, Rabbi Tirzah Firestone, Rabbi Bernard Presler, and, particularly, Sue Ann Fotsch, for their friendship and research assistance; Susan Dubitsky, Elisa and Richard Appelbaum, Nadiva Wilson, and Susan Corbett, for jumpstarting me into writing; Elaine Bivetto, for her administrative assistance; and Laurie Chittenden, for her assistance in the editorial process. I am also indebted to the members of Temple Adath Or and the guides and participants of LivingWaters, for supporting my work and joining me in living a magical, mystical life.

God always sends angels to assist in making miracles happen. The angels that God sent to help in the miracle of this book are my dearest and wisest friend, soul sister, and spirit mother, Florence Ross, whom I feel blessed and grateful to have in my life as she continuously holds the light through which both Phillip and I fly; my spiritual brother and professional partner, Howard Chess, to whom I am grateful for joining in my vision and for his patience, integrity, and adept facility for listening and making things happen with a reverence for the sacred; my childhood friend and professional counsel, Debrah Dopkin, whom I thank for playing a major part in my life during this past year, believing in me and helping me stay grounded. I am also grateful that God brought Edith Gordon (of blessed memory) and her husband, Manuel, into my life. Every writer needs a quiet place to contemplate and write. Manuel Gordon has graciously provided a serene residence in which to live while I write. When I asked him what I could do in return for his generosity, he stated simply, "Shoni, make this book *great.*" Thank you, Manuel!

The *greatness* of this book is due to Divine inspiration and editorial intervention. I cannot say enough adoring words about my editor at Simon & Schuster, Mary Ann Naples. She opened my heart, explored my mind, fully embraced my spiritual environment, and brought out the best of what God has given to me. I am indebted to Mary Ann for giving shape to my thoughts and ease to my words with a deep belief in and commitment to the message of *Miraculous Living*.

Thank you, Holy One of the universe, for having bestowed this miracle upon me and all who may be touched through the teachings of this book.

To my most treasured miracles,

Phillip, Marc, and Arik

Contents

Introduction, 19

Method, 23

INTENTION *31*

Meditation on Breath, *34*

Start on Empty, *35*

Cultivate Nothingness, *38*

Know That Your Soul Is Pure, *40*

Dismantle Your Filters and Discover
Infinite Energy, *43*

Bathe in Silence, *48*

Recognize That You Are Holy, *52*

Travel on Wings of Spirit, *55*

WISDOM *59*

Meditation on Clearing the Mind, *62*

Empty Your Mind and Increase Your Wisdom, *63*

Access the Great Mind, 67

Use the Right Mind in the Right Time, 69

Seek the Wisdom Beyond Duality, 72

Hear Wisdom Speak and Witness Truth Happen, 75

Ride the Divine Chariot, 77

Remember That Nothing Is Certain, 80

UNDERSTANDING 85

Meditation on Silence, 88

Separate in Order to Come Together, 90

Create Patterns, 94

Know God, 97

Connect, Focus, and Know Yourself, 100

Journey Beyond Reason and Logic, 103

Practice Mindfulness, 106

Recognize Transient Knowledge, Receive
Essential Knowing, 109

COMPASSION 113

Meditation on Light, 116

Embrace Infinite Love, 117

Make Peace with Suffering, 121

Cultivate Right-Making, 125

Become Grace and Compassion, *128*

Serve Selflessly, *131*

Let Go of Mistakes, *135*

For-Give, *139*

STRENGTH *143*

Meditation on Guidance, *146*

Practice Self-Discipline and Discretion, *148*

Cultivate Strength and Discernment, *151*

Seek Justice Without Judgment, *154*

Free the Sacrificial Lambs, *159*

Free Yourself, *162*

Accept Love and Fear, *165*

Journey Beyond Fear, *168*

HARMONY *171*

Meditation on Centering, *174*

Define the Midpoint and Mark Your Journey, *176*

Maintain Balance and Harmony, *178*

Live with Courage and Openheartedness, *182*

Dispel Confusion, *188*

Listen from the Heart, *192*

Pray and Heal, *195*

See, Hear, and Touch Beauty, *199*

SUCCESS *205*

Meditation on Awakening Consciousness, *208*

Maintain Focus and Priority, *210*

Practice Self-Responsibility, *214*

Motivate Yourself, *217*

Manifest the Power of Your Will, *220*

Economize Your Energy, *224*

Use Tools for Transformation, *227*

Exercise Personal Freedom and Envision
Infinite Possibilities, *230*

GLORY *235*

Meditation on Remaining Conscious, *238*

Let Go and Step Aside, *239*

Take God as Your Partner, *243*

Access the Glory of Your Soul, *246*

Bring Soul to Your Ego, *249*

Bring Joy to the World, *252*

Live Consciously, *255*

Use Essential Speech and Pure Action, *258*

CREATIVITY *261*

Meditation on the Flame, *264*

Recognize That You Are Born of God, *265*

Love Yourself, *270*

Cultivate Divine Sexuality, *274*

Care for Your Relationships, *277*

Find Your Soul Mate, *280*

Become Cozy with God, *284*

Travel Lightly and Breathe Fully, *287*

NOBILITY *291*

Meditation on Perfection, *294*

Uncover the Majesty of Who You Are, *296*

Expand Your Reality, *299*

Dream Bigger Dreams, *304*

Walk Your Talk, *307*

Return, Redeem, and Redefine, *311*

Welcome New Beginnings, *315*

Know That All Is One, *318*

LivingWaters, 321

Notes, 325

And the eyes of the blind will be opened,

And the ears of the deaf will be unblocked.

And the lame will leap as a deer,

And the tongue of the dumb one will sing.

For waters will flow in the wilderness,

And rivers will rise in the desert.

And the dry land will float as a pool,

And the thirsty ground will spring forth water.

And peaceful herds will gather in the place of jackals,

And it will be lush with grass and foliage.

And there will be a highway there,

And it will be the way,

It will be called the Way of Holiness.

Isaiah 35:5–8

Introduction

I know it is possible to live a magical, mystical life filled with unconditional love and freedom. I know it is possible to move beyond the boundaries of your background while acknowledging and honoring the best of what it has given you. And I know that who I am now has taken nearly a half century to cultivate, yet only a moment of consciousness to awaken.

When I was in my twenties I attended an interfaith peace gathering at which a journalist asked me my name and religion. My name was no problem, but to define myself by a religion was difficult. I was a universalist-humanist-Taoist-feminist-kabbalist who happened to be born Jewish. At that time, I did not want to be confined by the religion in which I had been so heavily indoctrinated, yet of which I knew so little.

For the first nine years of school, I had spent half of each day in religious studies. The curriculum of my childhood was based in the maxim "Sit, absorb, obey, do not question, and above all, fear God." God was an authority figure who was sometimes judgmental, sometimes compassionate, sometimes angry, sometimes jealous, always distant. The rabbis in my school and in the community were all men who portrayed God in male imagery and language. They taught me with integrity, and I was expected to believe as they believed. But as hard as I tried, I could not imagine a God who was not part of my own imagination as well as theirs. I felt locked into rules and rituals that seemed meaningless to me. As I blossomed into my own femininity, I felt even more isolated from the God I was told to love and accept.

I thought the Judaism of my childhood was chiseled in stone, never to be changed. In my naïveté, I thought there were only two choices: remain a traditional Jew or leave. During college, I left. Living a secular life was OK, for a while, but it lacked the luster and magic of being connected with a force beyond myself. It felt too one-dimensional. I knew instinctively that there was more in the universe and in myself than a secular worldview recognizes. I knew there was a Divine Force, and I needed to find Him/Her/It.

In the process of seeking God, I fell in love with and married, of all people, a rabbi. Yet this rabbi was different from the average rabbi; he too was exploring the edge of his religious boundaries. Together we sought God in art, music, and nature. Yet God still seemed beyond our reach. We fumbled and played with the rituals of our childhood and continued to search for meaning. I recall the anxiety of Friday afternoons when I was a child: my grandmother would yell for all to hear, "Stop what you are doing. It is now the time for lighting the Sabbath candles!" I had felt resentful of God for not giving me enough time to prepare my soul for receiving the light of Sabbath— time to bathe, dress, and wash off the week, so that I could focus in a beautiful way to light the candles. In our adulthood, my husband, Phillip, and I envisioned the serenity and sanctity with which we would like to kindle the lights and herald the Sabbath. We desired a way to begin the ritual that would be more liberating, more personal, more joyous; and we still yearned for an even closer connection to God.

One day, while our children were yet young and Phillip was yet a rabbi in a mainstream Conservative congregation, I was sitting in an afternoon class on Eastern philosophy at Barry (Catholic) University. My body began trembling with an awesome awakening. During the discussion on Taoism, my deep yearning finally broke through the filters of years of Orthodox Jewish indoctrination to a visceral awareness that God and I were one. The Way, the TAO, the Way of One—there is none other. God and air are one; God and sound are one; God is in everything. God is in me. *God is in me??*

I had heard that "the kingdom of heaven dwells within" was a Christian thing. So for a Jewish girl with a yeshiva background

—how could I say, "God is in me"? Dad, the rabbi, giggled; Mother, the rebbetzin, thought it was a new trend that would blow over. Friend, the rabbi, said it was idol worship and therefore forbidden. But my husband, the rabbi, knew that I was finding a new language of spirituality, and he held my hand as we led each other into a garden of renewed awakening and lifetimes of spiritually healthy living. The journey has led me to exploring Eastern traditions around the globe and has brought me back home to a new awareness that the Infinite is in everyone, everything, everywhere.

Along the path to finding God and the oneness of God in all things, I found many other spiritual seekers, from various backgrounds and faiths. What tugged at my heart the most was the inordinate number of Jews who, like myself, felt increasingly uncomfortable in their Jewishness. They, like me, were looking for a God with whom they could be cozy, a God who elevated rather than judged, loved rather than intimidated, crawled into their skins and helped them rather than hovering in distant skies. They, like me, were looking to the Eastern traditions to heal the wounds of alienation from a religion they had found limiting.

Along the journey to finding the God in myself and the oneness in the universe, I was drawn to Buddhism and Taoism, traveled in India and Nepal, and studied meditation and yoga. The spiritual practices in the Eastern traditions helped me to dismantle old filters and fears so that I could begin seeing my own heritage and origins through the lens of love. I was able to return and explore Judaism in a whole new way. And in the exploration I found that the Buddhist path of the bodhisattva —the dedication to serving goodness in all sentient life—was part of the magic and glory of mystical Judaism as well.

One of the first miracles that occurred was Phillip's handing me a book in which I found an article that spoke to my soul. It was by Rabbi Zalman Schachter-Shalomi. I knew I had found my teacher, and I lost no time in tracking him down. Rabbi Zalman Schachter-Shalomi taught me about the kabbalistic Tree of Life. I learned that the Tree was an ancient template for living a powerful, joyous, sacred life. When I journeyed the path of the Tree, my life changed. What had been chaotic became simpler; what had been confusing became clear; what had been dissonant became ordered; and what had been sadly ordinary became sacred and extraordinary. This sacred path is the most comfortable and joyous place from which I continue to choose to serve and to live. It leads me to a God who loves me unconditionally in all the moments in my life. As a result, miracles have happened and continue to happen in my life. This path is referred to in ancient kabbalistic teachings as the journey through the Ten Heavenly Gates of the Tree of Life.

The most wonderful aspect of the path is that anyone can access its wisdom in order to live miraculously. I invite you to walk with me.

As you journey through the pages of this book, may it add wings to your thoughts, meaning to your words, holiness to your actions, and infinite possibilities to your everyday living.

Method

Each of us chooses the mystical path that speaks to his or her soul. We arrive at that path from the various roads of our life's experiences. You, like me, may have thought your life was neatly mapped out and the direction your parents or society dictated for you was going to take you where you needed to go. Then something happened. It always does. You may have experienced the sudden loss of a loved one, the ordeal of a physical or emotional illness, the devastation of a failed opportunity. Or you may have awakened gradually to the fact that something is missing in your life, that the road you have traveled is too narrow and is leading you to a place you no longer wish to go. Whatever road you have traveled to arrive here, you now stand at a crossroads asking yourself many questions: Who am I and what is my life all about? I got this far—now what? What is my purpose here? And is anybody *up there* listening, anyway?

In the beginning of time there was a Tree that grew in Eden. This Tree bore ten branches, and each branch was touched by a particular power of God. When the mystics meditated on the symbols of this Tree, they saw each of the ten branches open to reveal one of the Ten Heavenly Gates. Each gate led to a path that connected the powers of heaven with the powers of earth, and the powers of God with the powers of each human being. Walking through the gates and pathways of the Tree, the mystics entered worlds of miraculous splendors that unraveled the beauty and wonders of nature and added joy, meaning, and purpose to their lives. The Tree that grew in Eden is a divine model of the pattern by which we too can live our lives. By approaching the ancient wisdom of the Tree, we too can enter worlds of splendor and joy, tap into the Divine pattern, and turn our most treasured dreams into wondrous realities.

Make no mistake: the knowledge you will gain on the path of the Tree is powerful, and if you truly put its ideas into practice, your life cannot help but change and become miraculous.

Each chapter of this book is devoted to one of the ten branches of the Tree and opens to one of the Ten Heavenly Gates. Each gate contains insights and meditations that will facilitate your excursion into newly realized territories of your spirit, your mind, your heart, your body, and your everyday life. As you journey through the gates of the Tree of Life, you will feel the miraculous benefits of living a life touched by God. What you will learn is what you have already known yet needed to remember, that *you are one with God and one with all life.*

The first three gates will take you into the world of knowledge and intuition. The journey begins in the Gate of Intention. All thoughts begin with Intention; Intention defines your purpose for entering the mystical journey. In this gate you will begin to let go—to release old and limited ways of being as you open to boundless new opportunities for growth and adventure. You will understand the bliss of emptiness and tap into the purity of your own intentions. You will recognize the infinite possibilities for uniting your will with God's, and feel more calm, more serene, more open to living in the fullness of all that life has to offer. With a refreshingly new openness, emptiness, and clarity, you will move forward to the second gate, the Gate of Wisdom. In Wisdom you will let go of the way you think things ought to be and open to a more expansive, dynamic, organic view of the way things *are.* In Wisdom you will open your mind to new ways of perceiving this universe. You will move beyond the five tangible senses to mystical encounters with deeper truths, more meaningful realities. You will tap into the Great Mind of the universe and open to the infinite possibilities for heavenly life here on earth. Then you will move onward to the third gate, the Gate of Understanding. In Understanding you will sift through the kaleidoscope of everyday thoughts and ideas and begin recognizing the sacred patterns and order with which you can consciously organize and define your life as a vital organism in this world. You will understand how to articulate your intention and access your wisdom in order to birth new concepts, attitudes, and beliefs that will make your life easier, more practical, and more meaningful. You will understand the interconnectedness of all parts of yourself while defining your unique role in the larger theater of humanity. In the first three gates, of Intention, Wisdom, and Understanding, you will receive insights that will help you to clear your mind, simplify your thoughts, and feel an inner sense of peace, while awakening your intuition and understanding to the fact that you are part of a much greater story of wonders and possibilities.

In the next three gates, of Compassion, Strength, and Harmony, you will be entering the world of emotions. Compassion is the soil in which Strength grows. Harmony is the equanimity that comes from balancing Compassion and Strength. As you journey through the Gate of Compassion you will know what it means to feel deeply and give generously while remaining free from expectations. In Compassion you will begin to see the light in darkness, the gift in each problem, the positive opportunity in every negative situation. You will compassionately give and receive unconditional love in a manner that desires, accepts, acknowledges, and nurtures the wonders and forms of life. Girded with the insights of Compassion, you will move forward to the fifth gate, the Gate of Strength. In Strength you will gain the courage to take risks and to access your own sacred power, while empowering others to do the same. You will become the sacred warrior in tackling your own fears and in moving beyond them. With insights into self-discipline, discretion, and discernment, you will clear a path through the obstacles and challenges in your life and act justly without the harshness of judgment. In the sixth gate, the Gate of Harmony, you will touch the spirit within your own heart and feel it balanced by the spirit in the heart of the universe. Through the insights gained in Harmony, you will be better equipped to maintain balance in your life and be at peace with yourself, regardless of outside influences or inner turmoil. You will be able to experience the beauty within yourself and empower the beauty in others. With the equanimity that comes in balancing Compassion and Strength with Harmony, you will continue your journey to the next three gates.

As your journey continues to the gates of Success, Glory, and Creativity you will enter the activity of the physical world. The seventh branch, Success, contains the insights necessary for creating excellence in your life. You will learn when to let go and when to hold on, while staying focused, motivated, and responsible. You will learn the importance of utilizing spiritual skills and tools in order to heighten your awareness and economize your energy. In the Gate of Success, you will take all the insights you received in the previous six gates and integrate them into your life in a way that will help you to live more consciously and act with greater freedom and joy. Programming Success into your life will help you to move forward to the eighth gate, the Gate of Glory. In Glory you will design your life and beautify your world with spiritual abundance, joyous meaning, and positive purpose. You will create an everyday structure that can partner God and hold the wonders, splendors, and miracles hidden in the universe of your experiences. The ninth gate is Creativity. Here you will access the creative forces that give birth to humanity, to accomplishments, and to new relationships with yourself and others. In Creativity you will bring soul to your ego and joy to the world, while becoming more intimate with your Self and more cozy with God.

The tenth and final gate is the Gate of Nobility. This is the gate that holds the dignity and reverence that embraces life. Nobility is the earth; it is the ground from which all life is born, upon which all life stands, and through which all life passes and is reborn. In Nobility you will continue to recycle, return, redeem, and redefine your life.

In journeying through the ten gates of the Tree, you will prompt, push, guide, pull, and gently set yourself free to live continuously in the moment and stand in your divinity.

I suggest that you journey through the gates and read the

insights in the order that they are presented. Each gate moves you toward the path of the next. Each insight builds upon previous insights. Take your time. Contemplate and engage yourself fully in each insight before continuing on to the next. As you use the insight in your daily life, you will begin to recognize the many choices you have that you never recognized before. Before reading each insight, take some quiet time to pause for the meditation that is included in the introduction to each chapter. Meditating on your experiences will help you further understand and integrate the mystical insights into your everyday life. As a result, you will see more clearly, hear more keenly, and feel more intimately. After you have completed the book and come to an appreciation of the mystical concepts within it, you will be able to open the pages at random for recurring inspiration and direction.

I hope that, as I share with you the abundant treasures of this spiritual journey, you will recognize that you are a spark of God, with direct access to the wonders of the universe as you unite and reunite with the Divine. May the insights you gain in reading this book enhance your understanding of spirituality and its practical application for living a spiritually healthy life-style. As you continue to live in the truth of your spirit, others will be encouraged to live in the truth of their spirit. Then the legacy of the Tree that grew in Eden will continue to eternity. Blessings on your journey.

In writing this book I used gender-neutral language wherever possible. The quotes that appear in the beginning of each insight may contain alterations from the original text to achieve that end. Where I referenced Hebrew texts, the translations are my own, taken directly from the Hebrew words or the essence of the teachings as they appear in the sources cited. In some quotes I also added words in italics that I felt enhanced or expanded the meaning of the passage.

Also, you will see that the journey in this book is described with an openness toward other spiritual traditions. Though at first this might be disconcerting, as you journey the path it is my hope that you will understand and welcome the openness.

INTENTION

Traditionally, when a man or woman became a king or a queen, one needed to have a halo that others could recognize in order to call them by their title. So they had a crown made that glowed and shone. When they wore the crown on their head, it said, "Look at me, see how I shine." However, as children of God, we are all empowered light bearers. When we touch the Infinite, there is no need to wear the crown. We already radiate the light of God.

Rabbi Zalman Schachter-Shalomi

The Tao that can be told is not the eternal Tao.

The name that can be named is not the eternal name . . .

Ever desireless, one can see the mystery.

Ever desiring, one can see the manifestations.

These two spring from the same source but differ in name.

Lao Tzu

W‍HERE DOES CONSCIOUS living begin? With intention. Intention is the desire to make something happen before it comes into being. In the Gate of Intention you experience the desire for potential before it is born, the desire for air before it becomes breath, the desire for thought before it becomes idea, the desire for sound before it is heard, and the desire for an image before it is seen. You were born from God's intention, and what comes through you is born from your intention. Before you enter a new territory, whether in your mind, body, or spirit, there needs to be intention. Before an idea, a word, or an action occurs, all aspects of who you are call to you and ask, "What is your intention?" When you know your intention, your spirit knows its purpose, your mind defines its goals, and your body acts accordingly.

With clear, pure intention you can accomplish any goal. The purest intention comes from a sincere desire within you to join your will to God's will. When you unite your intention with God's intention, heaven unites with earth and infinite possibilities are born.

How do you know when your intention is joined with Divine intention? You know it when you are open and receptive to the infinite possibilities of God living life through you. You know it when you become silent and still enough to hear your inner voice. You know it when deep within your soul there is a resonance of joy, peace, and serenity.

Standing before the Gate of Intention, you are about to receive the insights that will help you to clear your mind, open your spirit, and walk gently through the boundaries of who you

have been, in order to become all you can possibly be. Stepping
into Intention, you step closer to God and join your will with
the Divine will. Union and reunion with God is the essence of
Intention, and it is available to you as you use each of the
following insights to unlock the first gate on your journey to
miraculous living.

Before turning to the first insight now, take some quiet time
and experience the Meditation on Breath. This meditation will
help you relax, center, go within, and experience God breathing
in you. To benefit from this meditation, read it slowly. Pause
between each sentence and experience what you have read. Then
spend a moment enveloped in the peace that results. Review the
Meditation on Breath after reading each of the insights in this
gate.

❧ Meditation on Breath ❧

Pause a moment and sit comfortably in a chair or on the floor.
As you slowly inhale and exhale, feel the breath moving into
your body. Allow your inhaling and exhaling to flow evenly and
freely. In the quiet stillness, begin hearing the sound of the
breath, and know that it is the breath of God as it enters your
body. Slowly inhale and feel the breath of God entering through
the top of your head and moving through your entire body.
Now see the breath of God as it flows through your entire
image. Hear, feel, and see the breath until the sound, sense,
and sight of it become one in your body. . . . Pause. Relax and
luxuriate in the breath, the calm, the stillness, the peace.

Start on Empty

In the beginning . . . it was formless and void.

Genesis 1:1–2

Great fullness seems empty,

Yet it cannot be exhausted.

Lao Tzu

Have you ever felt so full you could not move? You may have felt so full of food you could not eat, so full of thoughts you could not think, so full of noise you could not hear, so full of data you could not respond clearly. When you feel overstuffed, overwhelmed, and overwrought, it is time to go empty and start anew.

Pause a moment. Hear the sounds of your breath. Open your heart. Clear out the thoughts in your mind. And now relax and empty before you begin to think the next thought or read the next sentence.

Emptiness is the first step in going within and touching God. When you empty your mind of clutter, your heart of expectations, and your body of excess stimulation, you become an empty vessel ready to receive God. Only if you are empty can you reflect God's image, echo God's voice, and be filled with God's light. Expectations, fear, confusion, and chaos leave no room for anything else. As the Zen teaching shows us, if you present a full rice bowl to the universe, it cannot be filled; if you present an empty rice bowl, the universe will fill it. Let go, release, relinquish, and stand ready to be filled by the Infinite Source. Emptiness is the way to God.

Starting on empty can be difficult to do, especially if you live a fast-paced, overcharged life. Utilizing this insight is like using a new key for the very first time. Its edges are still rough, and it does not yet turn with ease. You need to be patient, turning the key gently until it meets no resistance—until it reaches the "emptiest" point in the lock and opens the door. Just as the key that unlocks a door reaches into the emptiest point of the lock, so too the first insight to unlocking the process of Intention searches for the emptiness within you. It takes patience to empty. Meditating regularly helps. You can begin with the Meditation on Breath (page 34). With repeated practice, you will find emptiness a most comfortable, serene, enlightening, and natural state of mind. Everything you need to say or do will come to you once you have emptied.

A state of emptiness excludes expectations. It means being empty of everything, even expectations of what will occur next. It is a leap into the unknown, with the faith that you will fall gently into the arms of God.

Before the world was created, there was emptiness and void. Then light entered the emptiness, and colors and shapes took form, and trees, plants, and animals came into being. Then God breathed into the shapes, and life came into being. From life came consciousness, and from consciousness came intention and the desire to be one with God.

All conception begins in emptiness, and once it is fulfilled, it never repeats itself. A mother's womb is empty before it is filled; it is full before it is emptied. Yet each conception is totally new. This is the way of birthing the child in a human, birthing new ideas and actions in yourself, and birthing the fullness of God in the universe.

There are times when you will hear an inner voice or have an inner vision of possibilities for a brighter future. It is so clear to you that you can see it, touch it, feel it. Yet it takes time for you to smooth your edges, untie your tangles, and be ready to heed the call or act on the vision. In the chaos of your everyday life, do you hear an inner voice or feel an inner urge that beckons you toward new visions for yourself and others? How do you respond? Are you ready to empty and be filled by the Infinite Source?

Review recent events in your life and consider the ways in which you have emptied and prepared yourself to receive the fullness of God. Notice the serenity that occurs as a result of being empty of yourself and filled by the Infinite Source. Take a moment now to relax your body and calm your mind. Emptying, releasing, and opening is a continuous spiritual practice for receiving God's fullness. As your skill increases, this practice not only unties the tangles and smoothes the edges of limited ways of being; it also brings you nearer to God and to your own Divine nature. As distractions, challenges, or anger flood your awareness, ask yourself, "Am I starting on empty?" Both morning and evening, and as often as possible in between, remember to pause and empty. As you empty, the clutter, chaos, and expectations of everyday living are replaced by a deep sense of peace emanating from the fullness of God.

Practice the Meditation on Breath (page 34)
at least one time today.

Cultivate Nothingness

You can not see My face and live.

Exodus 32:20

No one has seen God and lived.

To see God one must be nonexistent.

Hazrat Inayat Khan

You come from nothingness. In nothingness there is no separation, no differentiation; all is pure energy. Traveling home to nothingness is a state of consciousness. It is like dipping into the cosmic womb, the formlessness in which all creativity is seeded. It is the place of the unknown that calls to you and beckons for your transformation and spiritual growth. Whenever you move from familiar to yet inexperienced terrain, nothingness awaits your return. In Buddhism this place of void is the state called *bardo*. In mystical Judaism it is the *tohu v'vohu*, the formlessness and void that precedes creation, follows death, and is the transition state before rebirth.

Nothingness is not a deficiency, but rather a fullness beyond our capacity to grasp it logically. There is no category or container that could possibly hold nothingness. It is a state of infinite and immeasurable, not yet existing potential, and enters your reality through pure emanation. Where there is nothing, nothing can be hidden. So when you are feeling as if you are losing yourself, notice whether the loss is from reentering nothingness and attaching yourself to the Infinite Source, or from attachment to outside stimuli that limits the vastness of who you are. When you lose yourself in the spiritual state of nothingness, there is joy and exaltation.

Nothingness need not be frightening, for it is the light of God that is concealed in you. God's light is perceived beyond the five senses as you know them. The fullness of God cannot be limited to temporary, physical modes of perception. God's light emanates from spiritual qualities hidden in the potential that lies beyond what you see, hear, feel, taste, or smell. To empty into nothingness takes a willingness to go quiet, become still.

During their journey through the desert, the Israelites at times waited three days before entering a new territory. That they stopped and waited is an indication of the need to empty, return to nothingness, and become still in order to receive guidance to the next step. This pause gave them an opportunity to become still in order to be instructed by God before entering new territories.

With each new occurrence in your life, you are conceived in nothingness, bathed in stillness, and guided to the next step. With regular meditation you will be at home with yourself and with what is most familiar to you as one born of God. Before and after you practice the Meditation on Breath today, luxuriate in emptiness. By recognizing your origin and returning to nothingness, you will find deep serenity and the sense of feeling complete with who you are right now.

Practice emptying into nothingness by relaxing your body, calming your heart, and quieting your mind at different intervals throughout this day, especially when you feel yourself becoming stressed and distanced from your God essence. While practicing the Meditation on Breath, hear, see, and feel the breath of God leading your way to stillness.

Practice the Meditation on Breath (page 34)
at least one time today.

Know That Your Soul Is Pure

My God, the soul You placed within me is pure, You created it, You fashioned it, You breathed it into me, and You protect it in me.

Talmud

The form of the formless,
The image of the imageless,
It is called indefinable and beyond imagination.

Lao Tzu

By opening your heart and clearing your mind, you have begun to glimpse the importance of starting on empty. Realize that in emptiness there is purity. The Infinite Source, God, breathes light into the pure vessel of the human and fashions the soul. The soul at its highest level is pure light and pure energy, directly connected to the pure will of the Infinite Source. The soul is that part inside that knows God and plays life for God through you. The soul knows God as the Source of all that is, was, and will be. With recognition from you as its caretaker, the soul flourishes and awakens you to the Divine spark that dwells within the sanctuary of your body.

The purpose of your soul is to connect you with your Divine essence. As your soul merges with the Divine, there is only purity. There are times, however, when it is difficult to feel this purity. You may feel cluttered with chaos and confusion, and the perception of who you really are is filtered through self-doubt, old negative attitudes, and limited thoughts. Recognize that the soul can do no wrong. The only limitation to the soul is your own limited perception of who you are. You are not separate from the soul, and the soul is not separate from God. When you acknowledge that the God of love and compassion created you with a soul that is pure and with an intention for greatness that flows from connecting with the Infinite Source, the old filters give way to a more positive sense of self.

God and the soul are available to you at all times. Only when you are open and empty can you receive fully. If you are attached to how you ought to be or should have been, you close off the channel to the unique spirit that is within you. It is difficult to remain open and receptive, to reach out and touch the Infinite, in the residue of unexpressed emotions, unfulfilled dreams, and unlived lives. Opening to the spirit of God within you takes a willingness to be still, empty your own vessel, and be receptive to the abundance that awaits you.

In 2 Kings 4:1–7 we are told of the impoverished widow who came to the prophet Elisha for help. When she told him she had nothing in her house save a little oil, he guided her to give it all away. With explicit instructions, she was told to collect all the empty jugs from her neighbors and fill them with the oil. She returned home, collected the empty jugs from the neighbors, and began filling them with what little oil there was. The miracle was that the more she poured, the more oil there was. The oil supply increased to fill as many jugs as she had. When there were no longer any jugs, there was no longer any oil.

The story of the widow reveals the greater story that unfolds through a relationship with God. In emptying herself of her belief in scarcity and limitation, the widow bears witness to the abundance that is possible in opening oneself to God. In our lives, too, the more we empty and open to God, the more God's beauty, love, and abundance flow through us.

Increase your awareness of how it feels to house a pure soul and to stay open and receive God's beauty, love, and abundance throughout the day. As you practice the Meditation on Breath and inhale fully, focus on the sensation of God breathing in you. Notice that the more you open, the more you can inhale the purity and receive the abundance of all God has to give you.

Upon rising in the morning, bless God for having created you with a soul that is pure. In saying to yourself, "My soul is pure," you reach that place within yourself that acts with integrity, compassion, and openness. Practice the Meditation on Breath. As you inhale, imagine that God is embracing the purity of your soul with unconditional love.

Practice the Meditation on Breath (page 34)
at least one time today.

Dismantle Your Filters and Discover
Infinite Energy

And I looked and behold, there was a stormy wind . . .

a thunderous cloud, a self-consuming fire, and a glow

around it.

Ezekiel 1:4

The highest notes are hard to hear;

The greatest form has no shape.

Lao Tzu

What does it mean to be ready? Your whole life you are getting ready—ready to go out, to come in, to get it together, to take it apart, ready to be. It is easy to be ready when you know what is expected from you. But how difficult it is to be ready for the unknown. As new ways of seeing, feeling, and hearing call to you, they beckon you to be ready to step into territory you have yet to discover. Stepping into the unknown requires you to let down the barriers of your mind and the filters of your perception.

Within you is a Godspark waiting to be freed. It is encased in a shell, called *klippah*. A *klippah* is a veil that hides your potential yet to be born, aspects of your life yet to be lived, unknown territories you have yet to travel. *Klippot* (plural) are illusions of fullness that stifle growth, block creativity, and limit the flow of infinite energy. As you dismantle the *klippot,* your Godspark is released, your soul soars, and you open to new ways of being. Then you are ready to step into the unknown with faith and trust that God will lead the way.

Dismantling and moving through the *klippot* is a continuous process. When the prophet Ezekiel wanted to hear the voice of God, he had to dismantle four different *klippot.* He experienced the *klippot* as occurrences outside of himself that reflected inner states of his mind. As he dismantled each *klippah,* he transformed it from a negative to a positive experience that brought him ever closer to God.

The first *klippah* was chaos. Ezekiel experienced chaos as a stormy wind in nature that reflected the turbulence within his mind. Through silent meditation he dismantled the chaos and transformed the stormy wind into a calm, subtle breath that flowed through his body. Think of times when you too experience chaos in your life. Thoughts, relationships, and work can become chaotic. Chaos reflects itself in the stormy thoughts and agitated breath within you, as well as in the turbulent activity around you. In order to dismantle the chaos you need to go quiet, become still, clear your mind, and relax your breath. Silent meditation dismantles the *klippah* of chaos.

The second *klippah* was confusion. This Ezekiel experienced as thunderous clouds in nature and clouded thinking that led to confusion within. He dismantled and moved through the clouds of confusion by transforming them into an image of God's nurturing, protective arms that lifted and transported him to refreshingly new territories of his life and his mind. How often have you been trapped in filters of confusion? Confusion comes when we forget we are an extension of God and think that we are all alone, with no map or direction to follow. To dismantle confusion, remember you are never alone. The Infinite Source is always available to you. As you open to receiving the Source, God enters and shows you the way. There are times when I feel confused and I stop, go still, and feel the presence of God surrounding me. Sometimes I think the confusion is a blessing, because it reminds me to pause and reunite with God. In order to dismantle the *klippah* of confusion, you need to revive your relationship with God and your faith that, even in the confusion, God is caring for you.

Then Ezekiel experienced the third *klippah*, misplaced passion. This *klippah* came in the form of a self-consuming fire in nature and obsessive desires within himself. He turned the misplaced passion and self-consuming fire into a burning passion for union with God. The more he desired God, the easier it was for Ezekiel to dismantle the filters that kept him imprisoned, his obsessive passions. There are times in your life when you may feel the fire of passion and it feels wholesome and healthy. At other times, the fire of passion consumes you and you get burned in the embers of obsessive and possessive attachment to money, love, or power. When your passion leads to an obsession with things outside yourself, the passion is misplaced, and misplaced passion exhausts your energy. When God and godliness are your passion, you discover infinite energy. In desiring God, you welcome infinite possibilities, manifest infinite love, and receive abundant security and a wealth of blessings.

The fourth *klippah* Ezekiel dismantled was illusion. Ezekiel experienced illusion as a semipermeable shield of light that had the ability to reflect his purest intentions and truest thoughts. If his thoughts were positive and sacred, the light lit the path to the essence of God. If his thoughts were otherwise focused, the light would darken and block the path to the essence of God. In dismantling the final *klippah*, illusion, Ezekiel could see clearly both the purity of his thoughts and the path to God.

Consider the filters of illusion that exist in your own life. They are the illusions hidden in the many choices we make. You can choose to think positive thoughts or negative thoughts. You can choose to feel happy or sad. You can choose to see the positive in a negative situation or the negative in a positive situation. Whichever you choose, toward the light or toward the dark, the *klippah* of illusion will reflect your thoughts and desires. This *klippah* of illusion appears as light but is only a membrane away from the shadow. If you are stuck in the *klippah* of illusion, you need to be true to your own spirit and think from the most God-filled place within yourself. In dismantling the four *klippot,* Ezekiel eliminated the barriers and uncovered the veils in order to touch God and manifest miracles, just as you can in your life.

The *klippot* in your life enter in a variety of forms. They are the stumbling blocks and illusions that keep you from experiencing your own essence of God. Ezekiel left the template for you to continue your journey in moving through and removing the *klippot* of your life. Remember to empty, release, and open to new ways of integrating the silence, hearing the love, and freeing the light as you dismantle the *klippot.* Notice the positive changes that can occur when your perception crosses over the barriers to the infinite possibilities in the sensations of life.

The *klippot* ask, "How close do you really want to be to God? Are you willing to dismantle the filters in order to experience infinite energy?" As you dismantle the *klippot* within your own life, you will feel more energized and recognize that there is an Infinite Source of energy available to you. This energy comes from the Divine influx that permeates everything in the universe and is the source of all matter. Like electricity, it is always there. It is contained until it is released. All you have to do is flip the switch, turn it on, and release the flow.

This Infinite Source of energy is available to you as you become available to it. It is here for you when you step out of your own limitations, open the *klippah,* the shell, and release what has been contained. According to the Zohar, the kabbalistic *Book of Splendor,* when you hold on to the Divine Energy and push through the narrow feeling of otherness to the side of oneness, the glory of God is raised up in all realms of existence. Rabbi Zalman Schachter-Shalomi describes this as a light going on and a new dawning arising in all the worlds.

This idea of being available by *pushing through* the narrow side of otherness, as a newborn pushes through the narrow walls of the birth canal, is called *itkafia.* It is the determination not to imprison the Divine Energy in a *klippah.* According to Rabbi Zalman Schachter-Shalomi, to push through in *itkafia* is to declare that you will not permit the three garments of the soul—

thought, word, and deed—to become hooked to a narrow energy system. You will walk on the side of Oneness and bring a new dawning to all the worlds.

How have you noticed yourself lately? Witness the source of your energy. Where is it in your body? in your life? Tiredness and weariness are indications that you may be getting stuck in a *klippah,* imprisoning the Divine energy as though it were something other than you. In what way are you available to the Infinite energy? In what manner are you going to open your *klippah,* permeate the illusion, and energize the light toward goodness? The quality of your intention is important to the dawning of a new way of being.

Notice the many ways Infinite energy becomes a possibility in your life. It is possible in the way you care for your soul by the thoughts you think; in the way you nourish your body by the foods you eat; and in the way you nurture your relationships by the actions you take. Infinite energy is stored in the *klippot* of everything you touch. The more *klippot* you open, whether through eating whole foods, thinking holy thoughts, or having more wholesome relationships, the more the Infinite energy is released into this world.

Practice the Meditation on Breath (page 34)
at least once today.

Bathe in Silence

In seeking Wisdom, the first state is silence, the second listening, the third remembrance, the fourth practicing, the fifth teaching.

Rabbi Solomon Ibn Gabirol

To talk little is natural.

High winds do not last all morning.

Heavy rain does not last all day.

Lao Tzu

As you walk the path of Intention, landscapes of light open to sanctuaries of silence. In stillness the silence welcomes you to explore the inner chambers of your being. Silence invites you to refuel your energy, clear your mind, relax your body, and return to the Source of your Divine nature. In silence, all becomes clear. Silence is the motor of the brain coming to a halt in order for you to have a look inside. When you observe the thoughts that continuously run through your mind and the energy that forever spills over into the world around you, you find a layer of chatter and static. A lot of energy is being expelled with little renewed. As you give yourself time in silence, you will notice how the silence regenerates your energy and revitalizes your whole body system. Whether you are alone or in a group, consciously diminish your speaking and gently move into silence for several moments. Observe the silence. At first this may feel uncomfortable, for you are most likely used to filling the silence with chatter. However, in the quiet you can listen more closely to the nuances of sound and comprehend more clearly the inner meanings of what is being said. In silence, you can glide between listening to the words and witnessing the energy behind the words. There is less need for approval and more compassion for others. The pressure to perform for others is diminished, and the desire to receive from God is increased. In silence you are able to hear the inner voice of God speaking to you. With increased practice, when alone and with others, you will find the silence comforting, revitalizing, and enlightening.

When a task is ahead of you and you are unsure of what to do, it is time to go silent. When you are overwhelmed in clutter and fragmented in responsibilities; when your energy is depleted and your throat is parched from too much talk; when you can no longer think clearly and your head is spinning, it is time to go silent. In the hours of the morning, the moments of the day, and the days of the week, take a vacation of silence. At first it may feel awkward; you will be ambivalent when the phone rings or the doorbell chimes and you feel compelled to answer. In time, however, you will learn the benefit of setting up guidelines for those around you and for yourself. These guidelines will help you glide into silence and luxuriate in the sound of your own breath, the sensation of your own energy, and the image of being surrounded in silent serenity. You may want to designate one hour a day, or several hours once or twice a week, as a start.

When Jonah resisted the prophecy for which he was ordained, he fled in terror to the seas. There he boarded a boat, got tossed in a storm, and was swallowed by a whale. As soon as he was cast into the sea, his soul ascended to the upper realms, where it was guided, and the moment the wave swam him into the mouth of the whale, his soul returned. He entered the whale as though he were entering a temple of God, and the eyes of the whale became the windows through which he could view the depths of the sea and the inner levels of the meaning of life. This was his time for silent introspection. This was his incubation period before facing his return and the destiny for which he was born, in the outside world. When he was spewed from the whale, he was ready to proclaim the prophecy from which he had previously fled.

Sometimes you are forced into silence by circumstances of loss, illness, or other avenues of solitude. Do not view the silence as confining or constraining: rather, sense it as an opportunity for spiritual development and accessing awareness. In silence you get to hear your own language, and words of promise and anticipation. You also witness yourself walking those words into living actions and enlightened service. People often come to me with difficult dilemmas and overwhelming challenges, and they need to make decisions from the truth within themselves— about divorce, abortion, job loss, life-threatening disease. And sometimes all the chatter in the world does not help them make the timely and sensitive decisions they so desperately need to make. I guide them into a very deep meditation, in which they can go silent, hear the truth from the depths of their own souls, and find the answer they need to turn the corner in their lives.

There are times in my own life when I need to go quiet, and I have retreated into silence. When I first began practicing silence, I would turn off the ringer on the phone and put a note on my office door for one hour each week that said, "I am in silence." It did not mean that I was not working, rather that I wanted to stop speaking. Anyone who needed me would put a note on my desk. Do you know what happened when I stopped talking? I had more energy. And then the one hour a week became one morning a week. And I found that I was more productive. I could do all the work, all the writing, answering, planning, administrating, and managing without getting caught in the chatter. I wrote notes to others and they wrote notes to me, and I felt so much more focused and energized.

Then several years ago I wanted to see what it was like to go silent for a whole week. A friend lent me his apartment, and I went there for a whole week of quiet. It was my own personal retreat, and do you know what I found during that week? That I could enter places in my imagination that I had never explored before. And from those imaginal explorations came dreams and visions that eventually guided me toward creating a community, a spiritual health spa, and writing this book.

You may not be able to go silent for a whole morning or for an entire week, but you could do it for five minutes every hour, or just one or two moments now. I tell highly stressed professionals, like doctors, lawyers, and fellow colleagues, to pause and take one moment of silence between clients or at the beginning and end of each meeting. In that moment you can touch, guide, and open the space for miracles to happen.

Spend some time today in silence. Designate the time and luxuriate in it, conscious that this is sacred time for yourself. Practice silence in the privacy of your home or in the solitude of nature. As you become more adept in the silence and more aware of the benefits, you may want to introduce it in fellowship with others. Utilize the silence when chatter dispels calmness, problems avoid solutions, and noise breaks concentration. In silence, the ego is still and the soul echoes your entrance into the inner chambers of God.

Practice the Meditation on Breath (page 34)
at least once this day.

Recognize That You Are Holy

You are holy; for I, YHVH your God, am holy.

Leviticus 19:2

Thus the sage knows without traveling;

The sage sees without looking;

The sage works without doing.

Lao Tzu

There is holiness in all of existence. Rabbi Abraham Joshua Heschel, the twentieth-century mystic and scholar, said that everything is attached to God and is close to a reality "that lies beyond all thought and feeling." Holiness cannot be seen, yet sees all. It cannot be touched, yet touches all. It cannot be heard, yet its melody sings throughout all creation. It is both in the world and of the world. Holiness is being in union with God and encountering spiritual union in all dimensions of life.

You are holy regardless of what you think, say, or do. According to Psalm 24:1, "The world is filled with God." You are holy because you are filled with God; and as God is holy, you are holy. God told Moses to tell the Israelites, "You are holy; for I, YHVH, your God, am holy." You are holy because you are born of God.

Through the garments of the soul, holiness enters this world. The soul is clothed in thoughts, words, and actions. How you fashion the garments of the soul in your everyday life affects your awareness of holiness in the world. Your thoughts, words, and actions affect your soul. How you care for your soul affects God. And God affects the world. Therefore, your awareness of the sanctity within yourself and the sacredness of all existence affects everything, everywhere. When you recognize your holiness, you think, speak, and act in holiness.

Holiness envelops you in the five physical directions: right side, left side, front, behind, and within. You are surrounded by holiness in the form of angels you may not see yet who see you; angels you may not hear, yet who hear you; angels you may not touch yet who touch you deeply. Each direction in space is inhabited by a different administering angel of God: Michael on your right, Gabriel on your left, Uriel in front of you, Raphael behind you, and the Shekhina entering from above the head to dwell within you.

Holiness lives in the realm of pure emanation. It emanates from the subtleties that come in caring for the soul, in loving humanity, in being aware of the miracle in each moment and in living fully with joy. Imagine a world where everyone and everything acts in the awareness of their holiness. Most people recognize the holiness of milestone moments—the birth of a newborn, the blossoming of a flower, a magnificent sunset. Yet holiness exists also in the ordinary moments and interludes of everyday living. Every moment is a miracle unfolding, and every person is holiness in action. Can you recognize the sanctity of the chair in which you are seated? It was designed by people who were created in the image of God, utilizing products from the universe of God. Can you recognize the cashier at the supermarket or the receptionist in your office? They too are as fragile, mutable, and holy as a newborn, a rose, a sunset, or even you.

Imagine yourself moving through this day in the awareness that you are encountering God each second in everything you think, say, and do. Even as you speak to another or another speaks to you, the words are but garments of your souls fashioned in holiness. As you become aware of the sacredness of all existence, witness the generosity of your thoughts, the sensitivity of your words, and the sacredness of your actions.

Practice the Meditation on Breath (page 34)
at least once today.

Travel on Wings of Spirit

You saw that which I did to Egypt, and how I lifted you
on eagles' wings and brought you to Me.

Exodus 19:4

Keep watch over them and do not lose them; you will be
connected to absolute unity above, and the vitality of absolute unity is connected to heaven.

Huainanzi

This insight is about using your imagination. Pause a moment.
Feel the breath of God breathing into you. Sense yourself enveloped by the presence of God. Imagine God's arms as wings
lovingly wrapped around your body. Now, with each inhalation
and exhalation, imagine yourself being gently lifted onto the
wings of the spirit of God.

Through your imagination, God and the universe of infinite
possibilities come alive. You can imagine who God is, the world
God lives in, and what God means to you. The heavenly spheres
translate themselves to you through imagination. They come to
you as symbols hidden in the forms of different images. They
come to you as angel wings, lights, and auras hidden in the

gates, corridors, palaces, and gardens of your inner life. And they lovingly embrace you in the wings of their spirit.

The Shekhina, the Hebrew Goddess, has wings that transport your soul from one state of consciousness to another. When you are initiated into the tradition of Judaism, you enter on the wings of the Shekhina. When you are in sacred union with your lover, the wings of the Shekhina embrace both of you. And with your final breath before death, you recline into complete tranquility in the loving embrace of Her wings.

Prophets and mystics throughout time have meditated on the midpoint between the sculpted wings of the cherubs on the holy ark in order to traverse transcendent states of consciousness. Mystics today wrap themselves in prayer shawls in order to feel themselves wrapped in the wings of the spirit and transported to higher realms of being.

Wrap yourself in imaginary robes of light and sense being held on the wings of Shekhina as she enters your body and emanates through you to your auric field, protecting and guiding you during the day. Upon retiring at night, be conscious of Her presence and renewing powers. Whenever you empty, open, release, and relinquish, feel all the administering angels of God surrounding you and lifting you to ascended levels of being. You are lifted on the wings of the great spirit, the Shekhina, God.

Whether awake or asleep, you ascend and descend the spiritual ladder of life embraced, lifted, and held by the wings of the spirit of God. The spiritual ladder has four rungs on which you step into the four worlds of experience. The lower rung is the physical world. The next is the emotional world, where dreams begin. The third rung is the intuitive world, where imagination is sparked. And on the fourth, you step into the world of pure emanation and light, where all things are possible. As in Jacob's famous dream, the angels are continuously ascending and descending the rungs of the spiritual ladder of life. If you want to travel on the wings of their spirit and ascend the ladder, all you have to do is intend it. When your intention is pure, they assist you in moving beyond the boundaries of your physical world into the heart of your dreams and the realms of your imagination. In the imaginal realms all things are possible.

Practice the Meditation on Breath (page 34)
at least once today.

WISDOM

How many are Your deeds, God,

You have made all of them with wisdom.

Psalm 104:24

Look, it cannot be seen— it is beyond form.

Listen, it cannot be heard—it is beyond sound.

Grasp, it cannot be held—it is intangible.

These three are indefinable;

Therefore they are joined in one.

Lao Tzu

NOW THAT YOU HAVE passed through the Gate of Intention, you stand on the threshold of Wisdom. At the entrance to the Gate of Wisdom there is no platform and there are no steps. In Wisdom there is nothing to hold on to, nothing to understand, nothing to form. Wisdom is thought before it is fully formed and experienced before it is processed and perfected. Wisdom is what drops in when you have an insight that solves a problem, adds a new dimension to your life, or reflects a new way of being—an insight that you know is so right you can feel it in your gut even though you cannot give it any rational explanation. As you open to wisdom, you will receive an abundant stream of new perceptions, creative thoughts, and innovative ideas.

Stand in the Gate of Wisdom as though you were standing in the center of a kaleidoscope of shapes and colors whirling around you. Enjoy the sumptuous variety of hues, values, and tones fashioning a variety of curves and lines into new and imaginative forms. If you attempted to define or pick out one shape from the whole, you would stop the flow of formations. Similarly, Wisdom is the wellspring of intuitive, perceptive thoughts before they are analyzed and rationalized. Wisdom envelops your creative mind and frees your self-expression. Forms, shapes, patterns, sensations, and sounds are continuously stimulating your mind and increasing your intelligence.

According to the kabbalists, there are three aspects of intelligence: Wisdom, Understanding, and Knowledge. First, Wisdom disseminates thoughts; it drops new ideas into the creative part of your brain. Then with Understanding you receive the new idea and, in the analytical part of your brain, rationally consider its properties and implications. Finally, through Knowledge you accumulate the knowledge necessary for implementing the new idea. In order to receive the three aspects of intelligence, it is important to remain open and receptive as you walk through the Gate of Wisdom. The insights you receive in this gate you will comprehend more clearly in the third gate, Understanding.

Before turning to the first insight in the Gate of Wisdom, take some quiet time now and experience the Meditation on Clearing the Mind. This meditation will help you remain relaxed, open, and receptive to new ideas. To benefit from the meditation, read it slowly. Pause between each sentence and experience what you have just read. Then spend a moment or two enveloped in the peace that results. Review the Meditation on Clearing the Mind after reading and contemplating each of the insights.

⊸ Meditation on Clearing the Mind ⊸

Pause a moment and sit comfortably in a chair or on the floor. Feel the breath moving into your body as you slowly exhale. Allow the inhalation and exhalation to flow evenly and freely. In the quiet calm, become aware of the gentle wind that calmly carries the breath in and out of your body. If distracting or absorbing thoughts arise, be mindful of them gliding through your consciousness with nonattached, effortless observation. As the thoughts come and go, in and out of your mind, bring your awareness back to the gentle rhythm of your breath. Always return to the breath. Allow the awareness of your breath gradually to clear your mind. Pause. Relax and luxuriate in the tranquil clarity of an uncluttered, empty, relaxed mind. Wisdom births new realities.

Empty Your Mind and Increase Your Wisdom

... it is not the intention that you come to a stop with some finite or given form, even though it may be of the highest order. . . . The less understandable they are, the higher their order, until you arrive at the activity of a force which is no longer under your control, but rather your reason and your thought is in its control.

Abraham Abulafia

Empty and be full;

Wear out and be new;

Have little and gain;

Have much and be confused.

Lao Tzu

Imagine a cup filled to capacity with water. Now imagine a hole in the bottom of the cup. What happens? The cup can no longer hold water. Instead, an immeasurable amount of water can now flow through the cup. When the hole is plugged the water stays; when the hole is open the water flows. If the cup were to remain plugged, the water would go stale. In the delicate interplay between empty and full, the water remains alive.

Just as an immeasurable amount of water can flow through an open cup, an infinite amount of wisdom can flow through an open mind. When you cling to an old idea, thought, or perception, you plug up your mind and stop the flow of new ideas, thoughts, or perceptions. In order for wisdom to flow through your mind, you need to unplug the limitations of old perceptions and empty your mind. An empty mind attracts infinite wisdom.

There are times when attachment to thoughts creates a traffic jam of chatter in your mind. It may not be easy for you to empty your mind of daily chatter. At such times you are guided to pause, relax, and to meditate. However, there are times when meditation is difficult, especially when your mind is clinging to thoughts, and thoughts are clinging to emotions, and emotions block you from accessing Infinite Wisdom. This is when prayer, study, and music can assist you in the process of releasing thoughts, relinquishing ideas, and emptying the mind.

When you start on empty you need to let go of everything, even the desire to empty. You cannot *endeavor* to empty, you can only empty—just as you cannot endeavor to think, but only think. As a result of letting go, you ascend to a much deeper level of consciousness. At the highest level of emptiness, nothing is understandable, and there is only a feeling of being enveloped in a radiant force. You arrive at the activity of a force that is no longer under your control; rather, your reason and thought are in *its* control. With practice, the journey to emptiness leads you to deeper and deeper levels of consciousness, where you can feel thick veils being removed and giving way to the subtleties of your spirit enveloping you in light.

When your mind is at its emptiest, it is at its most complete. The nature of your mind is emptiness. There is a moment before thought comes into existence that is filled with emptiness. Emptiness births stillness, stillness births clarity, and clarity births new ideas. When the sea is in motion, the sediment from the sea floor is mixed with the water and all is clouded and muddied. When the sea is calm and the water is still, however, the sediment falls to the bottom and the clear water rises to the top.

The same is true of the mind and its process of thinking. When the mind is calm, empty, and still, clear thoughts rise to the top and wisdom is received. In the vast emptiness, your mind is open, reflective, radiating intelligence, and seeded with enlightenment.

In our society, we are reluctant to empty our minds because we're afraid we may lose what is in them. But when your mind is filled, you become confused. Being confused may, at times, seem like a natural state of mind; it is not, however. Confusion can come from clinging to thoughts, which blocks the natural flow of new information from entering your mind. When your mind is empty, it does not cling, wander, or fade. It stays open, porous, and free. Profound insights occur when a free mind relates, integrates, and attunes to the dynamic, organic rhythm in all things, seen and unseen, known and unknown.

Most people go through periods of fixation with a belief or set of ideas, or of obsession with a relationship or loss. When this happens, your mind stubbornly clings to thoughts and the thoughts stubbornly cling to constricted sensations that block you from thinking clearly or living freely. You become imprisoned in a clinging mind locked in its own constricted energy. It is no fun. When your mind is in this state, wisdom cannot enter, thoughts cannot penetrate, and only slow rhythmic breathing can relax it. With regular practice in conscious breathing, you can help your mind return to its natural state. Imagine the breath as entering your mind, alleviating the attachment in order to free the energy and enable you to reaccess the process of clear thinking. Throughout your day, remember that the nature of your mind is to be empty, free, clear, and relaxed. During conversations, meetings, and times for reflection, maintain the rhythm of your breath, maintain the clarity, and new ideas will come to you.

In the emptiness, infinite thoughts flow through effortlessly and infinite wisdom emerges. In the emptiness wisdom is freely disseminated, understanding is easily received, and knowledge is effortlessly disbursed. Practice emptying your mind at different intervals throughout the day and follow the Meditation on

Clearing the Mind. Become aware of how, with regular meditation, it is easier to empty your mind. Recognize the new wonders and awareness that drop into your ordinary experiences each
time you let go and empty.

Practice the Meditation on Clearing the Mind (page 62)
at least once today.

Access the Great Mind

When a thought passes through the mind of a good person

it becomes divine and proclaims: O thou art divine.

Rabbi Levi Yitzchak of Berditchev

A man's *or woman's* mind may make him *or her* a Buddha,

or it may make him *or her* a beast. . . . Therefore, control

your mind and do not let it deviate from the right path.

Buddha

In kabbalistic terminology there are two aspects of mind. There is *mokhin d'katnut,* literally "smallness of mind," small mind, and *mokhin d'gadlut,* "greatness of mind," Great Mind. Small mind is limited to the local individual experience without tapping into the greater source of consciousness. Small mind fades, wanders, and wavers. The Great Mind, *mokhin d'gadlut,* opens to rapture, ecstasy, and creativity. The universal consciousness emanating from Great Mind sends thoughts from on high and seeds them in your mind.

How do you tap into the root of the Great Mind? First, realize that all wisdom and thought comes from the metaphoric mind of God. Every thought is attached to an aspect of wisdom that emanates from its own specific place on high. Whatever you are thinking this very moment has its corresponding wisdom in the source of the Great Mind. Second, all inspiration that finds itself in the human mind is also categorized on an infinite number of levels, depending on the openness and receptivity of the smaller mind. If your mind seeks wisdom from the deepest level and is open to receiving wisdom on that level of depth, then the wisdom thought that is stored in a comparable level of the Great Mind is detached and drawn down to your mind. This is the path of wisdom as it flows from the heavenly realms to the experiences within your mind.

Knowledge that is generated in *mokhin d'katnut,* the smaller mind, is both temporary and finite, whereas wisdom that is conceived from the *mokhin d'gadlut,* the Great Mind, is eternal and infinite. As you stand in the Gate of Wisdom, your awareness of the potential to merge with the Great Mind is awesome. In this heavenly gate you stand on the precipice between the infinite and the finite, the eternal and the temporal. You have the opportunity to receive wisdom on many levels from the Great Mind and to make it part of your laboratory of experience.

Your potential for connecting with the Great Mind is dependent upon the level on which you find your mind. Where is your mind now? Is it on a level that brings you closer to God, or one that distances you from God? Or do you waver in the spaces in between and fall into cerebral inertia? To paraphrase the verse in Isaiah, according to the Rizener Rebbe, God asks, "Are not My thoughts there in order to give you what is in your thoughts? Why then are not your ways as My ways?"

God's desire to give the greatness of mind to you is waiting for your desire to be open and receive. The more open you are, the greater the opportunity there is for you to merge with the Great Mind, to merge your thought with Divine thought. When the channels are open for free-flowing ideas between you and God, then the Source of thought thinks thoughts in you that you are receptive to thinking too. As a result, heavens rejoice and God sees you and calls you the embodiment of the Name and exclaims: "O thou art divine."

Practice the Meditation on Clearing the Mind (page 62)
at least once today.

Use the Right Mind in the Right Time

Thoughts exist in the mind in groupings, like bundles one
on top of the other. When a person needs a fact, he *or she*
remembers it by drawing it from its place in his *or her*
mind. This itself is a great wonder, for where was this
thought located until then?

Rabbi Nachman of Breslov

If you perceive space,

The fixed ideas of center and boundary dissolve.

Likewise, if mind perceives mind,

All mental activities will cease, you will

remain in a state of non-thought,

And you will realize the supreme

bodhi-citta *(awakened mind)*.

Sri Tilopa

Once Rabbi Hayyim of Krosno was watching the street performance of a tightrope dancer's act. His students asked him why
he was so enthralled. "This man," he said, "is risking his life
and I cannot say why. But I am quite sure that while he is

walking the rope, he is not thinking of the fact that he is earning a hundred gulden by what he is doing, for if he did, he would fall."

Amidst the kaleidoscope of images, experiences, and sounds in your mind, a still point in space and time draws you quietly into the observation of your own mind and the contemplation of its thoughts and ideas. When an idea or thought emerges out of the parcels of your mind, it is as a result of the coupling of similarly motivated thoughts on high. As one thought leaves, the remaining thoughts rearrange themselves in a different pattern in your mind. They self-organize until the next thought or idea drops down. All discoveries, inventions, visions, and inspirations occur like this. When your mind is empty and open to merging with the Divine mind, the appropriate thoughts are drawn to you. However, there are times when you may have sought an idea and it seemed to delude you. Perhaps you were not open, or it was not yet the right time for the inspiration to occur or for the task to be fulfilled according to God's plan.

How do you know when the right thought or idea is in the right mind at the right time in the Divine plan? In linear time, you will not know. Beyond time, it will not matter. Your real task is developing spiritually. Your challenge is to be less concerned with time and more concerned with staying clear and focused. This means letting go of expectations and enjoying wisdom and mindfulness for its own sake, rather than attaching it to outside expectations. Between the kaleidoscope of stimulation and the still point of contemplation, there is a mystical moment where right mind and right time effortlessly merge.

By turning down the static in your mind, you are better able to hear, see, and touch the Divine mind. In the process of fine-tuning your own receptivity to the wisdom of the supernal realms, your soul sings, visions appear, your mind is touched by God, and intuition happens. When the Israelites were bathed in revelation at Mount Sinai, it was because they had "fine-tuned" themselves beforehand. They traveled from a confining slave mentality to an empty, clear, freedom-based abundance consciousness. And when they stood reborn in glory at the foot of the mountain, the first sound they heard was the Aleph, the sound of silence. In the sound of silence, they intuitively touched the Divine Mind.

Pause and reflect for a moment now. Where is your clarity? Where is your focus? Is it inside the mind? In the static or in the still point? How are you reacting to stray thoughts? Pause again, empty the mind, and focus. As you continue to awaken to right mind and practice the Meditation on Clearing the Mind, you will enjoy wondrous discoveries, creative inventions, playful visions, and deep inspirations. Remember, it is not coming from you, but from the Source beyond you, who leads, follows, and walks alongside your right mind in the right time.

Practice the Meditation on Clearing the Mind (page 62)
at least once today.

Seek the Wisdom Beyond Duality

If the Torah had not been given to Israel, we could have learned modesty from the cat, intimacy from the dove, respect from the rooster, and integrity from the ant.

Talmud

The ten thousand things carry yin and embrace yang. They achieve harmony by combining these forces.

Lao Tzu

Duality is a way of thinking. In the true nature of mind there is no duality. Yet there is a paradox, for in order to recognize oneness, you need to step outside of the experience for a moment. A fish in water does not recognize it is in water until it leaves the water. Yet once the fish is out of water, it needs to go back into it. In the same way, when you desire to know something or someone, first you need to step outside of what you are seeking to know; then you will also need to unite as one with it. For example, to know you, I would need to be distant enough to see, hear, and sense clearly who you are. Yet to truly know who you are, I would need also to experience you fully and step into that part of you who is me too.

It is easy to get locked into a perception of either/or. Either I am close to you or I am far from you. Either you are good or you are bad. Either I can do this or I can do that. Either/or thinking leaves no room for the possibilities inherent in having it both ways. With wisdom, it is possible to experience a full range of options. When you believe you are confined by another's boundaries and limitations, or that the mind is confined to the dimensions of the brain, or that good is separate from bad, or black is separate from white, then choices you make are limited. When you limit your choices, you limit your perception of life and your life becomes limited, narrow, and isolated. However, when you come to recognize that boundaries are illusions, and good and bad incline toward each other, and black and white are variations of light, the dualities dissolve and freedom reigns. When you free your brain and move your mind beyond boundaries, beyond duality, life is perceived as boundless, magical, energizing, and is shared joyously and freely with all life forms, in all aspects of intelligence, for the ultimate purpose of serving goodness and awakening sparks of light.

In Hebrew there is no separate word for "to be." Being is implied in every word. Being is always present in you, in everything, and everywhere all at once. When this is taken to mind and heart, then even in the most ordinary and simple actions you will be able to bring your wisdom in harmony with the wise actions of those around you.

In "The Seventh Beggar's Tale," Richard Siegel writes so beautifully of the essence of nonduality:

> You once asked me who I am,
> Where I've been and what is my knowledge.
> The answers stand before you.
> I am suspended in air,
> And I am supported by earth;
> I am carried by the water,
> And I carry the water;
> My thoughts reach up and are met by
> thoughts reaching down;
> I am falling in the vastness of love,
> And I support through the offering of love;

From where I am there is no mountain
and no valley except for
the mountain and valley.
I have brought down the Heavens
and I have lifted up the Earth
and I bind them to each other with love.
And where I am there is peace,
but can you say where I am not?
Am I not like you?

*Practice the Meditation on Clearing the Mind (page 62)
at least once today.*

Hear Wisdom Speak and Witness Truth Happen

(Wisdom speaks)

Hear, for I will speak in excellence

And my lips open to that which is straight

For my mouth speaks truth. . . .

There is nothing perverse or crooked in them.

It is plain to those who understand

And correct to those who seek knowledge.

Proverbs 8:6–9

Having striven for mind's nourishment,

Sharpening the spearhead of the intellect,

I discovered permanent parents

Whom I can never forget.

Chögyam Trungpa

Clear your mind and open your heart to the wisdom that births new realities in you. Wisdom is a way of life impregnated with truth. When your thoughts are in accord with Divine mind, truth happens. It is not a result of internal inclinations or external influences. Truth is independent and has the power to transcend your own limitations. You recognize truth by living in harmony with the essence of who you are. This is the meaning of the Talmudic statement that God leads a person along the path he or she has chosen. First you choose your truth and then God leads you there.

The Talmud teaches that wisdom is knowing the consequences of your actions. One way to know the consequences is to recognize the subject matter of your thoughts. When you think holy thoughts, you are lifted by the heavenly spheres; when you think lowly thoughts, you are lowered by the heavenly spheres. Another way to know the consequences of your thoughts is through the energy that is transmitted by the thought. Thoughts have an energy life all their own. Once you put out a thought in spoken words, it cannot be rescinded. The energy you put out reaches others and boomerangs back to you. There are some cultures where people are so sensitive to negative thoughts that they duck out of the way of angry or intimidating words aimed at them. The biblical story of creation describes the power of words: when God said, "Let there be light," the light came into being.

Every word you speak creates an angel in heaven that assists in turning your words into reality. Your thoughts, like control buttons, are linked to a spiritual servicing station in the heavens and dispatched here on earth, where they are filtered through subject matter and travel in a path of positive or negative energy. Be open in your mind and let great wisdom enter as you think your next thought and speak your next word. The consequences of that thought are waiting to be activated. This is truth.

Truth encompasses your life from beginning to end. Truth is the foundation and the midpoint upon which you stand. When you speak with wisdom, truth happens. How do you know you are acting in accord with wisdom? When "your lips open to that which is straight and your mouth speaks truth." How do you know if it is truth that you speak? When it is independent of manipulation and in harmony with the essence of who you are.

Practice the Meditation on Clearing the Mind (page 62)
at least once today.

Ride the Divine Chariot

At the highest level of holiness are those persons who have achieved a state in which their whole personalities and all their actions are inseparably joined to the divine holiness. Of these persons it is said that they have become a "chariot" for the Shekhina, and like the Chariot, they are totally yielded up to the One who sits on the driver's seat, the throne of glory, and they constitute a part of the throne of glory itself, even though they are flesh and blood, men *and women* like all other men *and women*.

Adin Steinsalz

Let the movements of the body ease into genuineness,
Cease your idle chatter, let your speech become an echo,
Have no mind, but see the dharma of the leap.

Sri Tilopa

You were born to receive the light of God and to become the vehicle through which miracles can happen. The more light you allow to flow through you, the more wondrous your reality is. The Divine chariot is a vehicle of light through which God and you draw nearer to each other. In this vehicle you are not in control, for God is in the driver's seat. In this vehicle you leap into the unknown with complete faith that God is leading you on the path you are meant to travel. When your every thought, every word, and every action are in union with God, you become the chariot in which God travels. When you are in total union with God, the angelic forces weave a web of light and energy around you from which the Divine chariot is built.

In obscured language the prophet Ezekiel describes his ascent to the Divine chariot. He begins his vision with the words "I was in exile." According to Rabbi Aryeh Kaplan, what Ezekiel meant was that the "I" within himself was in exile from his inner spirit. The I he was describing was the God-filled part of himself, the Shekhina, the feminine essence of God. He felt distanced from the intuitive, sacred, nurturing aspects of God within himself. He felt as though his I (the Shekhina) was in exile, and he was isolated from his true divinity within. The Shekhina aspect of God dwells inside each person and is as close to you as your breath. And in a world dominated by outside influences, She too feels exiled and beyond your reach. She travels in and out of your consciousness by way of the Divine chariot. To bring back the Shekhina and to reaccess your own divinity, you need to re-create the chariot. When you reunite with the Shekhina, you become the chariot and ascend nearer to God and to uncovering the immanence of God in every aspect of life.

If you have defined yourself in terms of your outside world alone, then your God-filled self, the I part of you that is the Shekhina, feels isolated and exiled. In this state of mind and spirit, it is difficult to travel the metaphysical, astral realms. However, if you let go of obsessive attachment to your outer world and of controlling the way you think things ought to be, you will find greater peace of mind and a deeper connection to the divinity within yourself. All you need to do is pause, empty, and open to the spirit of God within you. This peace of mind and divinity are the essence of the Shekhina that resides in you. The Shekhina and you are inseparable. Each time you remember this, you reaccess your divinity and become the Divine chariot through which your soul soars.

In the process of re-creating the Divine chariot, Ezekiel first reaccessed the Shekhina in himself. Then he stood on the river Chebar, whose name means "that which already was." As he stood on the edge of the river of the past, he became one with God, one with the universe, and one with the chariot. There he was guided by the angelic forces and was transported back to the beginning of time, where he experienced the wondrous visions of the many aspects of God.

You too have the ability to reunite with the Shekhina and become the Divine chariot. With pure desire, quiet introspection, and meditation, remove yourself from the illusion of outside influences and self-aggrandizing thoughts. Then redeem your feminine essence by entering that part of you that yearns to be a receptor vehicle for God. Next, check your intention by asking yourself, Who is in the driver's seat? At that place where you are no longer attached to outside goals and are no longer clinging to expectations or control, you can travel into the different dimensions of worlds within worlds of being and draw ever nearer to the ever-evolving wonders of God. When you become the Divine chariot, you soar to greater heights, grander visions, and more wondrous ways of being.

As you review your day thus far, consider all you have learned in this insight and expand where you have been to the place where you enter God and are enveloped in a Divine chariot of light.

Practice the Meditation on Clearing the Mind (page 62)
at least once today.

Remember That Nothing Is Certain

For the mountains may depart

and the hills be removed;

But My grace will not depart from you,

Neither will My covenant be removed,

So says the God who has compassion on you.

Isaiah 54:10

The Way floats and drifts;

It can go left or right.

It accomplishes its tasks and completes its affairs,

and yet for this it is not given a name.

Lao Tzu

A wise person knows that nothing is certain. According to the Tao, if you can hold on to something, you can lose it. Nothing remains the same. Please read the last statement again; it is a play on words. Nothing remains the same, yet *nothing* remains the same. Nothingness and emptiness are constant. The path to the Infinite Source begins in emptiness. Empty yourself of preconceived ideas and emotional expectations. Whatever transpired in the last second of time can no longer be, nor can it return in the exact same form.

There is no such thing that is certain, only God, and God is the foundation of nothingness. Each generation and each individual come to God in their own way with their own visions, messages, ideas, faith, and trust. Your vision or idea of God is the basis and the template for your own self-image. If God, for you, is limited and full of rules, then your image of yourself is also limited and regulated by dos and don'ts, shoulds and should nots. If your idea of God is an ever-changing, free-flowing, dynamic, and vital force of creativity, then you also become an ever-evolving, free-flowing, dynamic, and vital spirit. You and God mirror each other through the lenses of your perception. It is counterproductive to your growth and possibilities to try to hold on to certainty and contain your God image as anything less than infinite. Even in certainty there needs to be room for dynamism.

The only certainty that you can hold on to is in the light that God pours into the foundation of your being. Infinite Light knows no limits and holds no shape. The prophet Isaiah describes a God who assures you that even when you walk through the heavenly gates and touch the wisdom of the ancients, the soul of matter, and the heart of emotion, there is nothing to hold on to. The physical landscape of your life as you know it now will continuously change its shape and grow new forms as time moves on. Nothing stays the same; all things blossom, ascend, and steadily expand in their light and truth.

Nothing is permanent and most things that reflect profound experiences occur spontaneously and last only seconds in a lifetime. Can you think of moments in your life that you tried to hold on to? Moments of laughter, joy, ecstasy, or moments of deep mystical encounters and spiritual awakenings. Moments you thought would last forever have become but fleeting memories of the past. Yet in that one second you were transformed into a new way of being.

Be gentle with yourself, as God is gentle with you. You are not expected to change suddenly, yet the possibility is certainly available to you. Remember, everything changes and everything has God in it. You may feel insecure acting on your own or taking self-responsibility—especially if you come from years of structured rules and regulations that have guided your path. I can relate this to my own life and to my process in writing this book. At first I was concerned with writing a spiritual guide that would receive the sanction of my parents (now deceased) and teachers past and present. I thought I needed to include numerous footnotes to prove that I knew my subject thoroughly and was writing in accord with the strict guidelines along which I was raised. Then, in the process of writing, I changed. I stopped writing for my parents and teachers and began writing for my children and their children yet to be born. I stopped writing to conserve the rules and began writing to redeem the spirit. I stopped writing to preserve yesterday and started writing the truth of what I believe and how I live now. The journey I have outlined in this book is not only for public consumption; it is for personal living. I don't only think this journey; I live it. And the only thing that is certain about my life is that nothing is certain.

So often the very rules that promise liberation become restrictions in themselves. When you depend on the rule and forget the intention, the light remains hidden in the veils and filters of the *klippot* of form and structure. There is a substance of energy and light, hidden beneath the web of structure, that is crying out for you to release it. Certainty relies on uncertainty, and security is an illusion trapped in insecurity. Everything changes—and is just as it is meant to be.

The Infinite Creative Source awaits your awakening to the pleasures of this moment, which are hidden wherever you look. Notice where your sense of self is today. Is it in the insecurity, looking for outside sources to build a secure, stable structure around you? Or is it in the freedom to be self-responsible and empowered to live in the creative, dynamic flow of life? Is it in the need to hold on to things, or in the desire to receive and share who you are and who God is in you? The certainty that you seek can be found only in the nothingness of God and in the flexibility to move as life moves and to change as life changes.

Practice the Meditation on Clearing the Mind (page 62) at least once today.

UNDERSTANDING

God founded the Earth with wisdom and

established the Heavens with understanding.

Proverbs 3:19

To walk safely through the maze of human life, one needs

the light of wisdom and the guidance of virtue.

Buddha

As YOU STAND AT THE entrance to the heavenly Gate of Understanding, you are entering the final path of the mind. In this gate you will receive insights to help you understand, define, organize, and pattern your life. All the wisdom you have received through imagination, memory, sensation, and experience you will now weave into a comprehensible tapestry of forms and colors that can significantly change the foundation of how you think and act. Now is the time for illuminating your intention, asserting your wisdom, and bringing new concepts into your life in practical, meaningful ways.

The kabbalists describe the relationship between wisdom, understanding, and knowledge as one that is imbued with the tender beauty and miracle of fertilization, incubation, and conception. In wisdom a thought is conceived, and in understanding it is born. Understanding corresponds to logic in the world and the rational part of your mind. The wisdom that was fertilized in the intuitive part of your mind now penetrates and impregnates its rational part. Wisdom unites with understanding in order to birth knowledge. Understanding, like the womb, incubates the wisdom of the past and bears its fruit in the knowledge of the future. Knowledge is the fruit that wisdom and understanding have produced.

Your thoughts and ideas today create the patterns you will live by tomorrow. The patterns you create now lay the foundation for your future way of thinking and living. To understand your future, you need to understand the wisdom and intention inherent in the information of your past. As you carry the wisdom inherent in the information of the past through the Gate of Understanding, you will receive insights into ways of utilizing the wisdom in the future. You will do this by understanding the multiple images and possibilities of God, the potential power inherent in yourself, and the connectedness of your experiences to the oneness of the universe. You will begin to recognize what is important and what is not. You will perceive and formulate what is essential to you and discern what is no longer meaningful. After you pass through the Gate of Understanding you will have the knowledge you need in order to think consciously, act consciously, and move consciously into the next gate on this journey and the next stage in your life.

Before turning to the first insight in Understanding, take some quiet time now and experience the Meditation on Silence. This meditation will help you calm the inner chatter of your mind and remain focused within. With regular practice, you will find it increasingly easier to focus, regardless of the distractions in your life. To benefit from the meditation, read it slowly. Pause between each sentence and experience what you have just read. Then spend a moment or two enveloped in the peace that results. Review the Meditation on Silence after reading and contemplating each of the insights in this chapter.

ഏ Meditation on Silence ഏ

Pause a moment and sit comfortably in a chair or on the floor. Feel the breath moving in and out of your body as you slowly inhale and exhale. Allow the inhalation and exhalation to flow freely and evenly. With each inhalation and exhalation feel your mind begin to clear and your body melt into relaxation. Hear the leftover chatter of your inner world. Allow the sounds and chatter to float into the distance, until they become fainter and fainter. As the sounds become softer and softer, feel their muted echoes absorb into the whispered breath of the universe. Hear the serene sound of silence and feel the inaudible stream of light that moves through your being. Luxuriate now in the warm silence that nurtures your soul and feeds your mind.

Separate in Order to Come Together

All heavenly lights may appear as separate yet emanate
from the One Source and are one unified light. Whoever
keeps these lights separated in their own minds, separates
themselves from life eternal.

Zohar

Ever desireless, one can see the mystery.

Ever desiring, one can see the manifestations.

These two spring from the same source but differ in name.

Lao Tzu

Can you ever know for sure that what your mind is perceiving
is true, or that it is an illusion? To know the world in which
you dwell takes subjective patience and objective observation.

There were once two cousins who had lived all their lives in
the city. They had never seen a field or meadow until they
decided one day to take a trip to the country. Along the way,
they saw a farmer turn a beautiful field of green grass into deep
furrows of overturned dirt. Then they saw the farmer take good
wheat and throw it into the dirt. Having lived in the city all
their lives, they were astounded at the craziness of overturning
the beautiful field and then the wastefulness of filling the holes

with good wheat. One of the cousins decided that she had had her fill of the weirdness of the country and went back to the city. The other cousin stayed long enough to observe the miracle that occurred over the next few weeks. She saw the field sprout green shoots even more beautiful than what was there before. She was so excited that she wrote her cousin to come back to the country and see the miracle. The impatient cousin returned from the city and also marveled at the magnificent sight and began to understand the farmer's method of work—that is, until the wheat grew ripe and the farmer took a scythe and cut it down. The impatient cousin once again became bewildered and ran back to the city disgusted. And the other cousin, who had understood the in-between stage of growth, remained in the country. She patiently watched the farmer gather the wheat in the granary and skillfully separate the wheat from the chaff. Observing how the sown seeds produced a hundredfold harvest, the patient cousin understood the logic and saw the connections behind the different processes of farming. Things that seemed separate were only steps in the total cycle of growth.

Think of the ways in which you separate one thing from another in order to understand them better, then notice how you need to bring them together in order to effect change. You must take apart a broken engine to ascertain the problem, but only when you reassemble the pieces can the engine perform as it was intended to. In the same way, you may separate one relationship from another, or one task from another, or one thought from another; yet in reality they operate at maximum potential only when they are integrated into a unique whole.

The problem arises when, like the impatient cousin in the story, you leave before everything has come together and you miss experiencing the completion at the end of the process. It is wonderful to prepare ingredients for baking a cake, and even to taste the nuts and lick the chocolate. But unless all the ingredients are mixed together in the appropriate manner, the cake will not bake. This reminds me of my teenage years, when, like ingredients in a cake, I had an array of friends. There were friends from school, friends from temple, friends for Saturday,

and another group for Sunday. Now, as I look back, I recognize
that each group of friends served a different part of my own
personality. There were so many aspects of myself that were
disconnected. The spiritual, religious, social, and cultural parts
of who I was were isolated from one another, chasms apart. As
long as all the parts of who I was remained isolated and fragmented, so did my groups of friends. As I began maturing and
acknowledging the varied aspects of my personality, I began
feeling more whole within myself, and this was reflected in my
relationships. No longer did I need to separate and isolate one
group from the other, or one thought from another, or one
culture from another. The party began when I integrated the
friends from Sunday with the friends from Saturday and the
friends from school with the friends from temple. Now my
religious, spiritual, social, and cultural experiences are indistin-
guishable. Now my friends, like all other aspects of my life,
represent the interconnectedness of my belief system, personality, and lifestyle.

The choice is yours, as it was mine. Do you wish to remain
in the illusion that you can isolate one part of your life from
another, or are you ready to open to the broader possibilities of
integrating the whole? Countless couples I have counseled were
caught in the illusion that their spirituality and their profession
were two different things, or that their spirituality and their
marriage or relationships were two different matters. This is an
illusion. When you live the truth it oozes out of every pore of
your being, sparks every chamber of your mind, and flows
through every aspect of your life. Just as there is no such thing
as being "a little pregnant," there is no such thing as a separate
or isolated experience. All experiences incline toward one another, and in the interchange of life, all things affect one another.

The Taoists say that for every up there is a down; for every
in, an out; for every outside, an inside. Things, issues, and
relationships are really never separate; we only perceive them as
such. In the past, it may have been easier for you to have a
structure that dictated polarities, to separate right from wrong
and good from bad. Values and attitudes were tightly packed

and uniformly placed in neat little boxes. Yet what may be right for you today may be wrong for you tomorrow, and what may be good for another may be bad for you. With persistent observation, you will notice that the polarities of your life and of all life eventually incline toward one another.

As you touch the Infinite, the definitions of reality change. You no longer find yourself battling good and evil, so much as defining new boundaries to accommodate new experiences. Things in your life that may have seemed separate and disjointed are now perceived as only temporary images of reality. They are stepping-stones to enter a larger story of who you are, parts of a puzzle that fit together into a greater whole. If you live each part of your life mindfully, the separate parts will come together and reap fields of new possibilities and wonders for you. Imagine now the marvelous opportunities that await your patient recognition, the glorious wonders that await your curiosity and openness, the diverse experiences that await your enthusiasm, wisdom, and understanding. Enter the sanctuary of your mind. Let go of expectations and luxuriate in the calm serenity of polarities inclining toward one another.

Practice the Meditation on Silence (page 88)
at least once today.

Create Patterns

For every part in the body and in your life, there is a
parallel part in the many "faces of God."

Tikkunei Zohar

If you are without desire, if you do not dwell in extremes,

You will see the dharmas *(patterns)* of all the teachings.

Sri Tilopa

Begin noticing the patterns that evolve from your thoughts.
Being the recipient of Divine intelligence gives you the opportunity to create patterns that are unique to your own development. The patterns you create form and shape the path to your
destiny. One thought can reverse an image or turn a situation
inside out. Even a fleeting thought travels on a wavelength that
can assist or hinder your development. Pay attention to your
thoughts; they are the entry through which you pattern the
quality of your life.

Infinite patterns are available to you. It is for you to decide
which patterns suit your growth and assist you in expanding
your mind, opening your heart, and nurturing your body. Become the witness to your thoughts and the many ways in which
patterns flow through your consciousness. The pattern, or template, through which you operate pervades everything you
think, say, and do. You cannot run away or hide from yourself.

You can only become more enlightened to what you are thinking and the patterns you create in your life. Notice the choices that you make.

Even in a time of chaos and disturbance, the thoughts that form in your mind from the information you receive can help you move in a more positive direction. One thought leads to another thought; one direction leads to another direction; one action leads to another action. Positive thoughts lead to positive directions and result in positive actions that lead to even more positive thoughts. The universe of goodness is yours to have and to serve; it begins with the thoughts you entertain in the landscape of your mind and in the patterns of your behavior. Do not be discouraged if you fall off balance or move into negativity. When you fall into forgetfulness, you have the power in your mind to pause, empty, change the pattern, and redefine yourself.

Consider for a moment the pattern you are defining for yourself as you read this book. You are walking through ten gates patterned according to the kabbalistic Tree of Life. As the pattern becomes part of your everyday experience, it will shape and form the way you think, feel, and act. Integral to this pattern is the order through which you journey each gate. You began with Intention, received Wisdom, and are now in the midst of Understanding. As you continue the journey through the Ten Heavenly Gates, you will continue to unfold the pattern through which you draw closer to God and manifest miracles in your life.

By observing Nature, religious traditions throughout time have uncovered ways of moving from one pattern of energy to another and from one season of life to another. This is often ritualized through festivals and celebrations. During the longest nights and shortest days of winter, when the seemingly dead earth comes back to blossoming life, there are the festivals of resurrection and freedom. Throughout the year, there is the ongoing weekly pattern of stopping and re-creating time in the Sabbath. What religions have long recognized is the need for individual and communal pattern making and pattern changing.

Pattern making was the first task given to a human. God asked Adam to name the animals. As the animals were named, patterns of recognition were being created. Then the androgynous human was separated and could see itself as male and female. When Eve ate the fruit from the Tree of Knowledge, she created a divergent pattern through which humanity entered into a new world. In the formation of Adam and Eve, God created partners, Adam to Eve, and Adam and Eve to God. You are the archetypal intelligence of Adam and Eve. In you is the template to co-create with the Infinite. Co-creating is an awesome task; it places responsibility for the quality of your life and how it affects others into your safekeeping. When you co-create with God you grow beyond familiar but limiting patterns to creating new and more expansive ones. With Understanding you are empowered to create patterns and weave relationships in the thoughts you think. You now enter the landscape of God as a miner would enter the diamond caves, in search of multifaceted, reflective diamond thoughts carved into the patterns of ancient rocks.

As you continue to practice the Meditation on Silence, become aware of the overlapping interactions and the shape-shifting patterns that birth in the quiet landscape of your mind as it unites with the Divine mind.

Practice the Meditation on Silence (page 88)
at least once today.

Know God

Q Who is the Creator?

A The One God.

Q What is God's quality?

A God's Greatness.

Q Where is God?

A In the mind.

Q I didn't mean that . . .

A But you questioned me in terms appropriate
   to a creature and not a Creator.

Rabbi Bachya ibn Paquda

Something mysteriously formed,

Born before heaven and earth.

In the silence and the void,

Standing alone and unchanging,

Ever present and in motion.

Perhaps it is the mother of ten thousand things.

I do not know its name.

Call it Tao

For lack of a better word, I call it great.

Lao Tzu

To know God is to welcome the Infinite, the Finite, the Never-changing, the Ever-changing, the Living One, the Eternal One, the Everything, the Nothing, the Absolute, the Relative, the Immanent, the Transcendent, the Father, the Mother, the Brother, the Sister—and you can continue this list. No wonder it is difficult to know God.

In a world of infinite choices and clamoring chaos, filled with confused people of low self-esteem, it is understandably difficult for people to make choices about what their image of God needs to be. It is easier to perpetuate a limited God image that is familiar than to risk the unknown. So many people perpetuate the God image of their parents or grandparents, even though that image may not be a dynamic force, relevant to their lives today. They put the God of their parents in an old box and keep Him/Her/It hidden in a vast mountain of authoritarian rules. Over time, few, if any, remember the box; nearly all remember the rules. Rare are those who desire to dig deep enough to unlock the box and release God from the old images.

To continue your spiritual journey with integrity it is important to face the God of your origins. It is time to dig through the mountain and get God out of the box. It is time to empower yourself with an image of God that is dynamic, exciting, and relevant to your life—a God image that gives your life quality, purpose, joyful meaning, and an overall sense of invaluable enthusiasm. (Enthusiasm comes from the Greek *entheos,* "in God.")

Rabbi Zalman Schachter-Shalomi, founder and retired spiritual leader of the Jewish Renewal Network, explained the need for a new mythology that is more authentic to our experience. He said, "We can no longer drive by looking in the rearview mirror. This means we can no longer go forward by concentrating on what was done in the past. However, the new myth needs access to all the energies that have preceded us." Using computer language, he said, "When we get a new computer we ask if it can read the old files. The old computers cannot read the new files; even though, the new computers need the capacity to read the old files. We need the new computers to be 'upwardly compatible.' In the same way, the new mythology, like the new computer, needs to be 'upwardly compatible.' It needs to access the splendor of the past and pour it into a dynamic, living fountain for the future, with compassion, authenticity, meaning, and joy."

The prophet Jeremiah said, "You will seek God your God, and you will find that God, if you seek that God with all your heart and all your soul." You see, hear, and know God in your own experience rather than in another's knowledge or language. In mystical Judaism, God is a direct experience of a direct relationship. Another cannot bring God to you more authentically than you can on your own.

No one else can journey through life for you, but you are not alone. Your developing God image is a vital contribution to the oneness of God and the wholeness of society. God needs you, you need God, and we need one another in a most God-filled way of being. Expand your image of God and expand your life, your self, and the perceptions in your mind. "It is not in heaven . . . neither is it beyond the sea . . . but it is so close to you, in your mouth and in your heart." As you meditate on silence today, access the splendor, experience the freedom, and know the love. Then look into the mirror, see yourself, and recognize the part you hold in God.

Practice the Meditation on Silence (page 88)
at least once today.

Connect, Focus, and Know Yourself

YHVH made me as the beginning of the path.

The original of *God's* wonders way back then.

I was set up for everlasting, from the beginning,

Before there was Earth.

Proverbs 8:22–23

Knowing others is wisdom;

Knowing yourself is enlightenment.

Lao Tzu

If you are what you do, and you cannot do, does that mean you are not? If you are what you speak, and you cannot speak, does that mean you are not? If you are what you think and you cannot think, does that mean that you are not? Then who are you? And how do you know that who you think you are is really you? These are some of the questions I started thinking about after I heard a lecture by the psychiatrist and author Dr. David Allen. These questions helped me understand that thoughts, words, and actions are the by-product of a deeper essence within us. When we remove the surface layers of doing, speaking, and thinking, a luminescent part of God is revealed.

According to the kabbalists, knowing yourself has to do with knowing the source of the self and the purpose for which you were shaped and molded. When God originally birthed you, on the passage through the void you seized a little piece of God known as a Godspark. This Godspark, attached to God by a beaded thread of light, descended through the four worlds. The worlds of fire, water, air, and earth. In each world it was clothed in organic activity until it arrived in the physical world, robed in the muscles, bones, and flesh of the human form. (This story was told to me by Rabbi Mitch Chefitz.) Having arrived in this physical world, you are still connected to God by the invisible beaded light thread. This thread, called *kavv'chut,* is the conduit through which you live possibilities for God and God lives possibilities for you.

Everything is inhabited by a Godspark. Everything in creation is a conduit for the light and is looking to share it freely with a receptive soul. The invisible light thread is a loop from God to your Godspark and from your Godspark to the divinity in the universe. There are numerous bodies walking around this world looking for a linkup, a connection that can touch and recognize the deepest part of who they are. It would be easy to connect if we were all wired in the same frequency, yet that is not the case. You are attracted to those whose souls are most responsive to yours. Not everyone is traveling with the same light intensity or wavelength, in rhythm with your soul.

Know who you are. Although everyone is inhabited by a Godspark, you are a Godspark with a unique soul circuit, born to receive and spread your part of the light. No one else has your unique light. The aspect of you that is light is everlasting because it is connected to the Infinite Source. All you have to do is empty and open for receptivity; position yourself to be a conduit. Witness yourself and your connections to other people. As you integrate with others, remember the essence of who you are and the abundance of your light, so that you will steer your energy away from a limiting perception of competition, jealousy, and insecurity. These sensations mislead you into believing your goodness, happiness, prosperity, and even your health depend on outside influences. Maintain your focus, instead, on knowing yourself as a radiant Godspark born to receive the light, and share it with discerning wisdom.

Each person has his or her own unique task to fulfill in the direction they have chosen. For each direction there is another connection. Imagine a worldwide human switchboard where everyone is on-line waiting for the appropriate linkup. When you connect your invisible light thread to another's whose soul circuit is receptive to yours, not only is the world brighter; there is also profound recognition on a soul level that validates the essence of who you really are.

There are times when you may measure yourself in comparison to another and, in doing so, diminish your own true potential. When you diminish your own radiance the Godspark in you goes into hiding. It is like the story of the children who were playing hide-and-seek. One little girl was chosen as the designated hider. She hid so well the other children got tired of looking for her and went on to another game. It just so happened that at that very moment the holy Rabbi Mendel of Rimonov was walking down the lane and found the little girl crying with much sadness. When he stopped and asked her why she was so sad, between the sobs she answered, "I'm hiding but no one's coming to find me."

When you forget yourself and lose sight of who you are, the Godspark in you gets hidden under the layers that cover the soul, while you walk around with a loose thread, asking, "Who am I?" The Godspark tugs on the invisible light thread and waits patiently for you to remove the surface layers of thoughts, words, and actions in order to remember, rediscover, and reactivate its light.

First empty the mind of clinging thoughts, and then practice the Meditation on Silence. In the silence, you are better able to see the wisdom and hear the understanding beneath your words and actions. In the silence you access the invisible, inaudible light that is uniquely yours. Remember in the pauses throughout the day to rediscover your uniqueness and reactivate your light.

Practice the Meditation on Silence (page 88)
at least once today.

Journey Beyond Reason and Logic

> . . . and What if it isn't a What or a Why
>
> or even a How,
>
> There is no Because with which
>
> you can answer a What if,
>
> And if you try and say What if . . . not
>
> that's no answer,
>
> So,
>
> they got lost.
>
> *Rabbi Nachman of Breslov*

In the secular fields, reason and logic are prized above all else. In the spiritual realms, reason and logic cannot exist without wisdom and understanding. You know this from the times in your life when things sounded reasonable and appeared to contain the logical formula for success, yet what appeared rational on paper did not manifest in reality. There are also times when the unexpected occurs in the form of miracles, beyond reason or logic. Miracles are happening all the time. To see the unexpected you need to be wise enough to perceive it and reasonable enough to understand that the unexpected really does occur. An overdependence on either wisdom or reason diminishes the wonders that exist in each.

Both reason that includes wisdom and logic that includes intuition open you to more possibilities in the physical and emotional realms. If you were to act and react by wisdom alone, the world of relationships would be too remote to grasp. Reason and logic enable you to understand the probabilities of relationships, such as those between animate and inanimate objects, between the heavens and the earth, between the elements and the directions, between the mundane and the sacred, the profound and the simple, between one human and another.

In the world of reason and logic, things follow a certain order, and all behavior is expected to follow that order—like the order of passing the crown of a king to his nearest surviving kin, or the expectation that success has to do with achieving material gains and public power. Reb Nachman tells the story of a king who went against the reason and logic of his times. He was a benevolent king who adored his son, so much so that he decided to make his son king even while he himself was still alive. He called together all the people in his kingdom and threw a big party to celebrate his son's becoming king. During the celebration and festivities, the wise father spoke to his son in a most profound way that was beyond reason or logic. He told him that he could see into the future and saw that someday the son would not be king. And he explained to his son that the virtues of being a king had little to do with the office and more to do with the qualities of nobility within oneself. So he told his son to remain joyous, even without the kingship. The wise father knew that if the son could remain joyous even without the throne, he would indeed be made of the substance of kings. However, if the son was saddened by the loss of the throne, he was not made for being a king, and it would be just as well that he would no longer rule. Either way, the father would celebrate and be joyous for his son.

Now the son became king, and he did not feel adequate in fulfilling his royal duties, so he chose the wisest ones in the country to advise him, and for their wisdom, they were generously rewarded. The more wisdom the wise displayed, the more generously the king rewarded them. After a while, there was

too much wisdom and too little reason. With all their wisdom
the wise governed unreasonably. They got lost in their wisdom
and forgot about the Source of their wisdom and the need to
have faith in something beyond themselves. Even the king himself got lost in wisdom and fell into doubt and confusion. He
would ask himself, "Who am I and where am I going in the
world?" And as soon as he began to reason, he would lose
himself again in speculations of what if this and what if that,
and he could have walked around saying "what if" ad infinitum.
The only ones who remained logical, reasonable, and filled with
faith were the simple folk, for they did not attempt to match
the wisdom of the wise. In their simplicity they remembered
who they were, and that satisfied them. In their faith and simplicity they were the wisest of all.

How do you keep a balance between wisdom and reason,
intuition and logic, simplicity and confusion? With faith. Faith
is simple; you just know you have it. It is not an idea; it is a
way of living ideas. It is the thread that weaves wisdom with
understanding, reason, and logic. Faith is fed and nurtured in
your soul. When faith is close to you, it is as though you can
actually see what it is you have faith in. Your wisdom with
understanding feeds your faith. With faith as the container of
wisdom, reason and logic are lifted to higher levels of understanding, and the heavens rejoice in the knowledge of the earth.
Then the science of the heavens and the science of the earth
integrate as one.

Practice the Meditation on Silence (page 88)
at least once today.

Practice Mindfulness

As one grinds the incense another *repeatedly* states, "Grind thoroughly, thoroughly grind," for the sounds are beneficial to the spices.

Talmud

Therefore, all things are primarily controlled and ruled by the mind, and are created up by the mind . . . if a *person* speaks and acts with a good mind, happiness follows him *or her* like his *or her* shadow.

Buddha

Practicing mindfulness is an important skill in all mystical traditions. Mindfulness is awareness of the thoughts moving through your mind without clinging, analyzing, or judging. It is observing the mind with compassion, generosity, and nonattachment. Pause a moment and observe the thoughts gliding through your mind now. Breathe fully and evenly. Notice each time your mind is holding on to a thought. And as though the mind were an entity to itself, say to it, "Oh, that is interesting," and let it move on to the next thought and the next and the next and the next. With continued practice of observing without clinging, you begin to experience calmness and serenity. In that calmness, your negative thoughts will be diffused. Eventually you will become one with the thought, and neither you nor the thought will any longer exist as separate entities. This is different from attachment. When you cling or attach yourself to an idea or thought, you and the thought are separate and struggling for each other's attention. When you become one with your thoughts, there is no separation, no differentiation. Then there is no longer you or the thought. You and thought empty, each into the other, and release the energy that flows into peace and serenity.

In being mindful, you become keenly aware of how your thoughts, words, and actions are vehicles for union and reunion with God. When God is one with you in your daily thoughts, words, and actions, meditation naturally happens. Even in mindfulness there are moments and periods when you forget your God connection. To remedy forgetfulness, the holy Baal Shem Tov, the founder of Hasidism, suggests the following simple yet profound practice: frequently pause throughout your day, wherever you find yourself, and focus your mind on the awesomeness of God. He said that this practice is beneficial even if you are already engaged in a sacred occupation.

Practicing mindfulness includes the possibilities of hearing your inner voice. Once you clear your mind and are free from attachment, the soul sings her sweet melody through the pores of your body and a silent sound is heard, an intangible feeling is felt, an invisible image is seen. This is the sound of the breath of the divine Name, YHVH. In this sound you hear the refreshing stream of the living waters and you feel the flow of the life-giving nectar of God. To hear and feel the sensations of the audible stream is a meditation available to everyone. God has placed within you the mindfulness to observe it.

The kabbalists use study, prayer, music, movement, and breath to assist in practicing mindfulness. Studying devotional works or contemplating aspects of Torah can lead to joy and ecstasy. Using devotional prayers as mantras can lead to expansive thinking (*hitpashtut*) beyond the physical into the spiritual realms. Read the words, think them, and dream them, and then they will live as you observe them. Music was used by the prophets, as it is used today, for altering states of consciousness. And one of the most joyous techniques for attaining an enlightened state of mind is body meditation through ecstatic dancing. Clinging minds lead to constricted bodies. Free the body to worship God and the mind follows, and vice versa. Rabbi Nachman of Breslov, who was beleaguered by melancholy, said the only way to rise after a fall is to dance your way up!

Remember, as you practice mindfulness, that awareness, deep consciousness, and inner wisdom and peace do not come from discussion, but meditation. Practice being fully present, empty, and focused.

Practice the Meditation on Silence (page 88)
at least once today.

Recognize Transient Knowledge, Receive Essential Knowing

(Wisdom speaks)

In the nothingness I was brought forth . . .

before the earth and the fields

and before the beginning of the dust of the world . . .

then I was next to God as a nursling,

daily playing with and delighting in God.

Proverbs 8:24

Therefore the sage goes about doing

nothing, teaching no-talking.

The ten thousand things rise

and fall without cease,

Creating, yet not possessing.

Lao Tzu

As you practice the Meditation on Silence within the Gate of Understanding, you will notice how thoughts continually pop up, and like corn in a corn popper, one thought gives birth to two, two to four, four to eight, the many to the myriad. Then what you thought you knew in the first thought is no longer so, and the most recent thought is the catalyst for many more. This is the impermanence of your thought and the lightness of your spirit. This is why you find yourself thinking and rethinking matters. Notice how you study a passage and think you know it, but then you reread it sometime later and it means something entirely new. Whatever it is you thought you knew is no longer relevant, for new thoughts have entered that have already transformed the old.

Thoughts are continuously refined by other thoughts. When you attempt to cling to one thought because you think it is very good, you are limiting your experience. It is like one who loves good food. You can purchase the best food, but if you hold on to the food for any length of time, it will not taste as good and will most likely spoil. It is the same with thoughts, for they are transient. This is what is called transient knowledge—a very important insight in mystical living.

Essential knowing, on the other hand, has less to do with thinking and more to do with receiving fully. In essential knowing there is no attachment, only a profound recognition and acknowledgment. In Genesis 4:1 you read, "And Adam knew Eve, his wife, and she conceived." It is said that Adam "knew" Eve. In Hebrew the word for knowing, *yadah,* also implies sexual union and intimacy. It is the kind of knowing that occurs when someone you love knows you deeply and fully, without clinging to any one thought. It is the total experience of looking into another's eyes and seeing his or her heart.

In the dynamic flow of life, thoughts are forever being exchanged between the Great Mind and the small mind, between heaven and earth, between God and you. The Torah is an example of this unfolding interchange: even the Torah is dynamic and ever changing. The blessing that is recited before studying Torah is "Blessed are You, Holy One of the universe, for having guided us to immerse ourselves in the words of your Torah." The mystic seriously abides by this blessing and considers mental, intuitive, and emotional immersion into the words, substance, and forms of the Torah crucial for understanding the hidden meanings. The Torah is not a static, never-changing relic of the past, but a vibrant, mutable, expansive dialogue between you and God. The more you put yourself into it, the better you can see the fluidity, flexibility, and playfulness of God. Immersing yourself in the words of Torah means swimming in the dynamic flow of the ever-changing, forever-revealing wisdom and knowledge inherent in the universe of experience.

In the impermanence between old, new, and renewed thoughts, the spirit plays, for only in joy can light thoughts be born. Light thoughts, or transient knowledge, travel on light spirits that soar in the freedom of creativity and change. Observe your thoughts and notice how they have changed over time; observe old attitudes that have given form to new ways of ⁺hinking. Notice relationships that have been stifled by clinging old perceptions and imagine the possibilities available in ting, without possessing, new, ever-changing ideas. Pay at- ⁺ion to the obvious and then notice how it too is an illusion. you seize your thoughts and realize them more fully, you become aware of their impermanence, your own creativity, and your ever-expanding dialogue with God.

You transfer knowledge from the inner chambers of your mind into the activity of your outside environment. Knowledge enables you to remember thoughts, access wisdom and understanding, and birth new ideas. The essential knowing you are receiving now is not a rehearsal for things to come. Essential knowing is the crescendo that reverberates through all time. It is like the essential knowing you experience in love. When you are known by another, you are fully recognized and deeply loved with such a profound feeling that the attention of the one who is recognizing you does not waver and does not change. At that moment of deep recognition, you know that you are the whole world to the one who knows you. Such knowledge becomes an everlasting memory, forever engraved in your heart.

Essential knowledge connects your mind to your body and your heart. With essential knowledge your thoughts and ideas become emotionally charged. As you exit the first three gates, recall your intention, collect your thoughts, and digest a fuller understanding of who you are in the universe of your experiences. Reach deeply within the essence of your being, envision your spirit, hear your soul's melody, and receive your Self. Know your Self in the manner in which you would like another to know you. Sense who you are and how far you have journeyed in a life that is continuously unfolding wonders and possibilities. Recognize that when God desired to create the worlds, you came out of the darkness wrapped in light. See yourself as God sees you and know, with a profound, unforgettable feeling that is unwavering and constant, that you are known by God.

You are now about to move from the world of your mind into a whole new world, of feelings. As you walk lightly and tread consciously forward, you will utilize these insights in your relationship to others, to the earth, to yourself, and to the God in everything.

As you practice the Meditation on Silence today, hear the melody born of your soul. Go forth in silence and enter with song.

Practice the Meditation on Silence (page 88)
at least once today.

COMPASSION

You open Your hands and You satisfy every living thing.

Psalm 145

Thus, the mind has compassion for poor people, becomes a mother to all people, honors all people, looks upon all as personal friends, and respects them as parents.

Buddha

Y OU ARE ENTERING THE heavenly Gate of Compassion, where you are sensitive to your own and others' emotions. The wisdom, understanding, and knowledge you have gathered thus far on this journey will now serve you well in the external, emotion-filled world of Compassion. Compassion is the primary quality through which you conduct your life. Compassion is the ability to feel deeply and give generously while remaining free of expectations. When you have compassion for yourself and others you interact freely and lovingly with all of life.

In the Gate of Compassion, you receive insights into nurturing the godliness that dwells within your mind, heart, body, and life. With the insights in Compassion, you will learn how to make peace with suffering, change old behavior into new possibilities, and serve goodness for the love of service itself. You will let go of past mistakes. You will speak gently and live fully in the moment, with total acceptance of your God and your life. With Compassion you will recognize how your thoughts begin to manifest feelings, and the feelings create the potential to love unconditionally, accept, and free yourself and others. Journeying the path of Compassion requires you to continue being open, empty, and receptive. You will feel eternally desired, accepted, loved, nurtured, acknowledged, and received by God. In turn, you will desire, accept, love, nurture, acknowledge, and receive the wonders of God.

The heavenly Gate of Compassion is the entranceway to developing your strength of character and tapping into the harmony that dwells within your heart. First there is unconditional love; then there is strength and discernment. As you blend love and strength in your daily situations, you will bring a heart-filled way of loving into your life and into the heart of the world.

The Divine purpose for continuous creation is to bestow goodness among humanity. Therefore, everything that exists in the external world is for the purpose of developing and serving goodness within yourself and within all creation. As you journey the path of Compassion, you are anointed with grace and adorned with a positive image that impregnates the light of creation. The generosity and greatness of spirit with which you serve will help carry you through the strength and discernment of the road ahead.

Before turning to the first insight in Compassion, take some quiet time now and experience the Meditation on Light. It is short, simple, and transforming. It can be practiced in a moment, for several minutes, for long or short periods of time, anywhere you find yourself to be. This meditation will help you maintain simplicity while embracing yourself with the light of God and lightness of spirit. To benefit from the meditation, read it slowly. Pause between each sentence and experience what you have just read. Then spend a moment or two enveloped in the peace that results. Review the Meditation on Light after reading and contemplating each of the insights in this chapter.

ꙮ Meditation on Light ꙮ

Pause a moment and sit comfortably in a chair or on the floor. Feel the breath moving in and out of your body as you slowly inhale and exhale. With the third exhalation, lower your eyelids and feel yourself surrounded in light. Let the radiance move through every pore of your being, nurturing and caressing you with unconditional love. Relax and luxuriate in the sensation of being fully accepted, fully supported.

Embrace Infinite Love

When a person is filled with God's love, all things become
sacred, pleasurable and loving.

Rabbi Nachman of Tchernoble

The sage accumulates nothing.

Having used what *the sage* had for others,

The sage has even more.

Having given what *the sage* had to others,

What *the sage* has is even greater.

Lao Tzu

I am good to people who are good.

I am also good to people who are not good.

Because Virtue is goodness.

Lao Tzu

Practicing the Meditation on Light, you come to realize that no
matter what you may or may not do, the Divine within you and
the Divinity in the universe never stop loving you. Even when
you may think all love is lost, there is always a ray of light, a

warm sensation or an echo in your heart that lets you know you are loved. Even Job declared, "Behold God is mighty and despises no one." You were conceived in nothingness, seeded with Divine intelligence, then placed into the world to experience all you know, through the quality of love. Since the heavenly Gate of Compassion is the first step into a world outside the mind, it is an indication of the importance love has over the other attributes of strength, harmony, success, and glory. Love is the stepping-stone into developing a strong character and a meaningful life.

How do you know love? By knowing God and realizing God is love. In every worldly sensation, there is an element of infinite love. This love is unconditional yet not exclusive. The one love you yearn for most is unconditional love. The one love that is hardest to give is unconditional love. Yet all other forms of love are an illusion next to unconditional love. True love is free from expectations and empty of preconceived notions. In unconditional love there are no disappointments, for there are no expectations; there are no rejections, for there are no preconceived notions. Unconditional love is giving yourself fully and receiving fully. In letting go of your own agenda and expanding the possibilities for receiving and giving love, you are able to surpass stubborn obstacles and emerge through the narrow confinements of your perception to greater visions of holiness and goodness.

According to legend, the Baal Shem Tov celebrated with his disciples the birth of Rabbi Levi Yitzchak. The Baal Shem Tov had prophesied that a spirit would come into the world who would be the embodiment of love, more than all the souls in previous times or in future times. The Baal Shem Tov saw Rabbi Levi Yitzchak's destiny as a lover of the sacredness in people. As it happened, Rabbi Levi could never see darkness, shame, or evil in people. He saw only the light, the glory, and the good. It wasn't that he was naïve about the other side, but he preferred to see only the blessed light, "even if it meant closing one eye." He loved all humankind, regardless of the abilities or disabilities of people's character, mind, or body. This was not an easy destiny, for it required steadfast trust and faith, and above all it required him to step aside from his own self and let his divinity emerge. He wrote of himself, "Until I remove the thread of hatred from my heart, I am in my own eyes, as if I did not exist."

God's love is not exclusive. This love does not discriminate between peoples, traditions, cultures, or even religions. God's love is inclusive of all creation, in all time, in every way. For all is in God, and God is in everything and everyone. You may not always be conscious of the infinite love that surrounds you; however, as you consider the things that have come into your life, from the grandiose to the minute, know that God brought them all to you. The supports and the challenges, the obvious blessings and the miracles hidden in the shadows are all from the love of God. Sometimes you may get carried away in the light, or even in the shadow, and forget that it is the love of God that is encouraging your physical well-being, emotional growth, and spiritual ascendancy.

Many stories are told of the miracles of God's love. There may even have been such stories in your own life. These stories may sound simplistic at first, yet when you are awakened to the possibilities of miracles that emanate from God's love, you will begin seeing miracles pop into the ordinary occurrences of your everyday life. For instance, there is the story of the Brisker Rebbe, Rabbi Yitzchak Zev Soloveitchik, who never doubted God's love. No matter what the problems of his disciples may have been, he would assure his disciples that when push came to shove, they would be provided with what they needed by God. One day, the rabbi was running low on medication that he ordered from Switzerland; he was supposed to take two pills a day and had only two pills left. He did not know when the next shipment would arrive. When someone suggested that he take only one pill that day and save the other for the next day, he refused. He believed that if he needed two pills a day for his health, he ought to take the two pills that day and not worry about the next day. His motto was "When you need it, it will be there." The next day a package arrived with a new shipment of pills. Another time, during the war, when food was rationed, the rabbi also lived by his motto of eating the full provision on the day it was given, in order to have the strength for serving God that day. He believed that the next day would take care of itself.

How often do you diminish the moment to save for something later? How often do you hold back from giving fully in fear that you will not have enough for next time? When you believe that God loves you always, unconditionally, then you can trust God's love, which becomes a template for how you can love others.

Imagine a world in which there is only love. Imagine living one day in the awareness that you are loved and supported totally and, in turn, are totally loving and supportive of others. If your mind is clinging to thoughts of ways in which infinite love cannot work, then ask yourself if your attachments are keeping you from being free. Pause, empty, release expectations, relinquish limiting perceptions, and be open to new ways of receiving, loving, and freeing your image of God, yourself, and others in the cosmic exchange of infinite love.

When you set conditions on loving God, yourself, or another, you build walls of limitation that cast shadows. Light and shadow cannot coexist in the same vessel. Unmet desires, plans, and expectations can lead to walls of limiting emotions such as worry, anger, and fear. These walls dispel the light and invite the temporary shadows of illusion. As these emotions occur, become fair witness to your mind and its clinging thoughts. In becoming nonjudgmental of yourself and your thoughts, feel your muscles relaxing, your energy loosening, your heart opening, and your consciousness becoming meditative and empty. In the emptiness you touch the void. Luxuriate in the nothingness and vast emptiness. It is here that you will return to the path of goodness and God. Whenever you find you are losing yourself in being critical and judgmental, pause and restart on empty.

Practice the Meditation on Light (page 116)
at least once today.

Make Peace with Suffering

Show me what this, that is happening at this very moment, means to me, what it asks of me—and what You, God, are telling me through it. Oh, it is not why I suffer, that I wish to know, but only whether I suffer for the sake of God.

Rabbi Levi Yitzchak of Berditchev

. . . return to the simplicity of formless substance.

Without form there is no desire.

Without desire there is tranquility.

And in this way all things would be at peace.

Lao Tzu

It is wonderful to pass through life and not be affected by sadness, illness, or suffering. Yet suffering touches all mortals. Just like pleasure is part of the challenge of life, so too is suffering. Clinging to thoughts of suffering, just like clinging to thoughts of pleasure, brings on pain and more suffering. Whether the pain is from loss, illness, burdens, or mishaps, it is in the illusion of the attachment that the pain dwells. When you attempt to cling to something or someone, or attach yourself to a perception of how you should live life or to an expectation of what you desire to happen, and it doesn't work out, you feel separation, anxiety, and pain. The dilemma is in the illusion of the attachment. The more you attach to something, the more you think it separates you from all else and the more dependent you become on the attachment. In nonattachment, you and the suffering or pleasure are released from expectations and free to change. For example, when a person is suffering from pain, and all he or she can think about is the pain, the pain remains vivid and unrelenting. Whether it is loss of life, of relationship, or of possessions, your attachment to the loss keeps the pain prevalent. And the pain brings on other attachments, constrictions, and more suffering. This is why you notice that when people are suffering, they seem to attract more suffering. However, if they can accept the fact that there is pain but that the pain is only one of the many aspects of their life, then the pain relents and there is more room for pleasure to enter.

When you accept suffering yet avoid attaching to its dominating all parts of your life, you can make peace with the suffering and go on. Making peace with suffering is so often necessary in people with debilitating diseases. A tragedy or disease that short-circuits their life plans, changes their lifestyle, and creates havoc in their minds, needs also to bring a semblance of meaning to their lives. Yet when the patient accepts him- or herself and the blistering storm of emotions and frustrations as part of life, he or she is free to move beyond the disease and the disability.

My friend Louis learned that he was HIV-positive some years ago. He was a successful businessman at the time. The dread of the disease changed his lifestyle drastically. At first Louis reorganized his finances, retired from his firm, and sequestered himself behind the doors of his home, wallowing in self-pity. Fortunately, he was too intelligent, vital, and faithful to remain in the closet, hidden behind the cultural stigmas associated with a sexually transmittable disease. When he was finished feeling sorry for himself, he redesigned his life and his appearance in a manner that spoke his truth and increased the vitality of his days and added meaning to his life. His whole personality changed. He looked great, sounded jovial, and was most generous. Louis uncovered an inner spark and followed his bliss, regardless of the circumstances. He found his sense of purpose when he began working on political and social-action issues. He dedicated himself to campaigning for AIDS awareness and gay rights. All the years he spent as a successful businessman were not as powerful, purposeful, and life changing as the years he spent living with the AIDS virus. Over and over again people like Louis are picking up the threads of the torn tapestries of their lives and rearranging them in new, more meaningful ways.

The answer to being at peace with suffering is in the mind. When there is right mindfulness, without clinging thoughts, you will find peace. Right mindfulness is the ability to witness the many thoughts and feelings in your inner environment without holding on to or avoiding any one of them. It is the pipe through which water flows without obstruction. There is no need to avoid the suffering. Witness, accept it, and go on with the rest of your life. What you may find is that though suffering is universal, attachment to suffering differs with individuals. What is love to one may be fear to another. What is good for you today may be bad for you tomorrow. What is bad for another may be good for you. So in suffering, as in pleasure, as in all areas of life, there is no need for judgment. There is only the acknowledgment of the moment and the feeling.

There are times when you may have suffered and, as a result of stepping outside the suffering, were able to view it from another perspective. There are numerous stories of those whose lives were changed by a particular mishap, who as a result found more meaning and purpose to their existence. There are also times when an illness does not leave totally, and you may be challenged to find a way to live with it, without being attached to its cure or dismissal. Making peace with suffering assists your spiritual and emotional growth and develops within you attributes of courage, endurance, acceptance, and flexibility. The essence of suffering does not lie in the ability to circumvent it; it lies in the ability to be at peace within the adversity.

Though the Tree of Life encourages you to be at peace with suffering, you are by no means encouraged to pursue suffering as a means to spiritual enlightenment. The kabbalists have always frowned on self-denial and self-negation. You were created as a vehicle for Divine Light, born for greatness. There have been times when students thought the way to truth and enlightenment was through fasting and separating from all worldly goods. However, their efforts substituted attachment to material possessions with attachment to self-denial. This was the case when a man came to the Maggid of Koznitz. In order to cleanse himself from evil thoughts and actions, the man wore only a sackcloth on his thin body and fasted from one Sabbath to the next each week. The Maggid took one good look at him and said, "Do you think negativity is staying away from you? It is seducing you into that sack. One who pretends to fast from one week to the next, yet secretly eats a morsel each day, is spiritually better off than you. That person is only fooling others, while you are fooling yourself."

Observe yourself fully experiencing life, not hiding from it, but rather allowing the full gamut of feelings and possible situations. Accept what is. Begin loving your limitations as though they were a gift of a new perspective, wrapped in a beautiful package that is now available to you. In the kaleidoscopic view of life, nothing is isolated; all opposites incline toward each other. While experiencing life fully, you will notice that moments of bliss are hidden in the pain, moments of joy are hidden in the suffering, forms of life are hidden in death, and eternity is hidden in impermanence.

Practice the Meditation on Light (page 116)
at least once today.

Cultivate Right-Making

A righteous person can nullify critical judgments and create new worlds.

Rabbi Noam Elimelech of Lizensk

... do not treat lightly the things that enter into a *person's* life, ... receive them for what they are and then try to make them fit tools for Enlightenment.

Buddha

As you journey the world of emotions and desire to be at peace within, review the situations of your life and notice that for every negative encounter, there is a positive possibility. The ability to turn a negative into a positive is the essence of the mystical process of living and learning. In many schools students are taught to listen critically to the material their teacher is addressing, with the intention of finding the flaw or loophole in the teacher's argument. In this way the students can excel beyond what has already been accomplished. These students learn that if they work harder or ask more informative questions they will achieve more recognition and gain greater rewards, especially the reward of expanding their own egos. A Hasidic disciple, on the other hand, listens in order to emulate the rabbi and to walk in the rabbi's footsteps. In this way of learning, the first thing a disciple would do is not hear where the rabbi went wrong but instead, listen in order to make it right. This is what is called right-making.

As you observe a situation that is not quite right, ask yourself, "What would it take for me to move into the mind-set where I could make this right?" The object is not to find flaws or to use your mind and listening skills for critical thinking, but to reverse the process. Use your mind and listening skills in a right-making perspective. Wonders and miracles occur when you enter into a right-making relationship with another, especially one whom you love and respect dearly. Doors of perception that were otherwise closed begin to open.

Right-making is a do-it-yourself process. The intention is to start on empty and then build from there, rather than to start on full and tear down. It does not necessarily mean that you or another have done something wrong that has to be corrected. Right-making is the dynamic of living consciously with a positive attitude. It is both self-correcting and self-preventative; it enables you to correct errors in judgment after they occur and, more important, reverse negative thinking before it is externalized in words or actions. This is intelligent action that is the result of spiritual awareness and mindful training.

A creative mind utilizes right-making. Whatever the creative person sees, hears, or feels is automatically turned into something interesting, refreshing, and aesthetically appealing, without preconceived judgments. There was a young artist who, after a long absence traveling the world, returned home with his new craft as a silversmith. Proud of their son, his parents invited their friends to a showing of their son's finest menorah. As each one looked at the menorah, he or she was encouraged to tell the truth about what he or she thought of it. Each one reported another flaw in the menorah. What one saw as an asset another saw as a defect. When the parents shared the reaction of their friends with the young artist, he was elated. He explained to the puzzled parents that the reactions of their friends was a confirmation of his great skill as an artist. It took artistic skill to craft a menorah that was able to reveal to each one his or her own defects and assets. What appeared to some to be a defect appeared to others a unique asset of beauty. Depending upon the perspective from which they looked, they were able to see either a defect or a unique beauty.

Like a jewel, the student's menorah could be viewed from many different aspects, each aspect unfolding new ones. With each affirmation of beauty, the menorah and its light were lifted higher and higher, to the realms above. With each right-making affirmation, you transform a flaw into an asset and raise your spirit and the spirits of those around you higher and higher.

*Practice the Meditation on Light (page 116)
at least once today.*

Become Grace and Compassion

Moses said, "Let me behold Your presence!" And *God* answered, "I will make all My goodness pass before you, and will proclaim before you the name of YHVH, and I will be gracious with graciousness, and compassionate with compassion."

Exodus 33: 18–19

Faith gives them the wisdom to recognize the transiency of life and the grace not to be surprised or grieved at whatever comes to them.

Buddha

You are born with grace. There is nothing for you to do to deserve grace; it is an ordained state of generosity, goodness, and purity that already resides in your consciousness. When you are gracious to another, grace emanates through you and serves humanity and the earth. When you begin awakening to all the positive attributes that were embedded in your system before you came into physical form, you realize how blessed and fortunate you are. This fortune, which is coded on your very being, lies dormant unless activated. You already know the result of its dormancy as you look to the world around you and see the chaos, struggle, and confusion. You also observe it at times in your own mind, as you cling to ideas and thoughts that aggrandize the ego.

In becoming grace, you start from a place of emptiness. When you empty of expectations, you open to the wonders that happen in moments and nanoseconds of revelation. With God's grace active in you, nothing can go wrong. Every thought, word, and action, when joined with grace, will be formless and serve goodness. Observe the moments when you feel you are in grace and acting graciously. Notice the joy, openness, and serenity that result from gracious action. Graciousness is displayed in generosity and in hospitality. When you greet another and give generously, you are entertaining God. When you give generously, it comes back to you manifold.

To act with grace and compassion is the path of the mystic. To relate to another human in such a manner that that person's grace and your grace mirror each other helps to heal and repair worlds. To look into another's eyes and feel his or her soul in your soul is to touch the glory of God in the depths of grace. To hear a friend speak without judging or analyzing, or to hear yourself in such an unconditional manner, is to stand in the hall of the wisdom of centuries and feel its benevolent radiance flow through you.

To sit at the bedside of a friend when there is nothing for you to do but be there, without relying on your titles, accomplishments, or need to act or react, is the essence of stillness, grace, and compassion. In a world full of activity and busyness, it is difficult to sit still. Yet compassionate action sometimes means sitting without acting—just being.

Laura was only thirty-one years old, with a rare, deadly nerve disease. She was a patient in a hospice when I went to visit her. She was propped up on a recliner, her frail body covered with blankets, her eyes red and glassy and her mind wandering in and out of consciousness. She was nearing the time of transition from this world to the next. All that she had been in her short life she was no longer. Though I was a hospice staff chaplain, I

was there to be for her in whichever way was needed. When I
entered her room, I was neither a title nor a profession nor an
expert nor a woman, nor any of those things I may call myself.
I just *was*. The visitation was filled with peaceful silence. There
was no fixing, no fussing, no appeasing, no rambling. Only
blessed, peaceful silence. We looked into each other's eyes and
held each other's soul. In the deep interchange something happened in Laura and in me. I could feel a light lift and a glow
emanate throughout the room. If grace had a melody it would
have been composed from the silence of those moments. If compassion had a sensation, it would be the sense of serenity and
freedom that accompanied the peacefulness of that sweet, deep,
and God-filled interaction. It was hard to remember when I left
her room, for the "I" of me was no longer there. I had seen the
darkness, and it was comfortable. I had floated freely in the
emptiness, and it was joyous. I had seen into the soul of another
and was embraced by the light. Laura is a spirit that lives on in
me as a memory, a moment, and an eternity of how compassion
and grace look, feel, and sound.

There was a time when grace was equated with humility and
sin was pride. This idea no longer serves in liberating men and
women from old limiting perceptions. A little pride is necessary
for growth and a positive self-image. In a rapidly changing and
spiritually evolving world, you need to acknowledge and honor
your light, while remembering you are part of a multitude of
sparks seeking their Source. In the Jewish tradition, grace is a
God-given quality that empowers all people to act and react
with faith in themselves and in their God, in serving goodness
unconditionally. When pride is lifted from the ego and placed
with spirit, men and women have a greater understanding of
the importance of acting compassionately.

Practice the Meditation on Light (page 116)
at least once today.

Serve Selflessly

The essence of *selfless* service to God is to desire, whether in public or private, to serve for the sake of God rather than for the sake of winning approval of others.

Rabbi Bachya ihn Paquda

The sage stays behind, thus *the sage* is ahead.

The sage is detached, thus at one with all.

Through selfless action *the sage* attains fulfillment.

Lao Tzu

Selfless service begins with accepting the myriad possibilities available in life. You are cultivating a spiritual path that acknowledges the supports and challenges, the confusions and frustrations, as well as peace, joy, and serenity. This path has led you to a greater acceptance and deeper appreciation of yourself and others. Being willing to share in the fullness of life's emotions enables you to serve with compassion, openness, and receptivity.

Selfless service has less to do with the self than with service. It is giving of yourself fully. It is serving others for the sole purpose of serving God, by extending godliness and goodness into the world. Rather than seek self-aggrandizement and praise, you receive fulfillment in serving others unconditionally.

Serving selflessly means giving generously, regardless of whether the person you give to is appreciative or receptive. This is why the rabbis considered one of the highest forms of selfless service to be the act of purifying and burying the deceased—for this, there is no remuneration or response—and the highest form of charity to be the act of giving anonymously. In both, neither the recipient nor the benefactor is aware of each other. This exemplifies unconditional giving. In selfless service there is no payback, only the gift of giving unconditionally.

So often people attach to the ecstasy of the spiritual path and consider going to the metaphoric mountaintop and staying there. As you feel the peacefulness and joy of meditation and simplicity, you may also be experiencing ambivalence between wanting to serve humanity and desiring to stay spiritually untainted by the chaos and confusion of the world. However, the real work is not on the mountaintop; it is in the valley with the people. The path of mystical Judaism emphasizes that the real service to God and the vision of holiness is in the valleys of the universe: in staying nonattached (even to the service itself) yet compassionate, while remaining attached to the pure, egoless intention behind the service.

The spiritually evolved being in mystical Judaism, as well as the bodhisattva in Buddhism, is dedicated to remaining in this world in order to serve humanity. Standing in the Gate of Compassion, you waver between removing your consciousness from the outside world and retreating into the mind, on the one hand, and using your intelligence to remain and help heal the external world of life, on the other. However, you have journeyed through the path of Intention and have the insights and memories necessary to carry the much-needed crown of light into the streets of the world in which you find yourself. The crown you wear is invisible; it can be ascertained only through unconditional love and selfless acts of kindness.

The archetypes for compassion and generosity are Miriam and Abraham. Abraham displayed his generosity when he was recovering from circumcision and the three messengers came to his tent. He did not hesitate to invite them in and graciously served them. Then, in another episode, at risk to himself, he put his own life on the line, when he bargained with God to save the misguided people of Sodom and Gomorrah. In walking with God, he walked in trust with abundance. In Genesis 25:5 it states that "Abraham gave all that he had to Isaac." In giving totally, Abraham started a new movement. As he gave generously, divinity was always with him.

Miriam, Moses' sister, is also a legend of generosity and started a new movement to empower women and men during a most trying time in Jewish history. She persevered with generosity, regardless of the prevailing Egyptian environment. When it was declared that all male infants of the Hebrew slaves were to be killed, the men left their wives, for fear of impregnating them and losing the children. Miriam confronted her father with having acted out of cowardice instead of faith, and took the responsibility upon herself to safeguard the male child of her parents' union. When Moses was born, Miriam guarded his safety. And when it came time to place him in the reed basket in the Nile, Miriam guarded his security. When Batya, Pharoah's daughter, adopted Moses, Miriam brought her mother, Yocheved, as the nursemaid, once again guarding the infant's vulnerability. Years later, at the crossing of the Red Sea on the Israelites' miraculous journey to freedom, it was Miriam who organized and empowered the women to dance through the waters to dry land. In her generosity, she gave fully. In the giving, she lived fully.

In selfless service, you redeem the hidden sparks imprisoned in the *klippot* of the world. Redeeming or releasing the holy Godsparks is like lighting candles. There are so many candles waiting to be lit. Lighting the candles in selfless service, you need to remain nonattached. It is difficult to light the way so others will not stumble, then to walk away nonattached. Your inclination might be to stay and light more candles, watch them glow and burn. Yet the selfless one realizes that in the lighting of just one candle, a series has begun, whereby one candle will light another, and yet another, and so on. Meanwhile, you move forward to where God calls you, without attaching to any one set of candles. Your task is not to count the candles, only to release the sparks.

As you continue the journey through this gate, be conscious of the decisions you make and the intention behind those decisions. Remember that the journey to serving goodness starts right beneath your feet and is directed to what is now in front of you. It does not discriminate between what is right or wrong, good or bad, easy or difficult. In serving God through selfless service, your reward is connecting with God through selfless service to humanity and all the myriad creations of the earth. As you practice the Meditation on Light, know that you are enveloped in goodness, crowned in light, and attached to all that is God-filled.

Practice the Meditation on Light (page 116)
at least once today.

Let Go of Mistakes

Rabbi Isaac explains the statement in Isaiah 1:18, "Though your sins should be as crimson . . . ," by saying: The Holy One has said, even if your sins were as numerous as the years that have stretched from the six days of creation until now, they would still become as white as snow.

Rabbi Jacob ibn Chabib

If *one* looks upon the world with defiled eyes dimmed by ignorance, *one* will see it filled with error; but if *one* looks upon it with clear wisdom, *one* will see it as the world of Enlightenment, which it is.

Buddha

Mistakes happen. Even when you are enveloped in light and serve goodness, mistakes happen. But if you dwell on past mistakes you will become preoccupied with yourself. Even though the journey of the spiritual seeker is within him- or herself, your intention is not to remain in the self but to connect with the Infinite and to serve goodness in the world. When you dwell on past mistakes, you cling to energy that can be put to better use in serving goodness.

The day after his wedding, Rabbi Eliezer's new son-in-law visited him. He was distraught over past transgressions and needed to absolve himself with Rabbi Eliezer. He even felt that his beard and hair had turned white with the stress of not repenting enough. "O my friend," Rabbi Eliezer replied, "you are obsessed with yourself. Consider forgetting yourself for a moment and start thinking of the world." In speaking to his son-in-law, Rabbi Eliezer was speaking also to us. His concise words leave us with an essential message: Do not waste your energy on past mistakes; instead, put the power of your soul into moving forward toward your destiny. Self-reproach is wasteful and damages your spirit. It is important to stop blaming yourself or feeling embarrassed or ashamed of past mistakes and failures, and to return to your true nature. You were born of Divine will, inhabit a Divine nature, and are here to fulfill a destiny.

Each time you stray from the path, you have the flexibility and courage to return. Return, known in Hebrew as *teshuvah,* was built into the foundational structure of the universe. The ability to return, to turn around and turn about, existed before you were created and is programmed into your being. It is available for you to choose when it is needed and you so desire. The word *teshuvah* also implies a response: as you select to return or turn about, you need to know what it is you are turning to. You need to respond to the inner call with an intention and focus. As you let go of mistakes, you return to your own divine nature, to the uniqueness of who you are, and above all, to reunion with an unconditionally loving God. In returning, you access memory of the void from which you emanated, with a clearer sense of freedom in moving toward the destiny you were born to fulfill.

Reb Zalman Schachter-Shalomi tells the story of a disciple who had committed every kind of error and transgression and who was ready to be punished, even if it meant death, in order to be absolved from his guilt and free himself from shame. The disciple went to his rabbi to confess his reprehensible crimes against nature and humanity. With a squinted eye piercing through bifocal lenses, the rabbi carefully looked into the soul of the disciple, and after a few moments of silence that seemed like an eternity, the rabbi pronounced his decree: death. "However," said the rabbi, "you cannot be put to death yet; you need need to wait one year." There had to be one year of *teshuvah,* during which the disciple would right all the wrongs before receiving the death penalty. The year passed, and the disciple returned. When he came to the rabbi's study he was prepared to die. The rabbi pointed to a chair; the disciple seated himself and awaited his execution. Death was to be administered by pouring hot lead down his throat. The disciple sat willingly in the chair, ready to give his soul over to the hot lead. While mixing the liquid, the rabbi asked the disciple to recite the traditional confessional one recites before death. In a quivering voice the disciple recited the confessional, tears streaming down his face, images of the love he experienced in the past year filling his mind and remorse for a life wasted filling his heart. The rabbi dipped the ladle into the hot liquid and carefully brought it to the lips of the disciple. As he began pouring it down the man's throat, the disciple realized that instead of hot lead, he was drinking honey. The disciple coughed in surprise and then asked the rabbi why he had tricked him, for he was totally prepared to die. "When you are ready to die," said the rabbi, "there is no longer a need to suffer. Now you are truly ready to let go and live." The rabbi explained that all transgressions can be transformed into deeds of goodness, just as hot lead can be transformed into honey. In arriving at the place where you are no longer consumed with the past and are ready to die in the old, you are born anew.

Without the ability to let go of past mistakes and turn wrongs into rights, you would find it impossible to reside in this world. At the completion of this day, notice if you are carrying mental and emotional weights filled with misplaced judgments, misguided communication, false responses, failed attempts, broken promises, shattered expectations, or any other mistakes for which you blame yourself or others. Notice how heavy and tense your body feels just by thinking about them.

Now acknowledge that these mistakes were placed in your path in order to assist you in growing to the next stage of your spiritual development. Along with these errors comes the ability to return. Turn the wrongs into rights in your imagination. Travel through the dynamics of this day with a right-making state of mind. Then take this opportunity to return to your true nature, to the purpose for which you were born—to carry the light of God. Be aware that in letting go of mistakes you have cleared the path for your spirit to soar to the upper realms and carry you into the center of miraculous, Divine happenings.

Practice the Meditation on Light (page 116)
at least once today.

For-Give

YHVH, YHVH, God filled with compassion and mercy, slow to anger and abundant in love and truth. *The One* who administers greatness to thousands, forgives our transgressions.

Exodus 34:6–7

The world is always burning, burning with the fires of greed, anger and foolishness; one should flee from such dangers as soon as possible.

Buddha

Healers, teachers, leaders, spirit beings, literate souls, and illiterate souls all have much in common. They can all create new environments of experience and effect positive, healing transformation in this world and in all worlds by simply forgiving and being forgiven. On the deepest level, whether you are aware of it or not, forgiveness has already occurred. It is waiting for anger and shame to subside in order to be recognized.

In letting go of your errors and mistakes, you are handed the seventh insight in the Gate of Compassion, the insight to forgive yourself. There is little difference between forgiving yourself and forgiving another; the refusal to do either can inhibit the spirit, congest the mind, and constrict the energy flow. Yet being forgiving is a process and spiritual practice. You cannot summarily dismiss feelings like anger, frustration, disappointment, and resentment that keep you from the generosity of forgiveness. You can only observe yourself as you are immersed in the fullness of your feeling and be mindful of the waves of thoughts moving in and out of your inner consciousness and outer experiences. Notice how these feelings affect your communications. They affect how you react to the one who you feel wronged you, and how he or she reacts to you. Allow your feelings to reveal themselves to you free of judgment. Accept the feelings without defining or analyzing whether they are good or bad. Accept them simply as a part of the life you are now living.

God created the full range of feelings you are now experiencing. These feelings were created in order for you to live life fully. As you observe how you utilize and access these feelings, you come to know yourself more intimately. What you begin to recognize is that there is infinite energy flowing through you that is beyond what you are feeling. However, your feelings affect its flow and stamina. When you experience feelings that constrict your mind, tighten your muscles, and stress your nervous system, the energy flow becomes blocked. The blocked energy creates an illusion of competition. You and the one who you feel wronged you begin competing not only for who is right and who is wrong, but also for who will receive the most and the least amount of energy from this discontent. When your energy feels depleted, it is because you have used it up in clinging to your point of view and the fear of losing the competition. It is like playing tug-of-war: the energy is the rope you hold on to for dear life. With closer observation you may notice that the energy competition is all an illusion, for there is plenty of energy that emanates from the Infinite Source. Yet when you are blinded by anger and other limiting perceptions, you are also blinded to the real source of energy. The moment you let go and return to your divinity, you will notice that your energy is replenished by God.

"Forgiving" may appear as one word, but in its inner meaning, there are two words, "for" and "giving." Forgiving has less to do with another and more to do with giving to yourself —giving yourself the freedom to release tightness, let go of competition, unveil illusions of boundaries and limits. When you for-give you are giving simplicity back to chaos, joy back to anger, love back to fear, and expansiveness back to constriction.

From the moment you entered this world, you were given a light to carry, which increased or diminished according to your thoughts, words, and actions. In acknowledging your wrongs and mistakes, even your difficulty in forgiving others, you arrive at unconditional acceptance of yourself and your changeability. In the acceptance, you are better able to view with humor the predicaments you get yourself into, which may feel irreparable at the moment and may seem silly thereafter. In the process of forgiveness, you have the opportunity to witness, reflect, accept, let go, empty, open, and regenerate. Forgiveness is not so much for another as it is for you. For-giving is opening the generosity of your spirit and the wisdom of your understanding to a life that holds the truth of many interchanging and interconnecting forms of reality. All the variations of experiences are here for you to become more intimate with yourself, your God, and life on earth.

In forgiving yourself and others, you open to the strength that awaits you in the next heavenly Gate of Strength. With love in your heart, step through the light of goodness and enter the path of strength and discernment.

Practice the Meditation on Light (page 116)
at least once today.

STRENGTH

When you serve God through God's compassion, you empower yourself with greater strength, elevate your mind with higher thoughts, and soar with the angels. This is what is called "complete service."

Baal Shem Tov

Now, it's because I'm compassionate
that I therefore can be courageous.

Lao Tzu

WHAT KEEPS YOU MOVING, regardless of the obstacles, restraints, and snags along the way? What quality within yourself has assisted you in championing your own truth while nurturing others and promoting justice in the world? Strength. In the heavenly Gate of Strength you will experience strength that is expansive, not confining; supportive, not coercive; and liberating, not impeding. As you journey the Gate of Strength you will become the shaman who knows when to empty and when to fill, when to push forward and when to pull back. With Strength you will look within, face your fears, and move beyond them. You will have an opportunity to transcend jealousy, doubt, and insecurity through strengthening your bond with God and the godliness in all things. With discretion and discernment, you will traverse the trails and trials ahead. With discipline, courage, perseverance, and conviction, you will clear a passage through the fiery swords of challenge, where a new vision of holiness and power awaits your arrival.

The Gates of Compassion and Strength temper and activate each other. Strength and discernment energize compassion, fuel unconditional love, and build the structure for continuing freedom and serving goodness. They are the path of cutting through filters and entanglements with a shattering blast, rather than a gentle blow. The ones who see and hear through the lenses of strength and discernment are not intimidated by the many shades of reality or the extremes of emotions. Strength is the dynamic energy that accompanies the gentility of Compassion.

It is the mystery that makes unconditional love happen, and vice versa. The two paths work in tandem. Each gives the other what it lacks, and in the process, the heart emerges holding both high.

Strength is the courage that frees you from stagnation and the discipline that frees you from weakness of mind, body, and spirit. It is the negative-karma stopper that protects the new and facilitates change in the old. It is the decipherer of time and the keeper of the rhythm of the heart. For every act of compassion, there is a pillar of strength holding it up. For every act of altruism, strength injects the color of pragmatism. Strength sheds light on the impermanent and strengthens its commitment to the eternal by its ability to overcome obstacles.

Before entering the heavenly Gate of Strength and turning to the first insight, pause and reflect on the Meditation on Guidance. This meditation will help you realize that you are never alone. There is always a sacred being available within you who will help you overcome obstacles with wisdom, understanding, compassion, and strength. To benefit from the meditation, read it slowly. Pause between each sentence and experience what you have read. Then spend a moment or two enveloped in the peace that results. Review the meditation on guidance after reading and contemplating each of the insights.

⟡ Meditation on Guidance ⟡

Pause a moment and sit comfortably in a chair or on the floor. Feel the breath moving in and out of your body as you inhale deeply and exhale fully. With each inhalation feel yourself becoming profoundly calm and relaxed. With each exhalation feel yourself ascending beyond the vast emptiness of your mind into a sanctuary of radiant light. As you enter the sanctuary of light, you are welcomed by a spirit who has awaited your arrival. This spirit has come to assist and guide you on your journey. Before taking the next step, pause, ask, empty, open, learn, and receive what you need in order to move forward. Thank the source of guidance and return refreshed and renewed to this world in which you dwell. Guidance from the spirit who dwells in the sanctuary of light is available to you whenever you pause, empty, and become still.

Practice Self-Discipline and Discretion

It is written that every individual should choose one obser-
vance and keep it very strictly, with all its fine points . . .
however, you should not be abnormally strict to the point
of foolishness.

Rabbi Nachman of Breslov

The person who is attached to things will suffer much.

The person who saves will suffer heavy loss.

The contented *person* is never disappointed.

The person who knows when to stop never finds himself *or*
herself in trouble.

This person will stay forever safe.

Lao Tzu

Self-denial is frowned upon in mystical Judaism. Your journey
to God is a journey of wholeness and joy, not ascetic abstinence.
A disciple of Rabbi Yaakov Yitzchak, the Seer of Lublin, once
fasted from Sabbath to Sabbath in order to cleanse his character
and draw near to God. On Friday afternoon, an hour before the
fast was completed, he had such a thirst he thought he was

going to die. He leaned over a well, and in the last instant before touching the water, he thought he could withstand another hour of thirst instead of destroying the whole week's fasting. As he left the well, he was touched by the pride of having completed a difficult task; he therefore went back to the well so as not to be caught in the snares of pride. As he reached into the well, his thirst disappeared, and he did not break his fast after all. When Sabbath arrived, he was greeted by his rabbi, the Seer of Lublin, who called out to him only one word, "Patchwork!" What the rabbi meant was that no matter how difficult the task, asceticism is not the way to God. "Patchwork" indicates a fragmented journey. When the form becomes so stringent that it causes you overconcern, then the substance for which the form was created suffers. The opposite of patchwork is wholeness. How can you achieve wholeness? With self-discipline and discretion.

In the Gate of Strength, you are in partnership with your God image. As you move in leadership roles and become more empowered, it is increasingly important to maintain self-discipline. This means that you set up goals, boundaries, a structure by which you will achieve your goals, and the time frame in which you are to complete the task. And then you discipline yourself to follow through. However, this is only half of the story. The other half has to do with God's role in the partnership. You may have your structure in place, yet if it is not according to God's plans it will not come to fruition, or it will cause you undue suffering if you attach yourself to it. So the real strength is in disciplining yourself to be prepared, then letting go and letting God take over. In essence, the best self-discipline is in the spiritual skill and practice of nothingness. Discipline yourself to empty, open, and release old limiting patterns, clinging thoughts, and attachments to having things go your way.

As you increase in preparation, you attune to the fine points of discretion. Being discreet means being willing to be there for another without either diminishing the other's power or strength. It means having the patience to listen consciously without judging; to act appropriately without needing to change another; to serve with compassion without altering another's beliefs or attitudes; to accept without analyzing; to empower without intimidation.

Being self-disciplined and discreet carries over into all areas of life. In determining your own guidelines, you may find helpful the following guidelines for wholesome sacred living, from Rabbi Moses Cordovero:

1. Do not be forced into anger.

2. Do not harm the body by overeating.

3. Always tell the truth. (Stay away from gossip.)

4. Accept both the supports and challenges of life.

5. Mentally review your actions of the day before each meal and before going to sleep at night.

Each time you move into nothingness and empty, you will follow the above guidelines effortlessly. When you begin knowing when it is time to stop and retreat into nothingness, you will know the essence of discretion and the ease of discipline. Continue to meditate on guidance and allow the inner voice to lead the way.

Practice the Meditation on Guidance (page 146)
at least once today.

Cultivate Strength and Discernment

Do not distort justice, nor favor people, nor take bribes,
for a bribe blinds the eyes of the wise, and perverts the
words of the righteous.

Deuteronomy 16:19

Better stop short than fill to the brim.

Oversharpen the blade, and the edge will soon blunt.

Amass a store of gold and jade, and no one can protect it.

Claim wealth and titles, and disaster will follow.

Retire when the work is done.

This is the way of heaven.

Lao Tzu

With strength and discernment comes the need to pause, to
stop, and to remember your goal and its intention. There are
many issues at hand, many options for you to choose, many
trails to explore. Yet with the power of strength and the wisdom
of discernment, this is the time for you to pause and reevaluate
your direction. This opportunity occurs with each step you take
and with each gift you receive along the way, both large and
small. Strength calls on you to stop, and discernment beckons

your attention to the details of your life. When you are in the midst of growth and movement, it takes strength and skill to pull back and pause. In the stillness you will regroup your energy and peel back to what is essential to your growth. With discerning wisdom you will notice and experience what is relevant and integral to your growth and to serving goodness. You will also begin to see through the veils of illusion and the filters of shaded light to the real truth and brilliant radiance of what awaits you on your journey forward. Your destination is the eternal ecstasy for which you strive. It is the union with the Infinite to which you journey. Beware of the seductive self-aggrandizing, temporary pleasures that deter your passage and delay your goals.

Rabbi Zalman Schachter-Shalomi tells the story of his journey with Reb Hayyim Elya, who was discussing the probabilities of Elijah, the prophet of peace, appearing in the garment of a Jew. Reb Zalman thought Elijah could come robed in any garment of any tradition, not just Jewish. He said, "God sent Elijah into the world to help us become aware that there is righteousness in everyone, regardless of their religious inclination." As they journeyed forward, Reb Hayyim Elya noticed a commoner sleeping along the path. If their discussion held any relevance, this man could possibly be considered the Messiah too. As the man awoke, they began conversing, and Reb Hayyim Elya found out that this man, who was not Jewish, was selling goatskins used for scribing sacred texts and holy prayers. Being a scribe, Reb Hayyim Elya examined the skins. They were smooth and light, the most exceptional skins he had ever seen and handled. He was willing to buy them at any price. The man named a price that was way beyond what Reb Hayyim Elya could afford. However, the rebbe offered him whatever was in his purse, and the man agreed. As the rebbe began emptying his purse, instead of the copper pennies he thought he had, gold coins in abundance poured forth. He was dumbfounded by the wealth. Yet he had promised the man that he would pay all that was in his purse for the goatskin, and that is what he did, though the coins were well over the worth of the skins. They exchanged the coins for the skins and then the man announced he had reached his destination. He leaped out of the wagon and vanished into the forest. Reb Zalman turned to Reb Hayyim Elya and spoke. "What we witnessed was, first, that in the eyes of God, sacred text and holy prayers are worth more than gold. Second, that Elijah can arrive disguised as a Jew or as a Gentile, as a farmer or as a salesman."

It was destined that Reb Hayyim Elya would write sacred texts on that parchment, for whoever purchased that parchment from him received extra protection. And the parchment made from those goatskins held the healing power of Moses and the souls who accompanied him at the time of the revelation at Sinai. The benefits derived from the goatskins far outweighed their price.

As you walk the path of strength and discernment, attune your ears to hearing the voice of God in all sounds, and open your eyes to seeing wonders in many guises. Look for the mystery behind the obvious and discern the truth beneath the veil of illusion. And in the words of Rabbi Levi Yitzchak of Berdichev, ask God to reveal the essence to you: "Show me one thing. Show it to me more clearly and deeply. Show me what this, which is happening at this very moment, means to me—what it demands of me—what You, Lord of the World, are telling me by way of it." Meditate on guidance and you will hear.

Practice the Meditation on Guidance (page 146)
at least once today.

Seek Justice Without Judgment

And behold a young lion roared against *Samson;* and the
spirit of YHVH came to him with strength, and he tore
the lion asunder as one tears a lamb; and he had nothing
in his hand, and he neither told his father nor mother what
he had done.

Judges 14:6

What is valued in the Way is its formlessness. Be formless,
and you cannot be repressed or oppressed; you cannot be
measured or figured out.

Huainanzi

To journey on the path of justice you need to be strong and
remain formless. Justice is not as much right or wrong as it is
the middle path between two rights or two wrongs. There are
so many choices today and very little that is totally right or
totally wrong. What may be totally right for today may change
and become totally wrong tomorrow. What is totally right for
you may be totally wrong for another. Even death is not totally
right or totally wrong, and depends on circumstances. Life also

dances on the middle road that rotates between journeying toward and journeying from God. And you spend a lot of time on the axis rotating between these two directions.

The path of justice is neither straight nor narrow. The path includes sudden angles and slippery corners that change and transform as you change and transform. Whether you follow the side roads or the main drag, all paths have a line down the middle that is the most equitable vantage point for maintaining strength and remaining just. All paths eventually lead to the mountaintop of the spirit, where the noblest part of you visits with the most accessible yet formless part of God.

To visit God and access your nobility you need to start on empty and cultivate nothingness. God is nothingness. When your strength is in nothingness, then any challenge that approaches can be observed and countered with the spirit of emptiness and with faith in God. This action does not negate your responsibility; rather, it increases your calm, your trust, and your mindfulness in the face of challenge. As a result, your ability to respond sharpens. When you meet the turbulence with calm, you disarm your challengers. When you witness the opposition clearly, you remain calm; you neutralize their strength and loosen their attachments. This is true whether your opponents are outside or inside yourself.

In nothingness there is no judgment, only judicious action. When your mind is clear and empty it does not judge; it accepts the challenge or challenger for what or who they are. Where there is no judgment of good or bad, right or wrong, pass or fail, there is no fear. There is only the spirit of nothingness, the essence of God.

Walking the path of justice means doing the appropriate thing without criticizing yourself or another in the process. It takes strength of character to remain nonjudgmental in the face of fear or in the act of justice. Yet nonjudgment is sometimes the strength one needs to overcome obstacles. With nonjudgment you have the strength to show compassion to an abusive parent, a demanding boss, a manipulative competitor.

It takes strength to be nonjudgmental of yourself, even as you fall or falter; and to be able to get up, brush yourself off, and continue on the just path without self-criticism or self-denial.

When Samson was on his way to meet the parents of his bride-to-be, a young lion roared toward him. Not having any means of protection, Samson paused, and the spirit of God entered and gave him strength. He rent the lion as though it were a lamb. The passage in Judges goes on to say, "He had nothing in his hand, and he didn't tell his parents," who were following behind. That the passage mentions he had nothing in his hand indicates his simplicity and formlessness at the moment of attack. That he did not run and tell his parents is a further indication that when the spirit of God entered him with an other than human strength, his ego was not attached.

What happened to Samson has been known also to happen today. A mother who sees her child threatened by an oncoming car has been known to lift the car sufficiently to save her child. A sudden burst of strength that came through her system enabled her to do this.

How have you wrestled with the lions that threaten your security? These lions are those established norms that you may fear yet dare not battle. These are the lions of authority, inequality, discrimination, injustice, cruelty, intimidation, impersonalization. Or they could be the lions of poverty, disability, futility, and depression. These lions block opportunities for self-responsibility, self-determination, and self-improvement in areas that touch your mind, your spirit, and your body. So often we run from the lions and tear at ourselves and others with criticism, blame, and fear, all in the name of justice. However, when the spirit of God enters and gives you strength, you no longer need to fear the roar of the lion. Instead, you become a formless vehicle through which a Divine destiny is fulfilled.

It takes a wise and spiritually seasoned person to be able to sit in a cold, intimidating room full of power-driven, ego-filled politicians who are arguing over diplomatic protocol, and to remain formless, quiet, and alert. At just the right moment, the spirit of God fills her formlessness with the wisdom and understanding to speak compassionately and act justly. Then with one swift statement she disarms the untamed lions of bureaucracy. This is what my friend Florence Ross did at a diplomatic conference in the USSR during the Cold War, when she stood up in front of the American and Russian delegations and told them "to stop acting like little boys playing one-upmanship" and get on with the work of peace! Had she not remained formless, and instead been intimidated by her surroundings and filled with self-judgments, she would not have felt the spirit of God in the wisdom of her thoughts or words.

What does it mean to be formless? And how does that require strength and effect justice? When you are formless, there is no form to which anyone or any thought can attach. When you are nonattached, you are walking the middle point in the road, between two directions. This enables you to view both directions and all thoughts with right mindfulness. Right mindfulness that witnesses without judging encourages right action. Right action flows from a clear mind, with clear intention. Nonjudgment observes without analyzing, accepts without criticizing, and acts with virtue through right action. Right action is always just. In this way, through nonjudgment comes just action. And all of this can be accomplished only with strength of mind to act willfully. It takes greater strength to act with focus and restraint than to act uncontrollably.

In choosing the path of justice, remember that what fosters goodness, unconditional love, compassion, and freedom is what strengthens the spirit of God in you. As you continue the day, notice the areas over which you assert control. Is the control a manipulation of strength, or a manifestation of godliness? In projecting your values on another, are you acting justly, or authoritatively? In manipulating your own thoughts and the many parts of your personality, are you observing without judging and remaining calm, or are you impassioned, anxious, and frustrated? Pause, empty, and relax in the calmness of meditation, and notice how quickly you can neutralize the battling forces of your mind and your life.

Practice the Meditation on Guidance (page 146)
at least once today.

Free the Sacrificial Lambs

God said:

Let one who has a bullock bring a bullock. Let one who has a ram bring a ram . . . Let one who has a dove bring a dove. Let one who has none of these bring a flour offering. And let one who has no flour bring words.

Rabbi Tanchuma

If they could rid themselves of these discriminations and keep their minds pure with the light of wisdom, then they would see only one world in which everything is meaningful.

Buddha

The time for human sacrifice is over. Too many generations and too much negative energy were given over to the sacrifices of the past. Throughout the ages too many children and adults have been slain as lambs of God. They were led to their slaughter in order to appease the angers, jealousies, and fears of the gods and the people. There was also a time when humans were replaced by animals on the fire altars of the gods. The qualities of the animals were offered as a symbolic gesture of elevating those same qualities within the people, such as strength, humility, agility, and flexibility. Then the time came when the altars of fire were dismantled and the courts of injustice were erected. In the courts of injustice, humans sacrificed one another by blaming and maiming through thoughts, words, and actions. It is time to release the lambs of God and to extinguish the fires of destruction.

There is no longer a need to destroy one another to feed the flames of fear, doubt, and insecurity. With the insights you have gathered along the spiritual journey of life, you can now erect a new form of altar and a new way of being sacred in the world. As you build this new altar, you begin to understand what it means to be sacred. The word "sacrifice" does not mean to do without; it means to make sacred, to lift toward a higher purpose. In Hebrew the word for sacrifice is *karbon* (plural: *karbonot*), meaning "to draw nearer" to God. It is a gift of a quality or matter within yourself that you offer as a way of ascending closer to the Source, for serving a more meaningful purpose in your life.

The Divine attribute of Strength is considered the sacrificial shaman of ancient tradition. The archetype for Strength is Isaac, who was bound on the altar of his father, Abraham. In the time when fathers took their sons from the laps of their mothers into the wilds of ritual death, Abraham, whose name meant "compassion," bound Isaac, whose name meant "joy and laughter," upon the altar of his God. According to the biblical tale, Abraham was following an inner voice, doing what he thought God wanted of him, to sacrifice his son as a lamb of God. The morning he asked his son to accompany him to the far fields, he explained to Isaac and his mother, Sarah, that father and son were going to a great house of study in a far-off place. Little did Abraham know that the great house of study was waiting to teach him a new lesson in a new way of being, without human sacrifices. As soon as Abraham's knife neared Isaac's neck, an angel's voice called out, "Do not stretch out your hand against the boy." Awakening to the message, Abraham, rather than sacrificing his son, seized a ram in the bushes and offered that to God. As the bindings were loosened from the weight of his body, Isaac knew what it meant to die and be reborn. The time for human sacrifices had come to an end. The time for killing laughter and joy in the service of love had ceased.

As a symbol for the sacrificial ram, who is no longer sacrificed, there is the roar of the shofar, the ram's horn. The shofar is symbolic of the voice of God heard generations later at the revelation at Sinai. It symbolizes awakening to the end of the negativity that results from people intimidating one another in the fires of destruction for the name of God. It is the symbol of awakening to the end of jealousies, fears, doubts, and insecurities in the name of God. It is the sound of awakening to the spark of God that resides in every atom of creation, in every breath of the human, in every vision of the universe. The sound is both sharp and subtle, loud and soft. It can be seen as well as heard, and above all, it can be felt in the silence of the peace that abides within your soul.

The blood offering of your soul is in the words you speak and the feelings you communicate. May they be words that elevate another, illuminate your world, and radiate your image of God within. As you conclude this insight, consider the ways you come nearer to God, and let them be in the gifts you offer to a higher Source, for a purpose that serves the greater goodness of humanity.

Practice the Meditation on Guidance (page 146)
at least once today.

Free Yourself

Behold I will come to you in the thickness of a dark cloud,

where the people will hear Me.

Exodus 19:9

Mastering others requires force;

Mastering the self needs strength.

Lao Tzu

Freedom is within. It is liberation from expectations and limiting perceptions. In doing nothing, you are free from all things. In serving from a state of formlessness, you are free from results. In feeling the vast flowing emptiness, you are free from attachments. In emptying the mind, you are free from clinging thoughts. Your sense of freedom depends on the state of emptiness that exists within you.

When the Israelites were three months gone from Egypt, God asked them to recall the miracles and wonders of their passage. God had lifted them on the wings of eagles, and they ascended the upper realms. They remembered how in the heavens they were touched by holiness, showered in sanctity, and anointed as noble beings. They vowed never to forget the covenant with God, a covenant of memory, "to remember God." And they knew God's glory was embedded in each one of them as they passed through the light of that moment of freedom.

Freedom is wherever you choose to see and hear it, through the lens of your own perception. God can appear even in a thick dark cloud, much as happened to the Israelites. The dark cloud was a symbol for the people to accept all the possibilities and forms in which God can be found: the afternoon's sunlight, the rainy days, the dark ominous clouds of a summer storm. God is in all of them. The open, accepting reception of friends, the intimidating controls of authorities, the chaos and confusion of disturbing relationships—God is in all of them. As you remember the covenant of memory, then even in thick dark clouds, those who choose to hear hear the voice of God, and those who choose to see see the glory through the filters of the cloud.

Miriam Bokser Caravella, a writer who journeyed the Eastern Bodhisattva path and integrated it with her traditional Jewish background, used the following illustration of freedom in her book *The Holy Name*. A charitable person was visiting a prison that was overcrowded with a large number of inmates. Seeing that there was no running water, the charitable person sent in a truck to bring in fresh water to the prisoners. The fresh water greatly improved the situation in the prison. Next, a second benevolent person visited the prison. Disturbed by the quality of food that the prisoners were receiving, the second benevolent person sent in a truckload of quality food. The prisoners were grateful to this person also for improving their situation. Then a third benevolent person visited the prison and felt the chill in the air, and noticed that there wasn't an adequate heating system to keep the prisoners warm in the winter. So this benevolent person sent in a truckload of warm blankets to cover the prisoners in the cold, for which the prisoners were most grateful. Caravella explains that they had now improved their environment from being class C prisoners to being class A prisoners. Yet they were still prisoners. That is, until the fourth visitor came and gave them the keys to the prison, and this freed the people forever. This fourth visitor was the greatest benefactor, the one who gave them the keys.

When God came in a thick dark cloud and proclaimed that you could hear God even in the cloud, that pronouncement was akin to the benefactor's giving prisoners keys to the prison. The greatest freedom of all is to realize that you no longer need to live imprisoned by expectations and self-imposed limitations, for in that freedom you recognize your own divine nature. In the mansion of life there are many doors, but none as liberating as the door that leads to the throne room of God. In that room is the vast freedom of emptiness, the awesome sense of holiness, and the possibility of being everything.

As you meditate on guidance today, as you near the sanctuary of light, imagine you are entering the throne room of God, and from that place deep within yourself, hear the spirit of holiness.

Practice the Meditation on Guidance (page 146)
at least once today.

Accept Love and Fear

I heard from my master *the Baal Shem Tov* . . . that love and
fear can only exist together when one is serving God.

Rabbi Yaakov Yosef of Polonoye

Because the sage always confronts difficulties,
The sage never experiences them.

Lao Tzu

How often do you fear you are going to lose love, and how often
do you love in order to keep your fears intact? Recall times
when you have felt love and times you have felt fear. Notice
how open you have been in unmasking your feelings and accepting them as they arrive at the door of your heart. If it is fear
that knocks, then open to the fear. See it for what it is and
decide how long you will visit with it. Notice whether you let
it take over your mind or you maintain faith and trust in the
Source of your own power. Also be on alert whether it is your
fear or another's you are welcoming in. Too often another's fears
erode the serenity of your mind. This is especially true when
two people are intimately bonded.

It is difficult to not take on the fear or anxiety of your partner.
It is necessary for the health of the partnership to remain compassionate yet nonattached. When you feel yourself falling prey
to the anxieties and fears of another, this is the time to act with

inner strength, discernment, and spiritual insight. The insights you are receiving on this journey will help you.

When love knocks at the door of your mind, be mindful whether it is a guest or a guise. There are times when you think you are acting out of love, but in reality you are acting out of fear. For instance, when you treat someone less fortunate than you with kindness, are you doing it out of love for them, or out of fear of becoming less fortunate yourself? When you give your boss a gift, are you doing it because you love your boss, or are you afraid of losing your boss's favor? And how about when someone seeks a favor from you and treats you like his or her best friend? Is this love or fear? This mindfulness does not mean that you need to be mistrusting. It only beckons you to remain nonattached and compassionate. Be mindful of your actions and maintain inner balance.

It would certainly simplify matters to be able to say that there are two basic emotions, love and fear. Yet to know love as separate from fear is illusion. There is a saying within the Jewish mystical tradition that every spiritual initiate should have two pockets in his or her garment. In one pocket should be a piece of paper that says love, in the other pocket a piece of paper that says fear. The journey of life wavers between the two emotions, and the interchange between love and fear is in the one who wears the garment. The spiritual initiate begins to realize that these two emotions do not exist separate from each other.

Some traditions say that in one pocket the initiate should carry the statement "The world was created for you today." In the other pocket should be a piece of paper that says: "You are but a speck of dust in the vastness of this universe." Which message would go into the pocket with love and which would go into the pocket with fear? At first, you may think that being only a speck of dust is frightening. On second thought, being responsible for the world being created is an awesome and frightening task. Be aware also that what you choose today may change tomorrow. Both are true, and neither can be categorized as all love or all fear, all good or all bad. In the interchange, the two are interconnected.

The quicker you admit your fears, the sooner they will leave. You are in command of the feelings you choose to have. Witness your choices and transform your attitude from one of criticism to one of acceptance and transformation. Fear hiding in the mask of love will intoxicate your senses and spray toxic negativity into your mind. Yet fear that is exposed and transformed into love refreshes and cleanses your perception, enlightens your mind, and enlivens your life. Shower your fears with the clear waters of love, not the murky waters of denial.

Practice the Meditation on Guidance (page 146)
at least once today.

Journey Beyond Fear

Do not fear, for I am your protector;

I have called you by name, you are Mine,

If you pass through waters, I am with you—

through rivers, they will not drown you.

If you walk through fire, you will not be scorched—

through flame, it will not consume you.

For I am God your God, the Holy One of Israel,

   your Savior.

Isaiah 43:1–3

The Way gives birth to them, nourishes them, matures them, completes them, rests them, rears them, supports them, and protects them.

Lao Tzu

What is your greatest fear? The kabbalists say that there are two kinds of fears, external fear and internal fear. External fear is the fear of losing the things we value in the outside world, like honor, wealth, health, or life. Internal fear is the fear of losing a sense of the Divine within yourself, of disconnecting from what makes you sacred. The internal fear of losing your soul is the greatest fear, for without your soul you have no life. The Baal Shem Tov said the greatest loss is not the loss of heart, but the loss of God in your heart.

Fear is an illusion. If the greater fear is internal fear and the worst internal fear is that of losing your soul, then it is illusion. You can never lose your soul. If your soul is connected to God, and God is everlasting and eternal, then God can never be lost. Only in your imagination can you lose God, but God is not lost in the world. Yet internal fear, even if it is an illusion, motivates you to stay conscious of living a soul-filled life and to take advantage of the miracle of each moment. And it also beckons you to move beyond your fears.

Life is like a hallway with many doors leading to various rooms of experience. Some people remain in the familiar safety of the hallway, locked in their fear. These people are stuck in the hallway of life. They are afraid to venture forth through new doors; they do not grow beyond who they have already been. Others venture out of the hallway to enter the room of philosophers and skeptics; they spend their time discoursing on the qualities of life, yet evade the experience of living. Then there are others, who walk through the hallway of their fears and enter the room of believers and mystics. In this room they find a celebration of emotions and an array of varied experiences.

To enter the room of mystics and believers, you need to have a desire to envision the sacred, hear your soul, and detach from fear. This desire cannot be achieved through talk, but only through the profound experience of meditation. Meditation gives you a sense of the sacred, enables you to hear your soul, and effortlessly detaches fears from your consciousness.

Deepak Chopra, in his book *Unconditional Living,* explains that the experience of sitting meditation can be best described not by what you do, but by what you are not doing. You are not confusing your mind by dwelling on an idea. Your thoughts move effortlessly as you travel past inner voices to the silent observer within. In the slowing down, in the stillness and the silence, you become like a candle in a windless place. In the meditation process, you do not need to detach from your fears; your fears automatically detach from you. In this way, Deepak Chopra proclaims, even one meditation can change your life, for it allows you to release your fears.

My friend and teacher Dr. Joan Kaye was hosting a Tibetan student for several months. This young girl had never left the sheltering hills and ancient lifestyle of her Tibetan village. Needless to say, arriving in America was a culture shock for which no language could have prepared her adequately. But having been weaned on meditation, simplicity, and the power of emptiness, she adjusted to the radical change from expansive spaciousness to crowded cities, from slow and even-paced movements to the vigorous raciness of city streets, from the timelessness of the countryside to the timeliness of urbanity. Throughout her stay, she held on to a journal that her parents had given her when she left Tibet. In the journal they left her an encouraging note that would help her on her journey into undiscovered worlds. It was simply two words: "Look within." Each time she needed reassurance and guidance, she opened the journal and was reminded to look within.

When you look within, you face your fears and move beyond them. You see yourself as God sees you and hear yourself as God hears you. In the breath that you share with God, the rhythm of your heart calms, the thoughts of your mind clear, and the wings of your spirit soar. Then you recognize that in the ordinary there is a profound, extraordinary you. With the profound awareness of the divinity within yourself, you exit the heavenly Gate of Strength and turn toward the pathway that reveals the gate of your heart.

Practice the Meditation on Guidance (page 146)
at least once today.

HARMONY

Welcoming a person with a greeting of peace and harmony
is akin to welcoming God, for God is peace.

Zohar

Therefore the Sage says:

I take no action and people are reformed.

I enjoy peace and people become honest.

I do nothing and people become rich.

I have no desires and people return to

the good and simple life.

Lao Tzu

*Y*OU ARE NOW STANDING in the heavenly Gate of Harmony, the midpoint of your mystical journey through the Tree of Life. In this gate you become the bridge between the ordinary and the extraordinary, the mundane and the miraculous. In this gate there is no place to go and nothing to do, but only a deep appreciation for beauty and balance as they present themselves in your life. In Harmony you pause, reflect, and stand in the splendor of who you are. At the place where you now stand, heaven touches the heart of earth.

The heavenly Gate of Harmony is the path of balancing opposites and recognizing beauty. Harmony balances strength with compassion and wisdom with understanding, and instills them with a sense of the sacred. When you are swimming in chaos and free-falling into confusion, harmony helps you to pause and find meaning and peace. In the midst of chaos, turmoil, and confusion, Harmony opens your heart to the wonders of life and the miracles that abound within yourself. When Harmony touches your spirit, God embraces your heart. When you touch the divinity within your heart, you envision the sacred and experience a newly found enthusiasm toward life.

As you open your heart to Harmony, you enter the rhythm of the universe and become a steward of the sacred visions of humanity. You experience the heart within you that holds the dreams, visions, and memories of moments past, present, and future. Harmony helps you to move forward with strength and compassion. Harmony helps you access the intuition that dwells in the heart of your soul and to act on the inner voice that calls to you.

In this gate you will receive insights that help you remain balanced and calm, become more courageous, feel more open-hearted, and empower beauty in all that you see, hear, and feel. You will gain a deeper appreciation for the miracles that exist even amidst the chaos and confusion of life. You will understand what it means to be fully known, recognized, and heard. You will immerse yourself in the profound power of prayer, the impact of healing words, and the potency of love.

Before turning to the first insight in Harmony, take some quiet time now and experience the Meditation on Centering. This meditation will help you center and balance. It reminds you that you are never alone. As you become balanced, the God within you also becomes balanced. As you center, the world around you centers. To benefit from the meditation, read it slowly. Pause between each sentence and experience what you have just read. Then spend a moment or two enveloped in the peace that results. Review the Meditation on Centering after reading and contemplating each of the insights in this chapter.

⊰ Meditation on Centering ⊱

Pause a moment and sit comfortably in a chair or on the floor. Feel the breath moving into your body as you slowly inhale and exhale. Feel the breath entering from the top of the head and flowing down through the neck and spine. Allow the inhalation and exhalation to flow evenly and freely. Feel it flowing down the feet to the earth beneath you. With each inhalation and exhalation feel the muscles and limbs of your body relax more and more—relax the right and left sides of your face, shoulders, arms, hands, hips, thighs, legs, and feet—feel your body become weightless, filled with energy and light. Feel your mind clear and your body totally centered as it floats on the breath and the breath floats on the light that moves throughout your body.

Now see the light emanating from your heart space, sending its radiance throughout your inner world and then emanating to all that is outside of you. Now bless God, the Divinity within, for centering and balancing with you.

Define the Midpoint and Mark
Your Journey

Does not Wisdom call

And understanding put forth her voice?

In the top of high places by the way,

Where the paths meet,

she stands.

Proverbs 8:1–2

The Noble Path, that transcends these two extremes and leads to Enlightenment and wisdom and peace of mind, may be called the Middle Way.

Buddha

In identifying yourself, you have declared that you are not a hodgepodge of chaos. You have dimension, volume, and density that move as you move, change as you change. In the wholeness of who you are, there is an invisible thread of light, the *kav v'chut,* that links you to the Infinite Source. It is the spiritual bridge that enables you to cross over from the physical to the spiritual realms of being. When you are standing in the space between your self-image and your God image, the physical and the spiritual, the ordinary and the extraordinary, the mundane and the miraculous, both sides call to you. In the space between one and the other, the midpoint is born.

As you stand in the midpoint of your own life, God calls you to integrate what was with what is yet to be. A woman in search of herself once walked to the edge of a precipice. There she saw a tremendous chasm and thought there was no way forward. As she pondered at the edge, she looked back over the road she had traveled. She heard ancient voices, saw old ways of being, seasoned relationships, completed accomplishments, and discarded dreams. In the stillness of the environment, at the edge of her perception, she heard the voice of wisdom speak. It enveloped her in the sounds of deep understanding and self-knowledge. It showed her the ways in which she had denied her own growth and had scrambled the information in her mind. But most of all, it showed her that the path she had taken had laid a foundation for the next step on her journey: this was not the end, but only the midpoint of her life. At that moment of profound self-recognition, a butterfly landed in her hand and awakened her to the water filling the chasm at the edge of the precipice on which she sat. In the clear water she swam across the river to the next plateau of her life.

Whether you are at midlife or at a midpoint, there is always a rite of passage. The ritual happens in the center of your being, as you recognize where you've been and accept where you are. There is no rushing to where you will go next. There is only the profound recognition of who you are and that you are between two merging points in your life, each of which has led you to the illusionary precipice over which you are about to take a leap of faith. Be comforted in the knowledge that you will not fall in a chasm but, instead, will turn a corner that opens your heart to new vistas. Heed Wisdom's call as she whispers in your ear and tugs at your heart to meet Her in the highest places within yourself. Stand on the high places within yourself and embrace Her.

Practice the Meditation on Centering (page 174)
at least once today.

Maintain Balance and Harmony

God created this world to correspond with the upper world; and all things in the upper world have their counterparts in this world; and all things in this world have their counterparts in the sea; and all is a unity of one.

Zohar

Primal Virtue is deep and far.

It leads all things back

Toward the great oneness.

Lao Tzu

Life is an ever-changing, interconnecting, growth-oriented, dynamic, heart-throbbing, sensational state of awareness. For every up there is a down, for every in an out, for every right a left, and for every around a through. All things are in harmony in the universe of God, and all worlds balance one another. For every blade of grass, molecule of air, and vibration of sound, there are counterparts in the worlds within worlds within worlds. For every experience there are infinite possibilities. For every relationship there are infinite lifetimes of karmic residue and psychic mending. Nothing exists in isolation; the whole universe vibrates with interconnecting aliveness and integrating unity.

In the interconnectedness of the universe, you are linked to the Infinite Source through thoughts, words, and actions on the level of the earth, planet, and stars. In the ladder of life, your thoughts, words, and actions create angels that transmit your communication to the upper realms. From the Talmud you learn that every word of God creates an angel. The angels that are the words of God act as receptors, assisting you in implementing ideas and answering needs. The angels balance and harmonize the world of feelings with the world of pure emanation. Where there are feelings there is spirit. When the feelings release themselves from clinging thoughts and ideas, the spirit soars into emptiness. In the emptiness there is free-flowing receptivity. In the nonclinging receptivity there is boundless harmony and limitless balance.

God works through angels, and the angels work through stars and planets. All things, even a blade of grass, has a star over it encouraging it to grow. As the human is to the soul and the soul is to God, so too are the angels to the stars. They are the souls of the stars and work in harmony with all things. Whether you are moving forward or backward, up or down, in or out, there is tandem movement supporting and encouraging your growth, assisting your service, and implementing your union and reunion with God, in all worlds of existence.

As you stand in the center of the sacred circle of life, your heart holds the central pulse of the rhythm of the Tree of Life. All things that emanate from your heart and the heart of the universe are founded on the harmony of the universe of God. Einstein, as were the kabbalists, was so certain about the harmony of the universe that he based his whole theory of relativity on it.

In the sacred circle of life, there is neither separation nor disharmony. Polarities do not exist in isolation. Just as you do not exist in isolation of your parts, so too good and bad, in and out, up and down do not exist by themselves. They are perceptions of how you connect with life. If you perceive life as limiting and think there is not enough money, food, or love available for everyone, you will connect to life out of fear and compete for everything. If you have faith in the harmony and balance inherent in the universe, however, you will realize it is unnecessary to compete for anything when there are an infinite number of things and possibilities.

When a horse goes to drink from a pool of water and sees his shadow, he thinks there is another horse next to him. He gets concerned that if the other horse continues to drink, there will not be enough for both of them. So he shakes his mane in an attempt to chase the other horse away. In reality what he fears is his own shadow, for there is plenty to drink for many horses. The same is true when you don't have faith in the abundant flow of God in the universe. No one can take away what is divinely ordained to be yours. You are an important part of the harmony and balance of this universe of life. Rather than hide behind your own shadow, rise up and notice the beauty, harmony, and balance there is in the abundance of God's world.

Just as there is balance and harmony, there are moments of peace within the process of living, momentary plateaus upon which to rest your feet. Through meditation you are able to reach deep within yourself and step onto the still point that bridges the gap from where you were to where you are right now. Being in the now is being at peace with yourself regardless of outside influences or inner turmoil.

There is a house of God to which all peoples are invited, where you dwell for short periods of time in order to receive guidance and refreshment along the route of life. In that house, your mind is cleared, your heart is opened, and your soul is free. In that house you are unconditionally loved. The only entrance to that house is through your intention. When you place it in your intention to be in the house of God and your focus is clear, God takes you there. The peacefulness that envelops you in the house of God returns with you to the world in which you live. As the prophet Hosea said: "Return until God is your God." This means that you stay in the house of God until you feel the Divine influx envelop and flow through you. When you feel immersed in the *shefa,* the Divine influx, your eyes will focus on all things and see God. At that point of immersion you become a vehicle for holiness and return to your everyday environment in union with God. The peace that you find in the house of God is carried in you and is perceived through the lens of your perception and maintained by the equanimity of your life. Neither static nor permanent, it is an organic peace and equanimity that moves as you move, changes as you change, returns as you return.

Ultimately, the peace you experience in the still points of your life is found in the moments when you dwell in the house of God. As you step onto the plateau of the next sojourn in your life, be aware that the house of God is both the garment of the universe and the sanctuary within you. Buddha teaches, "Do not think that this world is meaningless and filled with confusion, while the world of Enlightenment is full of meaning and peace. Rather, taste the way of Enlightenment in all affairs of this world." May you reach the peace of the high places, in the deep recesses of the ordinary roads of your everyday life, and may you know that equanimity dwells therein. Then may you know yourself in the words of the psalmist and be able to say, "I am all peace."

Practice the Meditation on Centering (page 174)
at least once today.

Live with Courage and Openheartedness

Above all that you hold dear, watch over your heart, for from it comes life.

Proverbs 4:23

With an open mind, you will be openhearted.

Being openhearted, you will act royally.

Being royal, you will attain the divine.

Lao Tzu

In the midst of chaos, turmoil, and negativity, some people hide from their feelings and close access to their own hearts. Other people react with profound faith, open hearts, and a committed courage to go on. In despairing times and overwhelming situations, where do you get your courage to continue? You do not run away and hide; you turn around and touch the hand of God that holds your heart. You access the heart within yourself and your vision of the heartbeat of the universe, which has not lost touch with compassion, love, joy, strength, wisdom, and understanding. These are the divine attributes with which you were seasoned for delivery into this world. Your heart is the center spoke on the wheel of your life. It is the point of intersection of God's qualities inside of you.

The word "courage" comes from the French word *cœur,* meaning "heart." Courage is the ability to look within, touch your heart, and face yourself. It is the courage to open the passageways of your heart and walk through your fears, regardless of the pain, disappointment, or loss. It is the courage to see yourself through the varied lenses of perception and to love what you see. It is accepting how you feel and manifesting the right action for serving goodness, regardless of outside influences or internal turmoil.

You will notice that stories of courage usually take place during trying times, when people of vision refused to give up their dreams of a benevolent people in a world of holiness. Stories of courage start with one person who kindles the light within him- or herself, before sparking hope and faith in others. They include the story of David, who overcame Goliath; of Samson, who slew the lion; of Moses, who split the sea; of Deborah, who defeated the army of Sisera; of Rahab, who triumphed over the Canaanites; and of Miriam, who guarded Moses' life and led the women through the sea. None of the above went to a war college to learn strategy or skills in weaponry. Each one communed with the Infinite Source in the depths of his or her own heart. Their communion with God was not an occasional occurrence that happened during times of distress. It was a way of life in which their thoughts, words, and actions were in continuous union with God. Being openhearted and acting with grace, generosity, simplicity, and nobility of spirit were natural to their character.

David acted out of faith and simplicity when he held up his slingshot and killed Goliath. He didn't think he couldn't do it; he opened his heart, lifted his eyes to the heavens, and recited Psalm 121:1—"I lift my eyes to the mountains, from where my help will come." And God blessed him with success. When Samson slew the lion, he had no weapons in his hand; only the spirit of God filled him with strength. When Moses stretched his hand out over the waters, God's arm was holding his up, and then the sea split. When Deborah was about to confront Sisera, she was enveloped in the spirit of God and prayed in the words of Psalm 115:1 — "Not to us God, but to Your name give glory." When the Israelite spies came to Rahab, the harlot's, inn, she was overtaken by the unconditional love of God and risked her own life to hide the Israelites and save her family from danger. When Moses was born, it was Miriam who hid him in a basket in the Nile River; Miriam who brought her mother as a nursemaid to Pharoah's palace. It was Miriam who danced the enslaved women through the Red Sea to freedom. She had received prophesies from the time she was a young child. She instinctively acted on what she received from God, without doubting its validity. This is what brought a slave population into freedom. Each person of vision saw the challenges he or she faced, and rather than analyze the opportunities, sanctified the moments by stepping aside and letting his or her divinity emerge. Thus the periods of diversity became opportunities for deepening faith and expanding hope in a benevolent, sacred world.

The stories of courage continue in you as you open your heart and see beyond yourself to the dreams God is dreaming in you. Courage and openheartedness live in your visions of benevolence and holiness, your acts of compassion and love, your perseverance toward strength and discernment. With courage and openheartedness, your life increases in meaning and your contribution to this world extends beyond your time in this space. In your heart you set the foundation and draw a template upon which others can tread lightly and live deeply, following their own pursuits, their own image of God, and their own inner visions for serving goodness.

It takes courage to live fully. With all that is available to you from the many realms of experience and the worlds within worlds, it takes courage to select for yourself and become responsible for your choices. Moreover, it takes courage not to select what you may not want, regardless of outside influences. It takes courage also to live to the fullness of your potential being, which is as vast as your choices and requires you to have faith in yourself and trust in God.

So often you take a backseat when you would rather be in front, or walk around something when you would rather walk through it, or evade a problem when you would rather deal with it head-on—but you don't have the courage. Spiritual courage involves all the realms of existence. It is being courageous physically, emotionally, and intellectually, as well as spiritually. What does it mean to be courageous physically? How many times have you procrastinated before doing something that you know will support your growth? Perhaps it was because you did not have the physical skills necessary to complete the task; so you shied away from it. There is an ethical teaching in Judaism that says: "Though you may not complete the task, you are not absolved from beginning it." Even though the task is greater than you can handle on your own or at this time, you are still encouraged to begin it. Once you take the first step, the guides and messengers are dispatched to assist in walking you forward.

Emotional courage asks you to circumvent your fears and accomplish your desires before they become too great to handle. Go with a beginner's mind, innocent of negative perceptions and emotional blockages. Beginner's mind is free, easy, empty, and open; it does not analyze or criticize. It speaks its truth freely and succinctly. If women did not have the courage to change God language today to reflect both the masculine and feminine as well as the gender-free, then religions would still be locked in old limiting perceptions of God and narrow ways of being. If children were still taught to be seen and not heard, we would have missed a rich, positive, playful experience of our own inner child.

Intuitive and intellectual courage means having faith that, though your thoughts may differ from another's, they are valid. And thoughts alone do not speak your mind. There are other worlds within your mind that access information in unique ways. There are your dreams and your intuitions; have the courage to act on the inner voice that calls to you. And above all, there is the courage to be, without the need to do: the courage to enter nothingness and empty. Entering the void, for those who spend their lives being full and overwhelmed, is a very courageous thing to do. Not only is it courageous; it is necessary in order to receive the light of God that is programmed just for you.

It is impossible to reach total perfection of all there is in this world. However, you were born coded for specific tasks in specific areas of perfection. Not everyone enters this world with the same task or the same standard of perfection. What is perfect for you may not be perfect for another. Your area of perfection enables you to perform the tasks you were assigned before birth; another's areas of perfection may be in a totally different realm. Together, you and others complete the puzzle that is called humanity.

How do you know when you are being called upon by God to act courageously? When it feels right in your heart; when the task promotes your growth and serves goodness in this world; when you are being asked to do something that your consciousness cannot refuse; when there is an opportunity for union and reunion with the Infinite. How did David know he could overcome Goliath? He was only a naïve young boy with a shoddy slingshot, and he did not even question the odds. He had not yet developed the many guises of adults who cloak self-consciousness and inhibition in rational thinking.

Think of the life you are missing by not having the courage to be free. Freedom doesn't mean turning your back on responsibility; it means freedom to live courageously, fully responding to your abilities. Thank God for the courage to think innovatively, to feel unique, to speak with conviction, to act differently.

Rabbi Zalman Schachter-Shalomi explains that the sages ask: if the angels taught us everything we needed to know, why was this knowledge shocked into amnesia the moment we were born into this world? He answers: so that all subsequent study will lead you to remembering what you have already known. Since each one has a special angel guide, no one else's philosophy or experience can be quite like yours or satisfy your soul. So you are here to have the courage to remember on the inner plane of your soul what you already know, and to act on it.

Practice the Meditation on Centering (page 174)
at least once today.

Dispel Confusion

And Moses was not able to enter the tent of meeting, because the cloud dwelled there, and the glory of God filled the tabernacle. And whenever the cloud lifted from over the tabernacle, the Israelites went forward on their journey. And if the cloud did not lift, they would not journey until the day it was lifted.

Exodus 40:35–38

Oh, my mind! Why do you hover so restlessly over the changing circumstances of life? Why do you make me so confused and restless? . . . you are like a rudder that is dismantled just as you are venturing out on the sea . . . of what use are many rebirths if we do not make good use of this life?

Buddha

In opening your heart to new thoughts and innovative ideas, you use senses of which you were previously unaware. You may experience dreams, visions, sounds, and voices that, though awesome, could lead to confusion and anxiety. When you are raised and trained to perceive a three-dimensional world and then begin experiencing a multidimensional reality, it can be disconcerting at first. It is like the story of Flatland, where everything was perceived as flat, until a citizen of Flatland came up with the idea that there could be dimension in things. The squares could become cubes and the triangles could become pyramids, and so forth. This was difficult for the other citizens to accept, and they reacted with nervous belligerence and unfounded rejection. In the same way, there are perceptions you have about your life that, if viewed from new perspectives, could open you to more possibilities. It is like the case of the person who is used to going to the teller in the bank and then, one day, the bank is closed, and she is confronted with a whole new system of banking, the electronic teller. Not only doesn't she trust the new technology; she doesn't know how to use it. Yet once she learns, more possibilities for banking are available to her.

How do you react to new things, new thoughts, new ways of being? Think of the time when you may have thought all of this spiritual talk was nonsense, then one day you had your own mystical encounter. You may have experienced it in meditation, in nature, or in a life-changing event with a loved one. As you begin to change your attitude and discover new possibilities, you may find that the different aspects of your personality and the roles that you play may revolt you and cause you confusion and anxiety. Among the many components of your personality there is a skeptic who questions your motives; a pragmatist who thinks all this metaphysical stuff is pie in the sky; a socialite who is concerned about losing status; a procrastinator who thinks you are rushing into things; and a parent who wants to hold on to the old, tried, and true. These aspects relate to or reject one another within the inner world of your mind, as well as in the outer world of your relationship with others. These aspects within yourself and the people in your life cause fear of change and resentment. Your path as a spiritual initiate is to remain empty, open, and calm throughout the period of confusion.

Remember, many roads lead to the same place, and not everyone takes the path of the spiritual initiate. That spiritual road is reserved for the visionary and seeker who can walk in emptiness and maintain clarity. Rabbi Bunam once told of two merchants who went to the Leipzig fair. One went by the primary road, the other took the secondary trail, and both reached the same destination. Rabbi Bunam said that the same is true of the road of holiness. The purpose is to connect with God through serving goodness. It doesn't matter how we arrive or the time it takes to travel. It matters only that we arrive.

When you feel confused, you cannot think clearly and your mind is clouded. You may feel as though you are in a fog. Know that God is with you in the cloud of confusion. As a matter of fact, God uses the cloud as a guide for you. You learn this lesson from the story of Exodus. When the Israelites traveled through the desert, God appeared as a cloud during the day and a pillar of fire at night. When the cloud descended into the tent of meeting, all travel ceased. When the cloud lifted, the Israelites continued their journey onward to the Promised Land. Consider the symbolism. Clouds are made of water, and water is symbolic of change and renewal.

When you are traveling into new territories of the mind and expanding your perception, you experience change and renewal. As you are immersed in the changes within, it is difficult to see outside yourself. Just when it seems you are deepening your awareness and accelerating your understanding, something happens to set you back or halt your progress. This abrupt halt could be the needs of a family member or friend, a change at work, or shift in your own health. Then the cloud of confusion sets in. This setback is no accident. The setback is God's way of protecting you by carrying you in a soft, light cloud and covering you with veils of illusion until you are ready to continue. Remember that even the confusion is part of the spiritual practice. All initiates pass through this veil of illusion in order to move to the next step in their spiritual development.

In all spiritual traditions, confusion is a necessary step on the spiraling ladder of life. Confusion is the midpoint between the Rung of Love and the Rung of Power. With unconditional love for all the aspects of your personality, for the varying roles people portray in your environment, you accept the confusion and you luxuriate in the nothingness. In the opportunity to simplify and empty, you receive the inner power necessary to ascend to the Rung of Power. God helps you dispel the confusion and balance unconditional love with sacred power when you are ready. When God feels you are ready, God will lift the cloud and you will travel to the next step on your journey. In the meantime, luxuriate in the pause; rest, relax, and empty.

Practice the Meditation on Centering (page 174)
at least once today.

Listen from the Heart

In insulting another you insult yourself, for it is your own
defect that is being revealed.

Talmud

If our minds are filled with sympathy and compassion, they
will be resistant to the *negative* words we hear.

Buddha

Everyone has a deep need to be heard. As you journey the
path of kabbalistic insights, you become acutely aware of the
messengers and messages that pervade your environment. Each
person was born with a unique light that bears witness to a new
way of being, a new insight, that is vital for the growth and
continuance of the planet. When you are in the presence of one
who is ready to speak his or her spirit, it is important for you to
listen from your heart.

What does it mean to listen from your heart? It means to set
your ego aside. At the moment a spirit speaks, there is nothing
more important for you to do than listen. Let the thoughts and
distractions in your head clear. Let the expectations in your
mind vanish. Move into the vibration and frequency of the
person who is sharing his or her spirit with you. Empty, relinquish, and release to being open and receptive. In the emptiness,
you join your soul to that person's soul, your heart to their heart,

your mind to their mind. In the blending of yourself to the other, there is neither you nor the other; rather, there is only the spirit speaking and the heart listening. In the union of spirit and heart, you are fulfilling a vital portion of your destiny. As it says in Deuteronomy 28:1, "In listening, you listen to the voice of God."

In the process of consciously listening to another from the openness of your heart, you are helping to transform, re-form, and newly form worlds. In the re-formation of the world, you are given the steps to fulfill your own destiny. The road to enlightenment is both active and inactive. You may think that you are fulfilling your destiny only when you are in the midst of creative action. Creative inaction, however, such as conscious listening from the heart, is also one of the steps that lead you to the path of destiny and enlightenment. In fulfilling your destiny, there are times when you need to consciously dismiss your ego and welcome another's soul as though the world depended upon it. For it does.

How you greet and listen to another reveals much about who you are. It is said that there are two hallways in which a person is judged. In the realm of holiness, there is the hallway of innocence. In the realm of profanity, there is the hallway of guilt. The difference between the two lies in your own perception. If you judge another according to merits and goodness, then you are standing in the realm of holiness. If you judge another according to transgressions and misdeeds, then you will argue for that person's guilt and insist in placing him or her in a bad light. In doing so, you place yourself in the realm of profanity. In becoming aware of the realm in which you stand, you gain a better understanding of yourself and your own spiritual level. A conscious, aware person sees his or her own shortcomings before criticizing another. A holy being searches for the God in each one and serves that goodness.

The story is told of a wealthy miser who once came to his rabbi for a blessing. The rabbi walked him over to the window and asked, "What do you see?" The miser answered, "I see people." Then the rabbi handed him a mirror and once again asked, "Now what do you see?" "I see myself," answered the miser, puzzled. Then the rabbi explained that both the window and mirror were glass. When you look through the clear window, you see others. Yet when you look through the mirror, which is the same glass with a silver veneer on it, you see only yourself. In the same way, when you are listening from a clear heart, you can see through another's words to that person's very soul. However, if you are listening through a veneer of critical judgment and a filter of negative perceptions, you see only yourself and cripple the possibilities for a dynamic interchange that could form and re-form worlds of awareness and ways of being.

In listening to another you can transcend time and space and join the heavenly realms with the earthly realms. One night the wife of Rabbi Mendel of Lubavitch heard a loud thump in the bedroom. She ran to her husband's bed and found him lying on the floor uncovered. In reply to her concerns, he explained that in his sleep, his deceased grandfather had visited with him. His wife tried to calm Rabbi Mendel, but he explained that when a soul from the upper world and a soul from this world want to visit with each other, the one must put on a garment and the other must take one off. So the spirit of his grandfather spoke through the veils of a garment while Rabbi Mendel unveiled his. In the same way, when a spirit speaks to you, whether in this world or another, disrobe your ego and listen from the nakedness that is the purity of your soul and the openness of your heart.

Practice the Meditation on Centering (page 174)
at least once today.

Pray and Heal

Everything that would ever be, has already happened in God. Therefore, when you pray for healing of another you are attaching yourself to God, and opening the possibility for what has already occurred in God's realm to take place in this world.

Rabbi Elimelech of Lizensk

If one is sick of sickness, then one is not sick . . .

The sage is not sick because *the sage* is sick of sickness.

Therefore *the sage* is not sick.

Lao Tzu

What does it mean to heal, and how can you heal or be healed with faith? According to the Hasidic view, the world in which you find yourself is inherently good. Every person is the best of all people, and every occurrence is meant to happen. In this way, everyone and everything is accepted and is managed with faith. This is the kind of faith that heals and transforms.

When your faith comes from an accepting attitude toward illness and emanates from the infinite light, you can overcome all obstacles, both great and small. The inner light of God is kindled and rekindled in you with the assistance of prayer. Prayer, in each of its forms, transmits energy. That energy can emanate in the recitation of liturgy, in the articulation of your own language, in the silence of meditation, and in the many other ways in which you empty, open, and receive the inner light of God.

Healing, like prayer, is the transmission of energy and the emanation of spiritual light. It is not meant as a cure for disease, but as an aid in assisting you toward your destiny. The energy that kindles the inner light originates from God and may come through you or through another who willingly offers to be a vehicle for healing. Since the beginning of time, there have been people who kindle their inner light, are generous in sharing the energy that flows through them, and are available as vehicles of God for healing others.

A story is told of how Elisha, the man of God, brought a young boy back to life. In his travels he stayed at the home of a Shunammite woman of wealth and substance. In gratitude for her generous hospitality, Elisha prayed for her to conceive a child. When the child he had prayed for was grown, he fell, hurt his head, and died in his mother's lap. His mother, the Shunammite, laid him on Elisha's bed in her home and went to seek the man of God. Elisha returned with her to his room, where the child lay. First he prayed; then he stretched himself across the body of the child—mouth to mouth, eyes to eyes, hands to hands. The child's body became warm. Elisha then walked back and forth in the house, after which he returned to the bedside. Once again, he stretched himself over the child. This time, the child was revived and came back to life.

Rabbi Elimelech of Lizensk (1717–87) helps us to understand this phenomenon by explaining that you need to have faith, that the potential for healing is given through God to humankind. Your faith needs to include the understanding that God created you through Divine will and encoded you with the potential for forming new existence. This potential can create new worlds of experience, universes of existence that already exist in the Divine plan but are waiting for you to activate them. These worlds are new to you but not to God. Your task in healing is to bring the dimensions, worlds, and universes of God from potential into external realization. Therefore, when you pray and effect healing, you are not changing what has been; you are only activating what is meant to be. The healing itself is part of the already existing sequence in the Divine plan.

There have been many different prescriptions for healing, each rabbi having his or her unique remedy. The commonality between all of them is faith and prayer. When Rabbi Nachman of Breslov was ill, he found that faith in himself was an important aspect of having faith in God. After all, why would God create someone with a small image of him- or herself? Would God want such a disempowered partner? So Rabbi Nachman mustered his healing faith by first immersing in the living waters of renewal at the *mikvah,* then reciting ten prescribed psalms. These psalms begin with positive affirmations, then acknowledge the challenges of life with Divine intervention, and conclude with joy and celebration. They are Psalm 10, declaring that joy comes from God; Psalm 32, declaring that joy is forgiveness; Psalm 41, acknowledging suffering and receiving God's intervention; Psalm 42, acknowledging the spirit's exile and receiving God's intervention; Psalm 59, acknowledging danger and receiving God's intervention; Psalm 77, acknowledging affliction and redemption; Psalm 90, accepting human mortality and Divine immortality; Psalm 105, a prayer of thanksgiving; Psalm 137, reclaiming Jerusalem; and Psalm 150, praising God with music and dance. Rabbi Nachman stressed that these psalms are a *tikkun hak'lali,* a general remedy, that should be recited on the day that one feels diminished.

Since faith is a major ingredient in healing, and faith is believing in God, and God is love, then love also is involved in healing. Love is the intangible fuel behind prayer. Love is the energy, the light, and the sound that echoes from your soul and emanates from the center of your heart. Love is both an aid to healing and compatible with illness. Whether it heals or helps you accept your circumstances, love plays a vital role in the healing process. With love in your heart and with the loving support of others, you can accept and adjust to any outcome.

If love is God and God is nothingness, then returning to nothingness is also an effective process for healing. Clearing your mind and starting on empty will help you access the nothingness. Staying in a meditative state of mind during the healing process will help you detach from outside influences and expectations and assist you in remaining calm, accepting, and nurturing of yourself. Staying nonattached frees you to go within and access the energy and light that are needed for becoming a conduit through which healing flows.

Practice the Meditation on Centering (page 174)
at least once today.

See, Hear, and Touch Beauty

Whoever prays for others also sees his *or her* own

desires fulfilled.

Talmud

This is called the virtue of not competing;

This is called correctly using man *or woman;*

This is called matching Heaven.

Lao Tzu

There is an epidemic of low self-esteem today. So many people are walking around detached from their souls, looking for a tailor of souls to seam them back into one piece. Unfortunately, they search for another while looking through the limiting, highly critical filter, or *klippah,* of low self-esteem. How can you find another when you cannot see yourself? It's like trying to see in the thickness of a midnight fog. You cannot see yourself, let alone another. All you hear are the moans and groans of the search and a shoulder here and there of one person bumping into another. Yet even in the middle of the fog there is beauty, and there are wonders yet to be born.

The Talmud teaches there are three things that revive a person's spirit: beautiful sounds, sights, and smells. To be able to see, hear, taste, touch, and smell beauty in everything is awe-

some and inspiring. When you can accept the beauty in everything and move beyond that to endowing everything with
beauty, everything you come in contact with becomes beautiful
because you have made it so.

Rabbi Shlomo Carlebach once told the story of a man yet in
the upper realms who asked to see who his soul mate would be
here on earth. God showed him the picture of a beautiful young
girl who had a hunchback. The man was so taken by the inner
beauty of the young woman and knew how difficult it would be
for her to live with such a deformity that he requested God give
him the hunchback rather than her. So this man was born into
the world with a hunchback. Many years passed until he was of
age to marry. As was the custom in those days, his bride did not
meet him until the wedding day. Needless to say, she was disturbed by the distortion in her newlywed husband's appearance.
With the gentlest of care, he told her the story of when he was
yet in the upper realms and contracted with God to be the one,
instead of her, to have the hunchback. For the first time his
bride looked at him with such beauty and adoration. At that
moment her eyes and heart were opened and she could see, hear,
and touch the beauty in her husband as he had in her.

Can you look beyond the facade of another and empower that
person's beauty? Can you see beyond the affects and defects in
others and accept them as part of the beauty of yourself, the
wonders of nature, and the miracle of love?

Begin by experiencing the beauty in yourself. Look at yourself
in the mirror and begin seeing through lenses that color everything in beauty. Accept each part of your body as a beauty of
nature and wonder of life. Practice this with people you meet
during the course of your day. You will notice that when you
see beauty, the beauty is reflected back to you. This happens
with people, with animals, with plants, and with all the elements in nature.

To a mystic, everything is ordained with a heart, a voice, and
a vision of itself. In this way, the animate and inanimate worlds
are in correspondence with each other. You are in continuous

correspondence with your environment and all its elements. As you empower the beauty, the beauty empowers you. In the process, there is a deeper appreciation for every aspect of creation and for all properties of life and living.

In the Hasidic tradition the essential vision of creation is one of goodness and godliness. The psalmist said, "Only goodness and love will follow me all the days of my life" (Psalm 23:6). This means that goodness and love are patiently following you until you slow down, turn around, embrace them, and bring them home. When you are always in a hurry and operate from a state of crisis, you keep yourself imprisoned in a *klippah* of limited perception and narrow scope. It may seem as though you are forever rushing forward to keep ahead, yet are going nowhere. In slowing down and turning around, you will be able to smell the healing fragrances, witness the intimate miracles, and hear the music of the soul awaiting your arrival into a more pleasurable, effortless, empowered way of being. Pause, empty, and listen to the sounds of the wind, the melody of your soul, the heart of the one you love. Stop a moment and smell the leaves of the trees, the mist of the ocean, the fragrance of the food you are about to eat. Slowly open your eyes to the beauty that surrounds you and mirrors God.

The Baal Shem Tov used to empower everything in nature, as well as empower his students. He would walk past a tree, empower the tree, and listen to the language of the tree. The same with the birds and flowers and fields of grass.

Sometimes empowering others means you need to overcome your hesitance and self-consciousness in speaking to strangers, in opening a dialogue with people waiting in line at a sales counter, post office, or movie theater or even with those you see regularly at prayer services but have not engaged in conversation. Some of the best connections are made in the most unlikely places. If God wanted you to be empowered in solitude, you would be living on an island by yourself. However, you are here as part of humanity in order to receive the richness of empowering another to empower yourself. So next time you enter a restaurant, a waiting room, or even a sanctuary that is familiar to you, empower someone and see the miracles unfold.

We learn from one another what we need to know. Imagine there is a tremendous network of information that is routed to numerous destinations within different souls. As the information is passed along, it gets closer to its destination. If you hold information and do not share it, you do not leave room for other information to drop in. In the same way, with generous networking of pertinent spiritual information, more spirituality is emanated into the world and arrives at its designated destination.

You are aware when you receive the information that is meant just for you. It fits perfectly with what you need at the moment to help you grow and expand to the next step. It may come in conversation, followed up by a piece of mail or a flyer. Then you begin seeing the synchronicity in the events and the data input in your life. When the information reaches your destination, it is meant to be held only temporarily. For as you continue to grow, you will feed others the information and receive new input.

As in the fable of Beauty and the Beast, the world is full of spirits imprisoned in judgmental *klippot,* waiting for a look, a sound, a fragrance, a touch of beauty to release their divinity and kindle their Godspark. Be aware of your reactions to another as well as to yourself. In the world of the spirit, there is no difference between how you relate to yourself and how you relate to another. You are who you are, and how you relate is not separate from who you are. You are also not separate from your soul, and your soul is not separate from God. In other words, you are not separate from God, nor are you separate from another.

Be aware of your next encounter with any aspect of God's creation, whether it be animate or inanimate. Remember it has a soul that awaits your empowerment. As you see, hear, and touch the beauty in it, it will reflect it in you. Imagine a world where there is only the acceptance of all as beautiful. The standards of tomorrow rest in you today. Walk forward to the next heavenly Gate, Success, and experience a world that is possible to be.

Practice the Meditation on Centering (page 174)
at least once today.

SUCCESS

Success is an attribute of God available to all. The degree to which a person is ready to receive success is the degree to which God gives it.

Joseph Albo

The Tao of heaven is impartial.
It stays with good men *and women* all the time.

Lao Tzu

THE HEAVENLY GATE OF
Success represents triumph and indicates the victory that comes
in successfully mastering yourself and freeing your spirit as it
soars through the physical world. The benefits you will receive
in the heavenly Gate of Success serve the goodness of the universe and the beauty of nature. Success emerges in the physical
world and sets the framework upon which glory is rendered and
foundations are built. Success is the basis for practicing skillful
means and mindful living.

On the path you have traveled thus far, you have gained
insights for your inner development and received knowledge
through the Divine influx of infinite energy. Now you are set on
the road to manifesting all you have learned in a manner that is
congruent with who you are becoming. It is now up to you to
make things work and to access all the resources necessary to be
self-responsible and self-motivated. In the Gate of Success you
are free to be who you are, and at the same time encouraged to
blend your will with the Divine will through conscious living,
essential speech, and pure action. In the maze of life you are
given the tools to succeed and the opportunity to master the
subtle differences in levels of understanding and realms of experience.

In Success you maintain focus, order priorities, and develop
the direction that encourages faith and trust, while nurturing
commitment and dedication to a purpose beyond yourself. In
Success you view a world as it perfects itself, a life as it fully
manifests itself, and a soul as it triumphs within itself. Within
the next three gates, of Success, Glory, and Creativity, you will

be constructing, recycling, and re-creating the foundation upon which your life continuously stands. The more you give to what you are now doing, the more you will effect success in the universe of your experience and contribute to building the foundation for planetary transformation. With the assertion of Success you will dismantle *klippot* and conquer the spirit of freedom and empathy.

Before turning to the first insight, take some quiet time and experience the Meditation on Awakening Consciousness. This meditation will help you remain clear in your intention and conscious in your words and actions. It will help you awaken consciousness in the conversation of your life and touch the infinite possibilities for success and sanctity. To benefit from the meditation exercise, read it slowly. Pause between each sentence and experience what you have just read. Then spend a moment or two enveloped in the peace that results. Review the Meditation on Awakening Consciousness after reading each of the insights in this chapter.

ꝏ Meditation on Awakening Consciousness ꝏ

Pause a moment and move your attention into the breath. Slowly inhale and slowly exhale. Allow the inhalation and exhalation to flow evenly and freely throughout your body. Feel your body relax and your mind empty as you move into an awareness of the moment. Luxuriate in the peaceful, quiet stillness for a moment or two. Now become conscious of the next thought, word, or action waiting to emanate from you. It may be a thought about a task or a relationship, or a sense of what you need to say in a presentation, or an idea about an activity that is waiting for you to perform it. Think of your intention toward the next transaction you will make in mind, in word, and in action. With a clear intention become conscious of the sacred-

ness of your actions, the purity of your thoughts, and the conscious compassion in your words. Remain clear in your
intention, conscious of the words you speak and the actions you
perform.

Maintain Focus and Priority

When you want to achieve greatness, take one small step
at a time.

Baal Shem Tov

See simplicity in the complicated.

Lao Tzu

Focus requires self-discipline. No one else can do your focusing
for you. Whether your task is large or small, you must focus to
accomplish your goal. Every small task is a part of something
larger. Maintaining a vision, or sense of the larger perspective,
while dealing with the seemingly smaller priorities will help
you to maintain your focus. Remember that it is the small steps
that assist you in ascending the vast ladder of life. For some, the
first step is the most difficult. For others, the first step is exciting, while the ones that follow pose more challenge. This is why
some people hop onto the first step and jump off before it leads
anywhere; and others, who may lack the skill to focus, choose
not to ascend the steps at all.

Visionaries and prophets throughout time have maintained
their focus for a more benevolent, peace-loving, compassionate
world regardless of outside influences. They have held up dreams
of hope and courage amidst chaos and confusion. They created
the template for perseverance through strength and discern-

ment. You are surrounded by the lens through which you choose to view the world. If you choose to see through the lens of goodness, then goodness is the path upon which you will be led toward the destiny you are meant to fulfill. If you choose to see through the lens of challenges and negativity, then negativity will be the path through which you are led. God will come to you in the varied images through which you perceive God. Challenges and supports will fall on the trail of your life through the doorways or peepholes of your perception.

As you journey the roads of your life, do not lose yourself in the oblivion of fragmented pathways and alternate routes of being. If you choose to stop and pick up the scattered refuse thrown from every which way, it will be difficult to maintain focus on the larger purpose and destination of this highway. So often, people get caught in the litter of outside influences and momentary distractions and forget the original intention with which they journeyed a particular road.

At every intersection and doorway in your life there is one who guards the entrance. The guard, a messenger of God, appears in different forms. Sometimes it is a friend who encourages you to move forward. Sometimes it is a challenging or frustrating situation that places stumbling blocks in your path or pushes you off the road. Sometimes it is an inner voice or vision that beckons you to heed its call. In whatever form the guard appears, it challenges you to stay focused and follow the divinely directed course of your life.

In your life you are always confronted with decisions and priorities. How do you know when you make the right decisions and choose the appropriate priority? When your decisions and choices come from the truth within your spirit. Your inner spirit beckons you to go within, empty, open, and receive the focus that speaks to the truth of who you are. Your decisions are right for you when they access your unique talents and serve goodness in the world. When you are utilizing your talents and contributing to the goodness in this world, you are fulfilling the destiny for which you were born. Your task is like no one else's, yet it is a vital part in the puzzle of humanity. The more you focus and prioritize your intentions and goals, the closer humanity and the world will be to *tikkun olam,* world transformation. The world's transformation depends upon your own.

Practice simplicity in your mind by taking one idea and focusing on that one idea each day. Within that one idea, all other thoughts and ideas evolve naturally. For instance, if your one idea today is to remember God is with you, then everything that happens is affirmed through the idea that God is with you. If someone needs your assistance, you respond with the awareness that God is with you. If you receive new knowledge and understanding during the day, you respond with the knowledge that God is with you. All things that happen during this day will be enhanced by remembering God is with you.

There is great power in your mind and its ability to focus on a simple thought. By thoughts alone you can achieve abundant health and wealth. Rabbi Nachman of Breslov describes the power of thought in the following way: "When the external and internal thought, as well as the point of awareness, are fastened onto a thing and have taken hold of it—and they do so without disturbance or turning to another thought—this concentration makes things turn out just as first thought to be. This concentration must be down to the most minute detail and not merely in a general way. . . . But [the one] who merely scans, in a general way, is like the one who fashions only the outer form of a vessel without creating any open space on the inside."

Focused thinking has the power to heal. A woman who visited my women's spirituality group told of a remarkable incident in which the healing power of thought changed her life and increased her faith. She had had an injury on her hand that festered into an infection. The doctors told her that the infection threatened the rest of her body, and the finger that held the infection would have to be amputated. She came home in pain and in shock over the impending loss. Plans were made for her to enter the hospital the following morning for immediate surgery. Meanwhile, she consulted with a spiritual healer, who encouraged her to focus her thoughts on the infected finger and see it, in as detailed a way as possible, filled with the light of

God and being healed. The woman stayed awake the entire night and meditated on the Divine Light in the cells, the nerves, the muscles, bones, flesh, and even the hairs and the pores in the skin of the finger, and envisioned it as it healed. The next morning she dressed for the hospital, not aware of whether her thoughts helped heal the finger, for her hand was covered in many layers of bandages that she was not able to remove. At the hospital, when the doctor removed the multiple layers of bandages, he was astounded. The infected finger had healed.

Focused thinking is also a form of prayer. It guides you along your direction in life. The Baal Shem Tov teaches the power of concentration and suggests that it be accompanied by daily affirmations in the form of Torah teachings. He prescribed staying simple, pure, and openhearted in serving God through prayer and acts of goodness. He maintained that the way to maintain this simplicity, purity, and openness was to learn words of Torah each day. Take one thought, be it large or small, that comes from the place of holiness. Affirm that thought as Torah, and throughout the day, bind it to you through the words you speak and the acts of goodness you perform.

The Talmud speaks of a future time when external orders and commandments (mitzvot) will no longer be necessary, for you will be carrying the light of God within, and deeds of loving-kindness will be the natural animated spirit of all life. The power of your thoughts today prepares you for the next step in your life. As you move forward, you open to more profound ways of serving goodness and ascending nearer to the Infinite Source. As you travel nearer to God, there is more focus and direction in your life. The forward path leads you to new dimensions of yourself, your life, and your God image.

Practice the Meditation on Awakening Consciousness
(page 208) at least once today.

Practice Self-Responsibility

It is not in heaven that you would say: "who can go to
heaven for us and bring it back so we can hear and do?"
Neither is it beyond the sea, that you would say: "who will
go *(walk)* over water for us, and bring it back?" . . . but
the voice of God is so near to you. It is in your own heart
and in your own mouth, for you to receive and act on it.

Deuteronomy 30:12–14

The human person models himself *or herself* on the Earth;

The Earth models itself on Heaven;

Heaven models itself on the Way;

And the Way models itself on that which is so on its own.

Lao Tzu

The manner in which you choose to relate to God is the same
manner in which you relate to life itself. As you see God more
present in you, you become more present in life. God encourages
you to become self-responsible in your relationship to God. In
Deuteronomy, God tells you that no one can go to the heavens
or cross the seas for you; only you can do it for yourself. This

thought is repeated again in the book of Jeremiah, when God inspires the prophet to seek the God his God, and he will find that God image, if he seeks God. This means that you are responsible, and when you take the responsibility for looking for your image of God, then you will find God. In other words, you are responsible for seeking your own image of God; no one else's image of God can do. When you do your own seeking, you will find a God image that is both beyond you and within you. For when you seek the Source, you uncover your own Divine nature within.

As you take self-responsibility for your spiritual quest, you also become self-responsible for the guidelines you set along the way. No one path works for everyone. Rabbi Baer of Radoshitz once asked his teacher, the Seer of Lublin, to give him one standard way to serve God. The Seer would not tell him one path to take, for each person is drawn to a different road and needs to be responsible for following his or her own path with strength and discernment. The guidelines you determine for your path may or may not be those chosen by your parents or grandparents. Although you may select or not select to emulate the path of your parents, God encourages you to forge your own. With your entrance into this world came a new light and a new way of being that never existed before. You are an original, unique person who is in the world in this way for the very first time. Your uniqueness is important to the transformation of the environment, to new ways of seeing, hearing, feeling, and being in life. Every person is a new organism who is here to fulfill a destiny that contributes his or her uniqueness to a far greater story in a larger world than themselves.

There is no need to replicate, imitate, or impersonate another, not even the rich and the famous. There is need only for you to be yourself and take responsibility for acting in the uniqueness of who you are. If God wanted another Moses or Miriam, the film of life would rewind and we would be back at the Red Sea. That does not happen. Although you can access and remember times past, the steps you are now taking are into the future. Rabbi Shlomo Carlebach used to say, "When you go to the next world you are going to be shown two screens. On one is the movie of who you were, and on the other is the movie of who you could have been. Which one will you be satisfied with?"

Every day we all must make many decisions. These decisions can be about matters as minor as what to wear or as major as how to approach a new situation or build a new structure. Witness how you accept the responsibility for making decisions or give it over to another. When you choose to relinquish responsibility, notice if it in turn increases or diminishes you and your unique ability to contribute to a new way of thinking, feeling, or being in this world. You were born to live in the fullness of your own mind, body, and spirit. In the interchange and interconnections of life, maintain your own distinctive *response*-ability.

Practice the Meditation on Awakening Consciousness
(page 208) at least once today.

Motivate Yourself

Do not say, "When I have leisure, I will study." A fool puts things off until tomorrow. A wise *person* does things at once.

Baal Shem Tov

A person seeks a path that will lead him *or her* away from birth, old age, sickness and death, or from misery, sorrow, suffering and agony; and yet, he *or she* follows the path a little way, notices some little advance, and immediately becomes proud and conceited and domineering.

Buddha

Your motivation is important to the quality of your life. No one can breathe for you and open your channels to the quality of life that you can receive from God. When you bind yourself to the Infinite Source in every breath you breathe, every word you speak and action you perform, the quality of your life markedly improves and can become miraculous. But when you are not motivated, you will more easily lose yourself in the humdrum of everyday life.

When you are self-motivated, you continually learn, grow,

and ascend the spiritual rungs of the ladder of life. With each level you gain new perspective, expanded views, deeper appreciation, and a more profound love of God, yourself, others, and life in general. Spiritually, when you grow from one rung to the next and desire to grow even more, you are enveloped by the Infinite Source. Yet if you think that all you have learned or are able to learn at this moment is all that you need, you will receive only the surface layer and travel no further into the depths of the mysteries of that knowledge. When you are self-motivated, each thing you attain becomes the doorway to newer and more glorious insights. You are the soil in which God plants the seed, and the caretaker of the crop that is harvested.

It is not always easy to keep yourself motivated and positive toward growth. Motivation requires all the insights you have been given along the path of Strength. It takes focusing in on your dreams, visions, and desires for holiness and making them happen. It takes perseverance and persistence even when you may not have the enthusiasm you'd normally welcome. It takes courage not to give in or give up, and self-discipline to make your life count for something in measure and volume, beyond yourself. It takes a sincere desire for freedom to be yourself. The more you empower others to empower you and the more you praise God in all you see, the more quickly your heart will open to the fervor and joy of living in union with God.

You begin the initiative by being courageous enough to stand for what you believe, taking the risk to empty of expectations and being open to receive the Divine plan. Then God will pour the divine influx through your every pore and awaken you to wonders you have yet to see, hear, and experience. This is what the daughters of Zelophehad bravely did when they stood before the patriarchal hierarchy of Moses, Eleazar, and the princes of Israel. Their father had died on the desert journey from Egypt; since he had left only daughters and a wife, but no sons, the women wanted their rights to his share of land and property. Their courage to stand up to the reigning patriarchal system was displayed in their voices and perseverance. Instead of being confrontational, they accessed the studied discipline of the sacred warrior. They presented their request with firmness; they surmounted the issue with strength; and instead of shrinking back and forgoing their rights, they reached out and countered the hierarchy. As a result they gained more than the ordinary share of land and property: they received the double portion of the firstborn, as well as the regular inheritance of sons. Because of their motivation to stand for their rights, they changed not only their lives but the lives of the generations that followed them.

As you act with valor and become self-motivated you affect not only your life, but the lives of all whom you touch and those who are yet to be. Now is not the time to slouch. If you need to, take time to rest and go silent first. Then muster up your strength to move successfully toward your goals and upward toward your ordained destiny. There is work yet to do, tasks yet to fulfill, paths yet to travel, joys yet to celebrate, and ecstasies yet to absorb in the glorious splendor of the spiritual lifestyle.

Practice the Meditation on Awakening Consciousness
(page 208) at least once today.

Manifest the Power of Your Will

I call heaven and earth as a witness that I have set before
life and death, the blessing and the curse; therefore, choose
life so you and your children may *choose to* live *in holiness.*

Deuteronomy 30:19

Therefore, one who devotes himself *or herself* to the Way is
   one with the Way;
One who [devotes himself *or herself* to] Virtue is one with
   that Virtue;
And one who [devotes himself *or herself* to] losing is one
   with that loss.
To the one who is one with Virtue, the Way also gives Virtue;
While for the one who is one with his loss, the Way also
   disregards him.

Lao Tzu

In the heavenly Gate of Success, you stand as a free agent for the
manner in which you choose to live as a manifestation of Divine
will. With each moment of life comes choices and the freedom

to make your own decisions, though there is a paradox in your freedom of choice and God's knowledge of the preordained future. If God knows what you will do before you do it, how can you have the freedom to choose? If your thoughts and actions are already drawn into the blueprint of the future, where does free will enter? Is it a divine ploy that gets temporarily pasted onto the drawing board, or is it an actual overlay that can change the architecture of what God plans to build for you?

Rabbi Nachman teaches that before you were born, you were joined with Divine will and contracted to enter this world for the purpose of completing a mission. During birth, God placed inside your soul a mission, unique to you, for enhancing life on this planet. God has dreamed a dream in you, and the realization of that dream is essential to your well-being and the well-being of this universe. As a vessel of joy for God's light, your dream effortlessly unfolds. You will know your dream is real when what you do in life feels naturally good to you and serves goodness to others with ease. It is your destiny to live out the dream God is dreaming in you. The fulfillment of your dream does not depend on outside forces. It depends on your living willingly in the integrity and essence of who you are. When you are living fully, you are totally engrossed in what you are doing; you and the action become one. If you are creating, you become creation itself; if loving, you become love itself; if serving, you become service itself; and if thinking, you become thought itself. At the point of destiny you will feel total engagement between what you are doing and who you are being; total integration between God's dreaming in you and your dream; and total union between God's will and your will.

You are enveloped in God's will as a soul is enveloped in a body, or water is enveloped by air, or the universe is enveloped by the galaxy. These "envelopments" are called *makifin*. They are essential thought forms that hover outside the consciousness of your mind. These *makifin* are difficult for the mind to comprehend. They involve the kind of knowing that cannot exist separate from God. Therefore, in the worlds of knowledge, feeling, and action, out of necessity for existence, your mind cannot know anything without separating from it. For instance, you cannot know yourself while totally engrossed in yourself. In order to know yourself, you must step aside from yourself and become a fair witness to who you are. In the same way, to know as God knows is impossible in these worlds, because God knowledge is one with God; there is no difference. To comprehend the *makifin* would require that you live in formlessness, in the angelic realm of being.

So, as long as you cannot know what God knows, you have free will. Once you know what God knows, you no longer need free will, for the freedom will be one with you and one with God and one with knowledge itself. The envelopments hover around your auric field, just beyond your reach, as long as you choose life. Once you move beyond dualities and realize that life and death, up and down, in and out are all illusions, they join and become one.

While you are still part of humanity and not yet ascended to the angelic realms, you have the freedom to do as you will. You also have the ability to step outside of yourself and notice how the choices you make assist in your development to the next stage of growth. When the Baal Shem Tov was walking with a student, the disciple became thirsty and complained of his intense thirst. The Baal Shem Tov replied, "Do you think God brought you this far in your life to leave you dying of thirst on this out-of-the-way road? Don't you think God foresaw the situation and planned for it?" At that moment a man walked by, carrying a pail of water. When he was asked what brought him by the way, he explained that his teacher had fainted up the road, and he had walked several miles to a spring to fetch water. The student drank, the water carrier went on his way, and the Baal Shem Tov summed up the situation, saying, "Now you know, before God created the world, God willed everything that was to happen. There are no accidents; everything depends on your intelligence, spirit, and will to choose to be part of God's will."

As the heavens and the earth are your witness, in the choice for life you choose to bond your will with God's will and to stand on the crowns of all who came before and all who will come after.

Consider the areas in your life that have held your attention and interest. What were the things that were most fulfilling? Do you recall being so totally engaged in and fulfilled by an activity or thought that you had the feeling of losing yourself in it? Did you notice how effortless it was when you were so totally engaged in what you were doing? Become aware of your thoughts, words, and actions today. Notice which come with difficulty and which with ease; what distracts you and what engages your interest and feels wholesome in your body; what feels distant and what brings you closer to serving the will of God. You are born of Divine will; your life has value; and your dreams are meant to be.

Practice the Meditation on Awakening Consciousness
(page 208) at least once today.

Economize Your Energy

Who is strong? One who has the power over their
impulsions.

Pirke Avot

In caring for others and serving heaven,

There is nothing like using restraint.

Lao Tzu

Success implores you to remain focused and economize your
energy. Regardless of the circumstances you find yourself in, you
can succeed with focus and skill. When you are on a shortwave
radio and would like to get a fragile and distant channel, you
need to turn down the static of the other frequencies. Once you
have reached the correct airwave, if you turn up the volume the
static is most likely to return. This is true also in your life.
When you are in constant motion, coming and going, doing
and fixing, teaching and demonstrating, giving and nurturing,
your energy becomes static, and it is difficult to tune in to the
fine frequencies of the mind. Some people remain very busy and
attuned to crisis; they keep the noise level high so that they
cannot hear the void within themselves. What they are missing
is the delicious freedom inherent in the void and emptiness, the
peace and serenity inherent in the stillness.

Rabbi Jonathan Omer-man, modern-day scholar and kabbal-ist, teaches the importance of economizing energy. He tells the story of when he was incapacitated by polio and had to lie on his back for a year in the hospital. With only the ability to lie back and observe, he learned what it meant to economize energy. He could not affect the world around him, nor could he direct events; he could only lie back and watch. And what he saw was a view of the larger picture of life. He saw that his life was only a small part of a greater experience. In observing experiences outside his own, he saw how others coped. He noticed how other people reacted to the challenging events of their lives. He observed how some people could remain quiet and still in the midst of chaos. Then he examined his own reactions as an over-achiever. And with great inner strength and spiritual faith he used his time wisely by becoming still and going within. This stillness brought him to deeper levels of spirituality. He suc-ceeded in touching the depths of his spirit and the embrace of God. As a result, he has become a great teacher of the power of silence, solitude, and spirit.

Economizing energy takes belief in yourself and confidence that what you are doing has value. When you are confident and know your value, you tend to give more attention to moving with economy and fluidity, rather than in a tumultuous up-heaval of dispersing wind. Before a Chinese screen painter puts the brush in the bottle of ink, hours of stillness and contempla-tion go into the preparation. When her energies are in tune with the parchment, the brush, and the ink, she completes the painting in very little time, with a few well-placed strokes of the brush.

When your breath races faster than you do, you know it is time to stop, reevaluate, and economize. Many people have a difficult time stopping the adrenaline rush, drawing boundaries, and setting limits. To recognize when you are using more energy than you are receiving, when there is more chatter than silence, and more motion than stillness is the skill of one who walks the path of Success. Whatever exhausts you exhausts those around you as well. Whatever exhausts you overworks your guides and angels. When you overwork your resources, you lose what you are trying to gain.

When your thoughts, words, and actions are in tune with the ultimate Source, you will not deplete your energy. Working in union with God is effortless work and joyful service. This way of working is the skill of the one who knows how to sit, silence the static, and hear the inner voice. When you learn to economize energy, you realize that you do not need to be a salesperson of ideas. When your will is connected to God's will, when your thoughts are connected to the Divine thoughts, when your words bring you nearer to the Infinite, and when your actions are effortless, you are more apt to succeed. So often people run in all directions to accomplish one thing, or juggle many acts while performing one. And then they wonder why they do not feel fulfilled. When you get lost in expelling a lot of energy for a little gain, life loses its meaning. When you stop, you can economize by finding the one candle that can light all the rest. Then you have extended the light without blowing your own fuse.

You are here to carry God's light and release the Godsparks that are hidden in limiting ways of being. This can be done only as you dismantle your own *klippot* and see, touch, and hear your own worth. Your life has value; do not waste it in the fast-moving, eternally revolving door of illusion.

Practice the Meditation on Awakening Consciousness
(page 208) at least once today.

Use Tools for Transformation

In meditation on Torah or scriptural verse, one must repeat the thought many, many times, knock and pound on the door, until it will be opened. Sometimes a holy thought fleetingly passes through the mind and then one needs great accomplishment to pursue it.

Rabbi Nachman of Breslov

Empty yourself of everything.

Let the mind rest at peace.

Lao Tzu

A mind tool, also known in Sanskrit as a mantra, is a vehicle used for crossing over from one state of consciousness to another. Different teachers offer varied vehicles for traveling from one state of consciousness to another and for living in union and reunion with the Divine. Some teachers use aspects of Torah or teachings from other devotional works as a mantra leading to ecstatic states of union with God. Some use repetitions of prayers as a mantra to opening the doors to the inner chambers of the palace of God. Some, as did the prophets of old, use music for entering the mysteries and touching the essence of godliness. Some contemplate God by opening all the channels available in the mind, the body, and the spirit; in the integration, they live passionately with God in all realms of life. For some, body movement is the vehicle through which they access different states of consciousness and ground it in the physical world. The kabbalists consider dancing to be one of the most important techniques for attaining enlightenment. These spiritual tools are not unique to mystical Judaism; they have been used since ancient times by those who delved into the mysteries of time, space, consciousness, and God.

Today, all of these methods are available to you. They have been made accessible through Jewish Renewal, the study of kabbalah, and the reemergence and integration of mystical practices. Kindred spirits are entering into community and praying with one another in a variety of ways that utilize the mind tools for effective living in union and reunion with the source. For example, if you were to enter a prayer service in our community on Friday night, the eve of Shabbat, you would find yourself transported to another realm. All aspects of the worship service serve as spiritual tools for transforming consciousness and increasing opportunities for union and reunion with God. The service begins on the physical level with body movement, such as yoga or tai chi, followed by silent meditation or guided visualization. This practice relaxes and revitalizes the energy that may have been depleted from the workweek. The sacred movement and silence open the window to the soul, which echoes forth in a gentle melody where one voice is joined by two, three, four, and eventually hundreds of worshiping voices in the sanctuary. We chant all prayers in different melodies that we consciously select for raising energy and deepening the emotional connections within. When the energy is at its highest and the community of worshipers is most coherent as a group, we join in a sacred healing circle. During and following the healing circle, melodies soften and the community rises in silent devotion. The silence is penetrated by the sounds of joy and blessing as the service draws to a conclusion with prayer songs of affirmation and blessing. The energy that can build in a community that consciously utilizes the spiritual tools of prayer, study, music, and movement positively affects lives, heals bodies, empties minds, and transforms spirits.

Spiritual tools assist you in remembering who you are as a bearer of God's light. Along with community, there are also spiritual tools you can use in the privacy of your own solitude. Setting a sacred space or altar in your own room, where you place spiritual objects of significance, is a way of remembering to empty, open, and receive the light of God. Sitting alone in front of a mirror and gently smiling at yourself is a way of recognizing and receiving the light of God. Wrapping yourself in a prayer shawl during meditation and worship is yet another way of feeling and receiving God. Opening a prayerbook or a Bible to a random page and meditating on the phrase that meets your eye is yet another way to receive God.

All tools you use to generate your spirit toward receiving the light of God are valid. If it is in your thought, it was placed there by God for you. Make it work for you with confidence, sanctity, and dignity. Spiritual tools help you in living a more fulfilling, joyous, and healthy life. They serve as transforming cables in all aspects of living fully. Wherever your intention is at the time you use your mantra, that is where you will benefit in receiving God the most. Conscious use of spiritual tools assists in diminishing anger, in decreasing overeating, speaking only truth, and in maintaining equanimity throughout the challenges and supports of life.

Set aside time for silence and prayer each day. As you practice the Meditation on Awakening Consciousness today, follow your intentions and ask yourself; Are you living or being lived? And in the life you're living, is your soul dancing? Is your heart singing?

*Practice the Meditation on Awakening Consciousness
(page 208) at least once today.*

Exercise Personal Freedom and Envision Infinite Possibilities

With human cords I ever draw them forward,

leading them with strings of love;

and I was to them as those who lift off the yoke of their

jaws,

and I gave them food.

Hosea 11:4

The great Tao flows everywhere . . .

It nourishes the ten thousand things,

And yet is not their lord.

It has no aim; it is very small.

The ten thousand things return to it,

Yet it is not their lord,

It is very great.

Lao Tzu

Is there such a thing as freedom? Can you be personally free? Or does that idea evoke anxiety and pressure you to become more self-responsible? Recognize that freedom comes with self-responsibility. Recall how freedom calls to you to observe and accept life in the fullness of its possibilities. Freedom beckons you to dismantle the filters, or *klippot,* that imprison the feelings and sensations through which you express your freedom. Now is the time, as you conclude your passage through the Gate of Success, to set yourself free. Imagine for a moment that there are no restrictions constraining you. How would your life change? Would you experience more joy? Would you be more content? Or would you find other excuses for not being free? Notice the choices you make in your life and the excuses you make for not being free. Freedom is your responsibility and your choice.

Freedom comes from within. It is nurtured in your soul. It is manifest in the way you view life and in the obstacles you choose to remove or place on your path. Freedom embraces the totality of life, the struggles and challenges of everyday living. Do not be deceived into thinking that there is freedom in exchanging one set of rules for another, one religion for another, or one family or partnership for another. Freedom is a result not of outside influences so much as of your inner spirit. One can have all the luxuries and wealth in the world and feel imprisoned; another can be locked away for a life sentence and feel freed.

Rabbi Nachman of Breslov sent four of his students into an orchard to seek the essence of the mystery of creation. To convey the depth of the mystery, Rabbi Nachman instructed them to bring back the fruit of the first tree they saw. Anxious to understand the lesson, they ran over to the first tree they saw, ready to pick its fruit. As they neared the tree, they saw fruit that looked like precious gems, illumined from within with a sparkling glow that mesmerized them. They wondered if this was the right tree and if they were supposed to be picking such glowing fruit. The first student apprehensively warned, "This cannot be the tree, for it is too enchanting, and if we pick the fruit we may become enchanted too." This student was afraid even to touch the fruit for fear of its danger. The second student agreed and volunteered his view: "Maybe we stumbled on the wrong tree, and if we pick this fruit we will be sinning." The third student had much more confidence and disagreed with the first two. She insisted that this must be the tree from which

to pick the fruit, for it was the first one they saw. The fourth
student was bewildered by the beauty of the tree. She walked
around the trunk of the tree, carefully exploring its branches
and gingerly touching its fruit. Even though she could see,
touch, and smell the tree, she still had trouble thinking it was
real. She agreed with the first two and thought it was best not
to pick the fruit. She did not believe that such a magnificent
tree could be real. She was afraid of accepting the tree and its
fruit as a reality that she was free to have. When the students
left the orchard and rejoined Rabbi Nachman, he was grieved,
for he saw that they returned without having picked the fruit.
Even though he already knew the answer, he asked them as a
teaching, "Has any one of you brought back the fruit of the Tree
of Life?"

In passing through the garden of your life, how many times
have you stumbled upon a surprising revelation or a heartwarm-
ing situation that feels glorious yet different? Because it is not
familiar, it seems forbidden, or not real enough, or a betrayal of
old beliefs or old ways of being. You may want to taste it but
are influenced by those around you not to change. Notice the
times you may have been on the edge of changing from what
was in your life to what could be. Freedom lies in the possibilities of what is yet to be. To be free means to be free enough
within yourself to risk change, and compassionate enough to
stay mindful.

In any shift or change, you move from one center to another.
You can find unconditional freedom in allowing yourself and
others around you to shift their positions from one center to
another without losing the sacred circle of life. When you place
conditions on yourself or others, you are not trusting in your or
their ability to serve goodness from a new vantage point. This
restriction causes the attachments and clinging that lead to pain
and suffering. Moving freely from one center of being to a new
one is part of growth and change.

Freedom means coming to peace with the fact that change is
inherent in life. Enslavement goes against the nature of humanity and all God's creations. The Passover Haggadah teaches that

you are part of a new generation of humanity and empowered to consider yourself personally liberated from the narrows of ancient Egypt and the restrictions of slavery. Coming through the Red Sea was akin to a birthing ritual. With recall and memory, you continue to access a God who is free and encourages you to be free.

In practicing the Meditation on Awakening Consciousness you have now become aware of the importance of having a clear intention and remaining focused on the direction ahead. It is with the power of these insights and practices that you walk forward in confidence and expand to the infinite possibilities of glory that await your entry into the Gate of Glory.

Practice the Meditation on Awakening Consciousness
(page 208) at least once today.

GLORY

God's glory fills the universe.

Isaiah 6:3

For glory, God created *it,*

formed *it,* and completed *it.*

Isaiah 43:7

*E*NTER THE GATE OF Glory and design your life with spiritual abundance, joyous meaning, and profoundly positive purpose. In Glory you will create a way of life that holds opportunities for receiving aesthetic wonders and awesome miracles. In Glory you will feel the glory of God envelop your environment, encompass your spirit, and embrace your everyday living.

As you walk the path of Glory, you will let go, step aside, and let the spirit of God come through you in a creative, productive way. With the insights you receive in Glory you will learn that with God as your partner you can accomplish everything with greater ease, dignity, beauty, and spirit. You will learn how to access the different aspects of your soul in order to better define yourself and utilize your talents. You will learn the importance of your ego and how it relates to your soul in order to enhance your spiritual life. You will learn how to nourish your spirit, maintain a healthy, nonattached ego, and live a glorious, purposeful life. You will invite joy into your world, pleasure into your activities, and abundance into your life. With enthusiasm and vitality you will live consciously in both your inner world and outer environment. You will turn the humdrum motions of your life into a state-of-the-art way of living. You will stop the inner chatter of your mind and speak positive and essential words in order to lift your thoughts and elevate your environment. You will learn that pure actions invite the heavens to rejoice and sincere praise lifts up the spirit of the world. As you design, polish, and refine your own life you will extend your ability to affect the world.

Before turning to the first insight now, take some quiet time and experience the Meditation on Remaining Conscious. To benefit from this meditation read it slowly. Pause between each sentence and experience what you have read. Then spend a moment or two enveloped in the peace that results. Review the Meditation on Remaining Conscious after reading each of the insights or at the end of each day.

ᕲ Meditation on Remaining Conscious ᕲ

Pause a moment and move your attention into the breath. Slowly inhale and exhale. Allow the inhalation and exhalation to flow evenly and freely throughout your body. Feel your body relax and your mind empty. Luxuriate in the peaceful, quiet stillness for a few moments. Then as you move into the awareness of this moment, become conscious of your activities during the day thus far, and review how it felt to be you and to do what you did, speak what you spoke, think what you thought. Acknowledge those thoughts, words, and actions which were joined in partnership with your Divinity and those moments when you may have lost consciousness of this partnership. Use your imagination to change anything you may have wanted to change in your own thoughts, words, and actions today. When you have reviewed your day and feel complete with it, acknowledge yourself for all you did and continue to do, for all you are and continue to be. Now bless God for having created you with a soul that is perfect, and bring your awareness back to where you are right now.

With continued practice and daily reflection you can profoundly affect your actions and reactions in the conversation and design of your life.

Let Go and Step Aside

And *the angel* said: Your name will no longer be called
Jacob *(heel)*, but Israel *(God wrestler);* for you have wrestled
with God and with humanity and have proven yourself
capable.

Genesis 32:29

Therefore the Sage

Puts himself *or herself* in the background yet finds himself
   or herself in the foreground;

Puts self-concern out *of his or her mind,* yet finds that his *or
   her* self-concern is preserved.

Is it not because *the sage* has no self-interest,

That *the sage* is able to realize his *or her* self-interest?

Lao Tzu

Stepping out of your own way is liberating and leads to a more
joyful life. Who is in the driver's seat anyway? Believing that
you are is an illusion; God has always been the Force that steers
your path to glory. You may be reluctant to let go, and that
reluctance may lead you on circuitous routes to nowhere. When

you awaken to the guidance of the Infinite Source, the path is smooth and the journey becomes pleasurable, effortless, and blessed.

When I think of letting go and stepping aside, I think of the biblical story of Jacob and Esau. Jacob betrayed Esau and fled from his home in fear of Esau's retaliation. During the years of their estrangement, each one married, bore numerous children, accumulated large armies of employees, and increased his wealth. After many years, Jacob decided with his wives, Rachel and Leah, to take his family and journey back to his birthplace. In order to reach home, Jacob had to cross over his brother, Esau's, land. The night before he was to cross his brother's land, Jacob was anxious, for he did not know how Esau would receive him and his family. He wasn't sure whether Esau would be confrontational or peaceful.

Jacob knew that his destiny was in God's hands and what he needed to do was to let go of his anxiety by stepping aside from himself and letting God take over. He did this by spending the night alone under the stars by the river's edge. In solitude he was able to go within, empty of expectations, and move beyond his fears. Through quiet meditation and introspection he opened his heart and poured his soul out to God. As Jacob surrendered his will to God, an angel in the form of a human appeared to him. He and the angel wrestled until Jacob totally let go and fully surrendered his strength, his fear, and his will. The moment Jacob stepped aside, the angel embraced him and asked for a blessing. I often wondered why the angel asked for a blessing from Jacob. Why did the angel need the blessing when it was really Jacob who was hurting? I finally realized that the angel was really Jacob's higher self. And what Jacob was doing by the river's edge all night was trying to step outside his local self and let his divinity emerge.

At first Jacob did not recognize the angel as himself, so he wrestled. It was not until Jacob could step outside his ego that he could see his divinity and bless it. Once Jacob blessed the angel, his higher self, he was able to transform his anxieties into calmness, his fears into love, and himself into a more evolved spirit, an angel of God. His name was no longer Jacob, which meant "heel." His name was now Israel, "God wrestler," for he wrestled with God and proved capable of stepping aside and letting his higher spirit come through. Once he let his higher spirit emerge, Jacob was able to meet Esau with love instead of fear. When the brothers met, they embraced each other's spirit and walked together in peace.

Artists, musicians, and writers all have to cross a river of inner turmoil at one time or another. In crossing, they wrestle with their own inhibitions and fears, until they let go and step aside. With their new view they can see themselves in fresh, new ways. From this egoless perspective they can look at an empty canvas, an empty score sheet, or a blank piece of paper and begin to see a subtle angelic impression. In the emptiness they can see the fingerprint of God, the song of the spirit, the hidden story revealed. It is the creative person who steps aside from himself or herself and lets God through, who manifests otherworldly creations, celestial music, and spirit-filled stories. Even an ordinary person can accomplish extraordinary things when he or she steps aside and lets God in.

Letting go and stepping aside has become a continuous practice for me. In stepping aside I let go of control. I am more able to respond when I let go of control. I practice letting go and stepping aside whether I am counseling, teaching, or presiding at a temple meeting. I begin with a meditation, step outside of myself, and ask God to give me the wisdom to know what to say or do. I do this whether I am painting or writing. I meditate first in front of the empty canvas, then step outside of myself and ask God for creative inspiration. In writing this book, I spent more time getting myself out of the way than in writing. I wanted every word to be so pure, so real, and so God-filled. I knew God worked miracles in my life, and I wanted to share this journey so that you also could experience the wonders of God and the miracles of life. I would not put a pencil to paper or touch the keyboard on the computer until I let go, stepped aside from myself, and felt the spirit of God enter. When I step aside, whether in counseling, planning, writing, painting, praying, or even socializing, I feel more organized, whole, open, productive, creative, and *honest.*

Stepping aside from yourself, letting go of control, and moving beyond clock time, beyond boundaried space and beyond goals and expectations, is the sacred journey of the spiritual initiate. It is a journey that opens your creativity and utilizes your talents. It opens new horizons, greater acceptance toward yourself and others, and a deeper trust in the Infinite Source. In stepping aside, you let Divine creativity create beauty, splendor, and glory through you.

Practice letting go of control today. You can be responsible without being controlling. Quiet the chatter of your mind and speak only what is essential. When there are decisions to be made, move out of your own way, witness your divinity, and notice how essential matters get handled. The power you give away is a power of illusion. The real power is not in your ego; it is in your divinity. That power is eternal. As you practice the Meditation on Remaining Conscious today, note what occurs as you step aside from yourself and review the day from a higher perspective.

Practice the Meditation on Remaining Conscious
(page 238) at least once today.

Take God as Your Partner

Behold, the God that keeps Israel

neither slumbers nor sleeps.

Psalm 121:4

God created the world to partner humans.

Rabbi Samuel Ben Ammi

There are times when God seems so close, and times when God feels so distant. But the most difficult times are when you cannot feel God at all. At those times we tend to divide and conquer our accomplishments and experiences in terms of judgments. Some aspects of our lives seem good and some seem bad; some seem indifferent and some beyond repair. In this state of clinging to expectations and ideals, we do everything in our power to avert pain, suffering, and negativity of any kind. Ironically, our attachment to ideal thoughts, perfect relationships, and positive experiences creates even more suffering. When we let go, empty, and release expectations and attachments, we can return to nothingness. Nothingness is both the vast, limitless emptiness and the name of God. In returning to the nothingness we partner God.

What does it mean to partner God? Such a responsibility would seem overwhelming and awesome; yet in reality, partnering God is effortless and liberating. As you move beyond the old paradigm of God as a hierarchical judge sitting on a throne, you find a more contemporary, helpful Infinite Source. There is an unconditionally loving, accepting, joyous, and playful God who is hiding within you. With God as your partner, you design your life with dignity, embellish your environment with beauty, and embody your actions with goodness.

However, with the inundation of stimulation in your life and in your mind, it may be difficult for you to access the God within or even to appreciate God in things around you. First, you need to want to know God. Second, you need to give yourself permission to know a God who may be different from what your parents described. Third, you need to let go of expectations and open yourself to receiving God in the mysteries of life. For instance, allow yourself the freedom to feel God in a blade of grass, to see God in the sunset, to hear God in the cry of a child. Then notice how God appears in the many guises of your life. There is part of God hiding in the soil of a napkin, the pain of a scar, the rotting of a pipeline. God shows God's self to you in everything you choose to see. It is easiest to see God when you can look through eyes that do not judge beauty, through ears that do not criticize sound, through a touch that does not pull away from harsh surfaces. With the strength of nonjudgment and the compassion of unconditional love, you can find God everywhere.

Once a student came to Rabbi Levi Yitzchak and desired to have a taste of Gan Eden, Paradise, by spending Shabbat with him. The rabbi went to the home of the water carrier for the Sabbath meal, and the student followed behind, a bit perplexed. He was surprised that such a holy rabbi would spend the Sabbath meal with such a simpleton as the water carrier. When they arrived at the water carrier's home, the whole family, the parents, their nine children, and the guests crammed into the tiny space of their house. The student noticed that the home had a horrific odor. They made the blessings over the wine and the challah, and then the wife proudly presented the food. Since she had known that Rabbi Levi Yitzchak was going to visit, she saved the leftovers from Passover and held them aside until now, four months later. The student was again horrified that he would have to eat food that was obviously spoiled, as there was no refrigeration in this home. The woman had barely opened the jar of food yet the odor almost made the student faint. When she served the rabbi, he tasted of the food and saw heaven on earth, and exclaimed how the taste of the food was like Paradise. Each person at the table ate the food as though he or she were being served fresh produce right off a queen's table. But the student ran outside and regurgitated everything. He was bent over with nausea when Rabbi Levi Yitzchak came out to comfort him. The rabbi said, "You are not yet ready to taste of Eden." To taste of Eden and to partner God is to be able to go beyond judgment and to live fully, with emptiness and receptivity. It means to be able to live enthusiastically, imaginatively, and with egoless, selfless service to humanity.

Partnering God means living a vision of holiness and trusting that your vision is not an illusion but rather God's vision being lived through you. It means tapping into a memory divinely ordained and eternal. It means letting go of the pride connected with doing it yourself, and noticing how God helps. What you do in this life depends on your intention, and your intention depends on your nearness to or distance from God. You are being awakened to recognizing God as the Source of your thoughts and the end goal of your actions. In a life that is accepting of the full range of emotions and the vast varieties of experience, there is eternal living. As you partner God you live more fully, more freely, and more joyously. From the perspective of God, your options are infinite. From your perspective your options tend to be limiting. With God as your partner you will reach higher horizons.

Practice the Meditation on Remaining Conscious
(page 238) at least once today.

Access the Glory of Your Soul

The light of God is the soul of the human.

Proverbs 20:27

Know the strength of man,

But keep a woman's care!

Be the stream of the Universe!

Lao Tzu

The Baal Shem Tov once told the story of a precious vase stored in a clear glass box and kept on a high shelf in the reception area of a large estate. All who saw the vase were fascinated by it, yet they could not reach or touch it. One day, a group of people were waiting in the reception area. One clever person decided to climb to the top and retrieve the box that held the vase. This person piled one chair on top of another and carefully climbed them all until she reached the top. She gently retrieved the glass box and brought the vase to the table below, where the people could examine it more closely. They gingerly opened the box and with curious yet delicate care, each one stroked the vase. Each in turn gently rotated the vase upside down, then right side up. And when they looked within they saw a clear emptiness in the center of the vase. In the reflective sheen of the vase's glossed surface they saw a distinctively different vision of themselves and one another.

Your soul is the precious vase stored in the highest parts of your Self. It beckons you to retrieve it, hold it, feel it, and see within it a new vision of yourself. The reality of who you are and who your soul is in you is so much more than can be seen from a distance. In accessing the glory of your soul, you define and redefine the possibilities of who you are.

You are both a unique individual and an integral part of the world at large. You are the sacred container that embodies the spirit and reflects both the particular and universal aspects of your soul. Within your soul are all souls, and within each soul is a universe of God. When you nurture your soul and then step outside of yourself into the world, you are held in the compassionate, loving arms of the soul of the universe.

God sees, hears, and senses you through the aspects of the soul that live in your body. These aspects are referred to as *neshama k'lalit* and *neshama p'ratit,* the general soul and the particular soul. Your general soul is part of the universal soul of God; the particular soul is part of the private, intimate realm that is unique to your spiritual essence. When you are in the mode of the general soul, you seem more socially assertive and entertaining. People who are charismatic and serve goodness through the joy of entertaining large groups of people are said to have developed their *neshama k'lalit,* general soul. When you are quiet and in retreat, you are in the mode of the particular soul. People who are reclusive meditators and solo-journeying spiritual initiates operate from the mode of *neshama p'ratit,* the personal, particular soul. An excess of either aspect of the soul creates a deficiency in the other. You can travel to the mountain-top and receive the peace and solitude of the high spaces, yet there is still the need to return to the valley below and commune with God in community.

You are a magnificent being, intricately designed and superbly adorned. You are both the universal soul and the personal, particular soul. If you dwell on yourself as being the vast, whole universe, you may become lost and perish. If within this universe of being you continually define areas where you are most comfortable, then that is where you will be most yourself.

And it is in that place where you define yourself that the universe will be with you. Your defined area is the still point within your soul that continually withdraws, expands, disperses, and transforms.

Creating and defining a spiritually active identity requires releasing the filters of the clinging mind and ego and seeing yourself with the love, compassion, and enthusiasm with which God sees you, hearing yourself as God hears you, physically acknowledging yourself as God physically acknowledges you. You are a carrier of the glory of God, fully present, empty, and open to receiving the wonders of life. Access the glory of your soul and watch the miracles unfold the limitless possibilities of who you are and opportunities for who you can be.

Practice the Meditation on Remaining Conscious
(page 238) at least once today.

Bring Soul to Your Ego

The essence of sacred service dwells in the mind.
When a person's thoughts are connected to Divine
wisdom and nobility, even the simplest actions
become holy.

Baal Shem Tov

Attachment to an ego-personality leads people into
delusions.

Buddha

The glory of God fills your life through the interaction of the ego, the soul, and the Infinite. Many people embrace their soul and yearn to touch the Infinite, yet when it comes to their ego, they feel they need to suppress it. There are times when you may feel that the ego is not a healthy part of your spiritual life, and you may try to annul your own ego. This is not really possible, for no matter how you try to let go of your ego, it is still there waiting to serve you. Your ego cannot be dismissed from your personality. Your ego needs to work for you, and in this insight you will learn how to bring soul to your ego in order to help it enhance, rather than diminish, your spiritual life.

The ego, the soul, and the Infinite are deeply intertwined and responsible to one another, yet there are moments of forgetfulness when you may lose the sense of the connections between them. Consider the example of a store owner who employs and trains a manager to motivate and organize the employees. When the employees do not heed the direction of the manager, havoc reigns. When the employees disregard the manager's wisdom and expertise, ignore the store owner's goals, and consider only their own short-term needs, the store drops in sales. Then the manager no longer looks forward to the work and the owner reconsiders his investment.

Think of your body as the store of life. Acts of goodness are the products. God is the creator of the store. Your Creator has invested your body with divine attributes and installed a soul in you to manage, motivate, and inspire you to acts of goodness. But the soul knows only to serve God. It is not attuned to your emotional and physical needs. For the soul to be able to transfer wisdom, understanding, and knowledge to you on the physical and emotional level, it needs to employ the ego. The ego helps the soul disburse acts of goodness. And just as the soul serves God, the ego serves the soul. The ego helps the soul survive in the physical and emotional realms. The ego is the messenger that travels a challenging path between the soul and the outside world. The greatest challenge to the ego is to stay out of its own way. As a messenger, the ego cannot get its own pride caught in the web of communications. The ego serves as an important purpose for the soul and is healthiest when it stays empty and nonattached.

You are in control of your ego. When you use it as a sacred instrument for your soul and do not get caught in self-serving pride, you maintain equanimity in your life. This idea reminds me of the story of a man who once applied for admission into the Society of Meditators. The first question he was asked by the interviewer taking his application was, "Your intentions are benevolent, but have you attained equanimity?" The man was confused and so the interviewer asked, "If one flatters you and another insults you, are they both equal in your eyes?" The man thought, and replied, "No, my friend. The one that flatters me brings me pleasure and the one who insults me brings me pain. Yet I am careful not to carry a grudge or take revenge." The interviewer from the Society of Meditators concluded that the man was not ready and answered, "May you go in peace. You have not yet attained equanimity. You have not yet reached that level in your soul where the ego is non-attached to praise or insult, pleasure or pain. Therefore, you are not ready to enter the Society of Meditators. Go and practice non-attachment in your ego until you have reached equanimity. Only then will you be ready to connect on the deepest levels with the Source."

As you continue to meditate on remaining conscious, consider the many ways of maintaining and accessing equanimity in all the parts of who you are, in the many facets of how you live. Notice when you feel fear and anger, and recognize that they are the attachments of the ego that filter out wisdom and understanding from the soul. In the personal inner sanctuary of your body, you have all the parts necessary for touching God, nourishing your soul, maintaining a healthy, nonattached ego, and living a glorious life.

Practice the Meditation on Remaining Conscious
(page 238) at least once today.

Bring Joy to the World

And I saw that there is nothing better than for a person to rejoice.

Ecclesiastes 3:22

Stand before it and there is no beginning.

Follow it and there is no end.

Lao Tzu

Did you know that what you put into the environment today will be available for centuries to come? Create joy in your life today and you create vibrations of joy in the environment that will last an eternity.

Rabbi Nachman of Breslov taught that the only thing worth giving your children is joy. Teach your children joy and teach the child within you joy. Joy leads you out of confusion and into clarity. Joy transforms negative thoughts into positive learning experiences that encourage freedom and creativity. Make joy your greatest legacy.

Before I was ordained, I was asked by my teacher Rabbi Zalman Schachter-Shalomi, "What is the message you want to convey as a rabbi?" I answered, "Joy." I found joy in God and in Judaism. And I want to turn others on to the joy they can find in their many images of God and then to encourage them to find it within themselves and their heritage as well.

Joy is contagious. When you bring joy into your life, the world around you catches it. When you inspire every thought, word, and action with pleasure and joy, you bring heaven to earth. When you think uplifting thoughts, you receive uplifting responses. When you allow your thoughts to pull you down, you attract diminishing responses. Even within the deepest darkness there is a ray of light waiting to be lit; within the greatest challenge, there is a miracle waiting to be found; and within the greatest sorrow, there are memories of joy waiting to be grasped. In thinking positive, beautiful thoughts you have the ability to touch the Infinite and manifest miracles.

When there is joy in your heart there is faith in your spirit and abundance in your life. Joy adds and sadness detracts. The Baal Shem Tov tells a story similar to the following. There was a beggar who entered the courtyard of a monarch and tearfully asked for assistance. He was unceremoniously given a small donation. Then a joyous person entered the courtyard, praised the monarch, and requested a favor. She was fervently welcomed into the palace and granted a favor of greater value than the donation the tearful beggar received. In your own life, when you impoverish your spirit and hold back joy through low self-esteem, anxiety, and depression, you limit the benefits of the present moment and the possibilities of the future. Let go of the fear that blocks the joy of this moment. Rabbi Nachman of Breslov says there are those who are afraid to enjoy what they have today because they worry about tomorrow. There are people who create their own sadness by holding on to things they cannot control. What they are missing is the delicious joy and sweet ecstasy of this very moment.

The psalmist proclaims, "Serve God with joy and come before God with ecstasy." Those who live in the light of God do not deny themselves pleasure. Those who trust in God are joyous. They know ecstasy and are protected. In pleasure they find God. In finding God within yourself, you tap into a state of consciousness that ignites your spark, inspires your creativity, and vibrates with joy through every pore of your being.

Become aware of the joys and blessings that are yours today.

Realize the miracles that have entered your life as a result of being joyous. Notice the people who are attracted to you when you are joyous. Recall the opportunities that came your way because you were open to joy. Joy begets joy. Share your joy and feel the glory of God.

Practice the Meditation on Remaining Conscious
(page 238) at least once today.

Live Consciously

There is something that can only be found in one place. It is a great treasure, which may be called the fulfillment of existence. The place where this treasure can be found is the place on which one stands.

Martin Buber

A tree as great as a man's embrace springs from a small
   shoot;
A terrace nine stories high begins with a pile of earth;
A journey of a thousand miles starts under one's feet.

Lao Tzu

Consciousness is the tool with which you live a spiritually ful-filling life. An ancient story tells us of a woman who had a dream that if she went to a certain place in the valley between two mountains at sunrise, and could dig in the spot where the sun pointed, she would find a great treasure. So she arose before sunrise and journeyed to that place in the valley. When the sun came up it pointed to a spot, where she began digging for the buried treasure. She dug feverishly until the noon. When she lifted her head and wiped her brow she realized that the sun was shining directly above her head. Looking at her radiant image in the full sunlight, she understood the real meaning behind the dream. She understood that the treasure she was digging for was not in the ground; it was inside of her. She was the treasure!

When you are conscious you maintain an awareness of all the dimensions in which you experience life. You are aware of being the perceiver, the perceived, and perception itself. You recognize that you are the seer, the seen, and the vision simultaneously. As you awaken to consciousness you awaken to the glory of God as it abounds in the universal realms and in your own personal spheres.

Rituals are acts performed for the purpose of raising consciousness. However, there are many rituals you perform daily without conscious attention, such as washing your face, brushing your teeth, and combing your hair. There are also rituals you may perform with a little more thought, such as reading the newspaper, walking the dog, and washing the car. Then there are the daily rituals of greeting friends and coworkers, which you may perform with unconscious repetition. The rituals that you perform habitually and without consciousness can become opportunities for awakening consciousness.

Meaningful rituals can turn the ordinary, humdrum motions of your life into a state-of-the art way of living. A ritual that is performed consciously awakens you to the wonder and miracle of life. When you pay attention to the details as though they are endowed with enormous spiritual powers, your life becomes infinitely more interesting, magical, and new. The Zohar, the kabbalistic *Book of Splendor,* tells us that in the head of a small pin there are innumerable God-filled spirits. If there are countless spirits in the head of a pin, then how many more are there in a facial muscle, on the tip of a tongue, in a strand of hair? When you hold a newspaper, are you aware that you hold the tree, the seed, the soil, the sun, and the rain that are all part of what went into making that paper? You are also holding the vibrations of all the writers and their thoughts, as well as the issues themselves that are recorded in the paper.

Consciousness is not a means to an end. It is where the goal and the process are one and the same. As your consciousness is awakened, you access deeper awareness, giving birth to deeper and more meaningful ways of being. With consciousness, what was ordinary becomes extraordinary. What once was limiting and confined, with consciousness becomes open and spacious. What once was judgmental, with consciousness becomes unconditionally liberating. Perceiving an ordinary act in all the dimensions of physical, emotional, spiritual, and hallowed ways of being leads you closer to the destiny you were born to fulfill.

Awakening to consciousness is living fully, as heaven lives on earth. When Abraham and Sarah welcomed the three angels into their tent and fed them, they were fulfilling an important part of their destiny as humans. Through Abraham and Sarah, the angels, who were unaccustomed to eating, participated in a human activity that was hosted with aesthetic beauty, love, devotion, and gratitude to God. By eating, Abraham and Sarah enabled the angels and God to live through them as they hallowed their own natural needs. As you sanctify your actions, no matter how trivial they may seem, you enable the angels and God to live through you, and you bring heaven to earth.

Open your mind, free your brain, and regard the smallest, most trivial actions as though they were both the means and the goals by which you and God derive pleasure from each other.

Practice the Meditation on Awakening Conscious
(page 238) at least once today.

Use Essential Speech and Pure Action

When I weld my spirit to God, I let my mouth say what
it will, for then all my words are bound to their root in
Heaven.

Baal Shem Tov

Whatever words we utter should be chosen with care for
people will hear them and be influenced by them for good
or ill.

Buddha

Words and actions are very powerful. They can devastate or they
can heal. So powerful are words that they hold the balance
between thoughts and actions. There is gentle language and
harsh language, essential speech and useless chatter, conscious
talk and superficial rambling. Rabbi Levi Yitzchak wrote of the
difference between one who rebukes harshly and one who speaks
gently to the people. The gentle speaker elevates the soul of the
people and dwells in holiness. The rebuker who uses harsh
language intimidates and shames people. As for essential talk
and conscious action, Rabbi Pinchas said, "There are no words
which, in themselves, are useless. There are no actions which, in

themselves, are useless. But one can make useless both actions and words by saying or doing them uselessly."

Essential speech is direct, focused, nonwavering, and non-wondering. It is communication that economizes energy and minimizes the use of language. A lot can be said in a few well-placed words. A clear mind articulates in essential speech; a cluttered mind attempts to hide itself in useless chatter. Pause at intervals throughout your day and witness whether your speech is essential or chatter. When it is conscious, it is flowing from the spirit of God dwelling in your soul and guiding your words. Conscious, essential, gentle speech happens naturally when you clear your mind and start on empty.

It is essential to articulate positive thoughts and serve goodness in your actions. Even if someone has wronged you, consider carefully how you speak to them, for all souls are one. Your soul and another's soul originated as sparks from the Divine soul. When you diminish from the glory of another's soul, you are diminishing from the glory of your own soul. Have compassion on another as you would on yourself; see the glory, articulate the positive, and act with integrity.

In praising another person, remember also to praise yourself. In treating others, remember also to treat yourself with kind actions. Be gentle and compassionate in the manner in which you treat yourself as well. In the words of Rabbi David Wolfe-Blank, "Praise yourself. Criticism breaks down the spirit. Praise builds it up." Praise yourself as you would a child of God. With sincere praise and action that comes from the heart, the heavens rejoice and God renews your spirit.

The Baal Shem Tov was once passing a house of prayer and was hesitant to go in. He felt he could not enter the sanctuary because it was overcrowded with teachings and prayers, and there was not enough room for him to stand. This reluctance puzzled those around him: after all, how could a room be too full of prayer? He explained that the words of the prayers and teachings of the people were not coming from the purity of their hearts. Their words and actions were out of balance with each other. Therefore their teachings and prayers were not ascending through the ceiling of the room, and instead were crowding out the people and stuffing the room "from wall to wall and from floor to ceiling."

Words spoken from the heart in prayer and actions performed with pure intention ascend on high and draw down healing energy. Heartfelt words and pure actions create new worlds and heal old ones. Each morning in the liturgy you are reminded of the power of words to create worlds when you recite, "Blessed is the God who spoke and the world came into being." Following the private meditation prayer, the *amidah*, you recite, "My God, guard my tongue from negative language and my lips from speaking deceitfully." In the private meditation prayer, during the Sabbath, the following is added: "Those who speak loving words have chosen greatness."

When speaking in private or in public, your words are garments for the soul and tender the interchange between thought and action. When you lie down and when you rise up, weld your spirit to God and witness what your mouth speaks. For when your words are bound to their root in heaven, they speak what is essential. When your actions emanate from pure intention, they are healing, gentle, and conscious. To assist in staying mindful of your actions and speech, you may recite prayers or invoke your own blessings. Remember, words create worlds, and words with heartfelt actions create glorious ways of living.

*Practice the Meditation on Remaining Conscious
(page 238) at least once today.*

CREATIVITY

And God said: It is not good for the human to be alone, I will make a helper *to stand* opposite *the human*.

Genesis 2:18

The Tao of heaven is like the bending of a bow.

The high is lowered, and the low is raised.

Lao Tzu

YOU ARE NOW ENTERING the Gate through which the exuberance and pleasures of life are born, the Gate of Creativity. Creativity is the foundation upon which you regenerate and revitalize your life. Creativity is the force of God that dwells within your spirit and moves you to birth new life, new opportunities, and new accomplishments. With Creativity you can solve the most difficult problem and fulfill the most challenging goal.

In the Gate of Creativity you will sift through the heart of your experiences and mold these experiences to your particular needs. You will realize that although you are one with humanity, you are born unique to God and vital to this universe. Through cultivating Divine sexuality, you will open to loving your Self and your limitations with deeper faith and greater generosity. You will move beyond self-consciousness and become intimate (cozy) with God as a lover, a friend, and a nurturing guide. You will touch God by touching others in sincere, nurturing, and caring relationships. You will gain insights into finding your soul mate and, more important, in becoming a soul mate. The love, pleasure, passion, enthusiasm, and ecstasy that you birth in Creativity will bring you and those you touch abundant joy. The joy you create today is the legacy you build for tomorrow.

Before turning to the first insight now, take some quiet time and experience the Meditation on the Flame. To benefit from the meditation, read it slowly. Pause between each sentence and experience what you have read. Then spend a moment or two enveloped in the peace that results. Review the Meditation on the Flame after reading each of the following insights. You will find it a helpful experience in understanding and integrating the mystical insights. For the following meditation you may want to light a candle and set it before you, or imagine a candle set before you.

✣ Meditation on the Flame ✣

Pause a moment and sit comfortably in a chair or on the floor. Feel the breath moving in and out of your body and sense your body relaxing as you slowly inhale and exhale. Then keep your eyes open as you gaze at the candle in front of you. Gaze on the flame of the candle. Notice the different colors and their subtle gradations as they sparkle through the flame. Pay careful attention to the gentle movement of the flickering light. Feel yourself becoming one with the candle, one with the flame and its colors, one with the gentle flickering movement. Maintain your focus on the candle in front of you and begin noticing the image and sensation of the candle moving closer and closer to you. At the point where you can feel and see the candle inside of you, blow out the candle in front of you and concentrate on the flame within your body. Hear it flicker in your breath. See it radiate through your body to the base of your spine and down your legs. Then slowly feel it moving back up your legs to the base of your spine, to every part of your body. Watch it move through one body part at a time, until it envelops you with passion and emerges out the top of your head in a fountain of color, light, and energy. Spend a moment or two luxuriating in the energizing flow.

Recognize That You Are Born of God

God said to me, "You are my child,

for today I gave birth to you."

Psalm 2:7

The low is the foundation of the high.

Lao Tzu

You are born of God and you are as important to God as if you were God's only child. You are unique and integral to God's plan. Your being here is vital to the progress of this world. Just as you are born of God and are important to God, so too is every other person. You and every other person are an only child of God. How is it possible for every person created of God to be considered a priority? In God's world we are all number one, because we are all a part of one another. Each one of us is both a unique individual and part of the oneness of humanity. When you start thinking of yourself as separate from me, then you forget that you and I are born of God and are one with all of God's creation.

You are not only born of God and one with all of God's creation, but you are born in God's image. This means that every part of who you are, all parts of your body and all aspects of your personality, are imprints of the Divine image, important to God and vital to the progress of this world. At each moment in your life, in all the roles that you play, you are special and loved. Just knowing that you are born in God's image profoundly affects the way you live. When you remember that your origin is in God, you cannot help but live with deeper conviction in the fact that your life, and all life, is holy. When you acknowledge your special place in God's love and in God's world, you gain greater confidence in yourself. When you recognize that the image of God in you also exists in each and every person in creation, you step out of your inertia and awaken to the awesome wonders and miracles that are unfolding everywhere. When you remember how special you are, you validate your life and accept the fact that you are enough, do enough, and have enough. And with joy and enthusiasm, you live in the pleasure and abundance of God's world.

So often we forget we are born of God and think we are less than we are. And then we think everyone else is wiser, smarter, prettier, and more important than ourselves. I knew a woman who was intelligent, talented, and financially successful and had a seemingly beautiful life, until she forgot who she was and gave away her spirit in order to feed her low self-esteem. She did what so many others do. She relinquished her power and stifled her spirit, all in the guise of rescuing others. When her loved ones came knocking on her door she gave herself away, a little piece at a time. First it was her hypochondriac mother, who needed her attention. When her mother called, this woman would stop what she was doing and give a little piece of her time and energy to her mother. Then it was her demanding husband, who needed her help in his office. Again, this woman would interrupt her focus on her own work and profession and concentrate on her husband's work and profession, all the while giving a little piece of herself to her husband. Then it was her complaining son, who returned home jobless from college. Again, this woman would stop her own routine and rearrange her life in order to give another little piece of herself to her son. Then it was her younger sister, who had divorced and needed assistance. Once again this woman stopped what she was doing and worked even harder in order to give yet another little piece of herself to her sister. This woman thought everyone else was more important than herself. She thought her family's health, happiness, satisfaction, and self-image were more important than her own. Depleted of energy and bereft of her power, this woman collapsed into a depression. She realized that somewhere along the road of helping others she had lost herself. In giving herself away little by little and piece by piece, she forgot who she was. She was not born to be a martyr. Who was she? She was born a child of God and was worthy of living fully in her own light and not in the shadow of others. She forgot that her family was also born of God and they too had the power to live in the fullness of their own light. She forgot to let herself be the child who was worthy of being loved, nurtured, and treated as specially as she treated others, to be loved as much as she loved others, and to be honored as much as she honored others.

You are born of the God who is called "I Am That I Am." Underlying the many roles you play in life is the intimate knowledge that you are the "I am" of the "I Am That I Am" of God's name. Whenever you say the words "I am," you are not only speaking of yourself; you are also speaking of God's image in you. When you say, "I am not smart enough, I am not worthy enough, I am not pretty enough, I am not good enough," you are diminishing God's image that lives in you. God's image is your truest potential, and when you diminish it you are falsifying that part of God that is in you. When you affirm the fullness of who you are and say positive statements using the words "I am," such as "I am intelligent, I am worth it, I am beautiful, I am perfect as I am," then God's image and the sacredness of all of creation are affirmed in you.

You and God are continuously enveloping each other. Some kabbalists feel so enveloped in God that they no longer use the pronoun "I," but say "we" instead. Instead of saying "I am healthy and I am content," they refer to themselves as part of

God and say, "We are healthy and we are content." So often when I pray or meditate I feel I am not doing it alone, but "we" are praying and "we" are meditating. I feel the presence of God doing it with me.

Know and celebrate who you are at every moment and in every situation. Every part of your life is a part of God. You stand on the foundation God placed beneath your feet. Beneath the attitudes, the titles, the responsibilities, the supports, and the challenges of the roles you play in your life is the foundation on which the largest part of your essence touches the largest part of God's essence. When you have faith in the abundance of the godliness in you, you are happier with yourself. When you feel happy and wholesome and holy, it affects every part of your life. You experience increased success at work, greater serenity at home, and more pleasure at play.

Every moment, every hour, each day, you are born in God anew. In the Gate of Creativity, you are continuously being born anew in the metaphoric womb of possibilities and extending your foundation. Imagine yourself inside the metaphoric womb of God's world, incubating in the vast emptiness through which Divine light pours into you. With each inhalation and exhalation feel the empty womb contract and expand. Hear the pulsating rhythm and see God's perfect radiance shining through you. In the radiance the Divine voice whispers gently, "You are the child whom I birthed today." And you see yourself born into a reality that is beautiful beyond your imagination.

Everything is possible when you are born of God. Notice the different roles you play at work, at home, and in your leisure time. Does any of these roles conflict with another? What are the roles that bring you closer to God? Are there aspects of the roles that you play in your life and in your relationship with others that seem hidden from God or ungodly? If so, can you begin to recognize that the conflicts within your relationships and your life are due to distancing yourself from God's image in you? When you forget that you are born of God and that every part of you is pure and God-filled, it is time for you to pause, empty, release, relinquish, and remember you are the "I am" of the "I Am That I Am," and the "we" of the God that is in you.

Practice the Meditation on the Flame (page 264)
at least once today.

Love Yourself

If I am not for myself, then who am I? If I am only for myself, than what am I?

Hillel

Love the world as your own self;

then you can truly care for all things.

Lao Tzu

You are perfect as you are, yet the perfection of who you are is in constant flux. It is not a perfection according to outside standards. It is a perfection that unfolds new adventures and possibilities as you journey through life to the destiny you were born to fulfill. Moving into a new place requires a mothering of your own skills partnered with a belief in a Force deep within and beyond your local self. It requires you to love all parts of yourself unconditionally. Only with an inner loving environment can you nurture yourself to continue growing and birthing new dimensions.

Loving yourself is an ongoing process, not specific to an age or event. It is the reciprocity inherent in all you have ever been along with all you are becoming. Pause a moment now, and recall the turning points in your life. As you recall the turning points, you will notice the pattern they weave in determining your goals and your destiny. As you remember the milestones of your life, the energy of those events surrounds you as though the events were happening now, outside of time, inside you. The more positive the recall, the more loving the sensations.

Loving your Self means loving your limitations. So often people attempt to live in another's shoes, even though they do not fit. One woman who came into wealth commissioned a famous fashion designer to design a magnificent gown for a special occasion. When she put on the gown, at first glance, she looked beautiful. Then, as the evening wore on, the gown became too heavy, too tight, too cumbersome, and too wide to do what she most loved doing, dancing. What good was this designer's gown when it didn't enable the woman to be herself? Too often we all discount discomfort and hide limitations in order to appear as everyone else. But you are not like anyone else. You were born to fulfill a unique destiny as a unique being. Love yourself for your uniqueness. In loving yourself unconditionally, you create an environment of unconditional love in which others can benefit. The more you are comfortable with yourself and your limitations, the more comfortable others are with their limitations and with you.

Loving yourself means being comfortable with yourself and your quirks and idiosyncrasies. It also means being comfortable with other people's quirks and idiosyncrasies. The well-known rabbi of Lublin was so comfortable with himself that he would occasionally take a pinch of snuff during the prayer service. According to a fellow worshiper, this was not proper during prayers. The rabbi explained his actions with the following story. A great ruler was once walking in a street in the capital city and heard a haggard street singer singing a song and playing a harp. The music was so pleasing that the ruler brought the street singer back to the palace, where the street singer played all day, each day. The street singer played on an old beloved harp and would not trade it for another. Yet it often needed to be tuned, even during performances. One day a court official become impatient with the musician and snidely asked why the harp couldn't be tuned ahead of time. The street singer answered with confidence, "In the ruler's court there are many who can play and sing. However, if the ruler picked me and my harp, then it is apparent that its peculiarities and mine are acceptable as well."

Loving your Self means coming face-to-face with your own truth, walking through that truth, and walking through your fears. At times of increased turmoil and confusion, it means allowing yourself to question the very myths and beliefs that sustain you. We've been taught to believe that work has to be difficult. This is not so. What makes work difficult is forgetting that God is your partner. Then your ego attaches itself to the work and you get in your own way of success. When you get yourself and the clinging ego out of your way, then God enters and helps you. Haven't you noticed the times in your life when you push and tug at an idea yet, no matter how you try to succeed, it fails? Or other times, when you know what you are doing is divinely ordained, yet it seems to come with such difficulty and effort? This difficulty arises because your ego is too attached to the work and you need to get your ego out of the way and let God in. You know when the work that you choose to do is divinely ordained and your ego is not attached to it, because it feels so good. Even when you work for hours and return home tired, you feel satisfied and wholesome knowing that you are accomplishing something that is beyond your ego and feels sacred to your soul. You cannot help but feel fulfilled and joyous. The effort becomes effortless and the challenges become creative endeavors. According to Rabbi Nachman of Breslov, the fact that you may think you have to work hard for something diminishes your faith in God and in yourself. Your doubt shows you lack confidence in your partnership with God and in God's decision to choose you as a partner for the task. Even though you may think you have faith in God, your faith is diminished when you do not have faith in yourself. Rabbi Nachman calls this small thinking, and small thinking leads to small living.

Loving yourself means having faith in the fact that you are dear and near to God and that you can overcome any hurdle with confidence, grace, dignity, and compassion. As you walk through your fears, the truth and magnificence of who you are become more and more apparent.

To love yourself is to affirm the beauty and spirit of your body. In birthing yourself, do not forget the joy and pleasure available to you. You too need nurturing, loving care. Nurturing yourself can also mean feeling comfortable in being alone and pleasuring yourself. Sexual pleasure and sensual needs are important to your physical well-being. Combined with *kavannah,* spiritual intention, your senses become vehicles for enlightenment. Rather than deny your senses, cherish and hallow them as parts of God.

Everything that has occurred in your life thus far has laid the foundation for birthing self-love. In loving yourself, you are loving the mirror image of God. In feeling good with yourself, you are identifying with the greatness of who you are. When you are most comfortable with yourself and your aloneness, you are most complete with those around you. In nurturing yourself, you nurture the part of God that is in you. In loving yourself, you give yourself the strength to continue serving God and others.

Practice the Meditation on Flame (page 264)
at least once today.

Cultivate Divine Sexuality

> . . . and God opened her womb.
>
> *Genesis 29:31*

> Only the Way is good at beginning things
>
> and also good at bringing things to completion.
>
> *Lao Tzu*

In the mystical Jewish tradition, we understand and experience
sexuality as a divine act. Sex is the ultimate gift of reciprocity
between the male, female, and God.

This relationship of reciprocity is most commonly understood
in the giving and receiving that occurs during intercourse between couples. However, the scriptures also describe God as an
inhabitor of bodies, a sanctifier of souls, who fertilizes the barren
and parents children. In Isaiah 54:2–5, the prophet consoles
the people in a sensual manner:

> Enlarge the place of your tent,
> stretch out the curtains of your dwelling—
> do not hold back;
> Lengthen your tent ropes,
> fasten your pegs.
> For you will burst forth to the right
> and to the left . . .

Do not fear, for you will not be ashamed . . .
For your spouse is God who made you—
God of hosts is God's Name.

In many Eastern mystical traditions the foundation of spirituality is based on the foundation of sexuality. The lotus flower is the symbol of the yoni (vulva) in India and was considered to be the gate to the goddess's inner mysteries. Through sacred sexual practices, the mystics could achieve the flowering of revelation from the invisible light that emanated from the thousand-petaled lotus spiraling from the base of the pelvis to the top of the head. Like the Goddess of the Lotus, the Hebrew Goddess, Schekhina, is the Infinite Divine made finite. Her name in Hebrew means "dwelling place," and She dwells within the body and soul of each human.

As you open the space for receiving, the God of many images impregnates your body and soul in different ways. The kabbalists call the act of divine impregnation *ibbur.* In *ibbur,* God enters your body through incarnate souls. The kabbalists describe *ibbur* as an opportunity for a spark from heaven, in the form of a spirit of a past soul or saint, to enter the body and the life of a worthy person as an aid or guide. There are incidents when a person can pray for help from the heavenly realms and will be sent a spark of a saint or relative. These previously incarnate souls can enter your body and assist you with a particular task at decisive moments in your life. These divine impregnations can stay for lengthy or short periods, depending upon the tasks they came to help fulfill. You may not be aware of their presence, yet they walk into your body and transform your life. They raise your consciousness to higher levels of awareness and productivity. They can inform you of future events or guide you in the present.

In receiving this insight, you are receiving your own body, honoring your own sexuality, and opening to God as partner, lover, and friend. In the process, you touch a part of humanity that commingles with the benevolent energies of a living God and creates ecstatic, joyous living. As you practice the Medita-

tion on the Flame today, allow it to enter your body and imagine
it as the bursting light of the thousand-petaled lotus of God
impregnating your soul and spiraling sanctity in every part of
your body, from the base of your spine to the top of your head.
As you sanctify your Self, your sexuality, and your spirituality
in this world, you are further sanctified in the worlds above.

Practice the Meditation on the Flame (page 264)
at least once today.

Care for Your Relationships

Love your neighbor as yourself.

Leviticus 19:18

Love the world as your own self;

then you can truly care for all things.

Lao Tzu

The kabbalists say that before we were separated into human forms, we emanated from the same Source. Each of us was part of the Divine soul. This means that when you were one with the Divine soul, you were nurtured in the space beyond space, in a time beyond time. As the world turned and planets were set in space, and your time arrived, God birthed you from the Divine soul into this world. As you emerged from God's soul, you held on to a little piece of God, and this little piece is now your soul. You were born into the world at this time with a specific mission —to refine your little piece of God's soul. A refined soul remembers its energy comes from God. A refined soul radiates light, love, acceptance, and compassion. You refine your soul by nurturing your inner spirit and caring for your relationship with God in your life and honoring the multiplicity of God's images in the lives of others.

The way you refine your soul is reflected in the way you care for your relationships. We all yearn to have real, sincere friendships and to be a part of sensitive and caring relationships. You do not need to be everybody's best friend or have a million superficial acquaintances. You need only a handful of really sincere friends. Real and sincere friendships are easier to find than you think. All you have to do is pause, empty, and see the soul hiding behind the mirror image. Behind the artificial glitter and superficial spark there is a soul waiting to be recognized. When you see the soul in another and hear his or her inner truth, you cannot help but recognize that person's sincerity and feel love.

At times I meet people attending our Sabbath services whose souls are hidden behind pretensions and perceptions that detract from their true nature. They are people who are not comfortable with themselves and are looking for their reflections in others in order to validate their discontent. These people are annoyed when they walk into the sanctuary and find only images of goodness and love. How many times have you been at a low place in your own life and looked love in the face, yet refused to see or accept it? In order to receive love, you need first to open to loving yourself. In order to attract the relationship you want, you need first to reflect that relationship within yourself.

When you are in a loving relationship with the soul, whether yours or another's, there is no confusion with pride or ego. The soul recognizes that within each relationship there is the potential for soul enhancement and for creating benevolent forces of heaven on earth. All the attributes of God are within the soul of each person. As you relate to another, you are also relating to the God in them. As you relate to the attributes of unconditional love, strength, harmony, success, glory, creativity, and nobility, you are reflecting those attributes within yourself. Practice being the mirror today, whether you are at home, at work, or at play, and shine your light gently enough to see within the soul of another and deeply enough to reflect your own. Then recognize the sincerity and feel the love.

There are no rights or wrongs, no static structure for successful relationships, only the dynamic flow of serving God through serving one another. If you want to know God more, get to know yourself and your friend better, and be more revealing about your feelings. If there is any doubt whether something feels wholesome in a relationship, ask yourself: "Does this bring my soul closer to God in myself and another, or further from God?" The story of your soul is the story of your relationship to God, to all parts of your inner self, to those you love, and to those whom you are yet to meet. Mystical Judaism is not a static set of rules and regulations; it is the gift of being in relationship with a community of people, a community of angelic forces, and a universe of God simultaneously.

Practice the Meditation on the Flame (page 264)
at least once today.

Find Your Soul Mate

Everyone will find his or her soul mate, as it is written in
Ezekiel 36:26, "I shall give you a new heart and will place
a new spirit within you."

Zohar

Everyone yearns to find a soul mate. As you nurture a relationship with your own soul, you become more open to attracting a
soul mate. The kabbalists believe that before a soul is born
into this world, it is complete in itself. A complete soul is
androgynous, both male and female. Yet in order to enter this
world, the soul splits in two. The male and female are disen-
gaged from each other, enter the soul of the universe, and are
clothed in their independent bodies to fulfill the tasks for which
they were born. As each person grows in him- or herself and
refines his or her own soul, he or she is more apt to recognize
and attract the other.

What the kabbalists have always understood in the mystery
of relationships and soul mates was articulated in part by the
quantum physicist John Stewart Bell in 1964. According to
Bell's theorem, one atom of a molecule can somehow recognize
an atom to which it was once paired. This recognition does not
diminish over distance, nor is it affected by light, sound, or
gravity, or localized in space or time. Bell's theorem and the
kabbalistic view are both nonlocalized and extend beyond the

boundaries of worlds, times, and places. When you are aware of the spiritual and scientific dynamic of relationships, you know that meeting your soul mate takes profound soul recognition that can traverse lifetimes of inner development. As you practice recognizing God's attributes within yourself, you will more easily notice where you mirror them in another.

I remember hearing a fable in which a queen was testing God and wanted to be convinced that there was a divine plan in which each person would find his or her soul mate. The queen took the most beautiful maiden in her court to a distant island and hid her in the trunk of a tree. She provided the maiden with all the comforts of home except for human contact. The queen felt that if there was a true soul mate for the maiden, he would find her no matter where she was. As nature had it, a ship was caught in a storm and drifted to the island. The only one who survived the storm was a princely lad, who made his way to the trunk of the tree, where he rested his weary head. He felt gentle movement in the trunk of the tree and peeked within. There he saw the maiden of his dreams. As in most fables, this one ended happily ever after. The maiden and the lad fell in love, and upon their return home, the queen hosted a huge wedding. The queen's faith in the power of God and the destiny of souls was restored, and all were joyous.

For each soul there is a destined mate, but sometimes we meet our soul mate and don't recognize who they are. I once saw a movie about a man and a woman who were living in heaven and were deeply in love. The woman was called back to earth before they could consummate their heavenly relationship. The broken-hearted man made a deal with God. He convinced God to bring him back to earth to find his love, and agreed to do it within a limited number of years. The man came back to earth as a newborn and lived a meandering life in a distant town, while his heaven-made love was growing up in the sophisticated city. During the movie you witness their parallel stories and realize that time is slipping by; if the man is to rejoin his soul mate, he needs to accelerate his growth. At one point you see him walking past her on the city street and want to shout at the screen, "Look in front of your nose. She is right there! Don't you remember why you came back into life? To find her!" But of course, it is only a movie. When I saw the movie I could feel tears rolling down my face and I could not rationally figure out why, deep within my soul, this story struck a familiar note. After all, aren't we here to find our soul mate? How fortunate some of us are to do it within this lifetime.

I feel fortunate that I have found my soul mate, yet it did take many years for us to recognize each other. Unlike in the movie, we met first and then through years of relating to each other entered that place of profound and sacred recognition. We could not recognize each other during our formative years, when we were caught in a maze of spiritual immaturity, emotional inadequacies, and physical insecurities. We needed first to empty before we could leave room for God to enter and our souls to awaken. It took years to dismantle our own filters and disengage unhealthy codependencies. Then, with God showing us the way, we could see the awesomeness of our unique imprints on each other's soul.

As you move forward in becoming the person you were meant to be and begin to live in the true nature of your divinity, you will find your soul mate. True soul mates encourage each other to fulfill their unique purpose, both individually and together. They honor each other's spirit and share holy visions and spiritual desires to be one with God.

Some people say they found their soul mate across a crowded room and just knew this was the one. Others say they felt a thunderbolt or electrical charge and knew that person was their soul mate. Sometimes this is so, and sometimes it is not. I know of electrically charged relationships that ended up as volatile battles in divorce courts. I also know of unhappy marriages in which, if only the partners would open to each other's soul and live in the fullness of their being, they might find that their adversary in bed is really their soul mate in heaven. The person with whom you are now or whom you are about to meet may be the reason you were born into this life and may hold the possibility of being your soul mate. Become who you were meant to be and attract the one who has searched a lifetime to find you.

Practice the Meditation on the Flame (page 264)
at least once today.

Become Cozy with God

And you who cleaved to God, your God, each one of you
is alive today.

Deuteronomy 4:4

Truly, great carving is done

without splitting up.

Lao Tzu

The Way's presence in the world

Is like the relationship of small valley

streams to rivers and seas.

Lao Tzu

Standing in the Gate of Creativity, you have the opportunity to touch the Source and be one with the totality of life. Yet the choice is yours. Although the presence of God radiates through the entire universe and all parts of who you are, you have the choice whether to receive it or not. Your desire to receive God's light, touch God's essence, and cleave to all that is holy is the highest goal, greatest challenge, and ultimate reciprocal partnership you can have. Yet you are endowed with independent choice. Although you are born of Divine will, it is your own will that maintains the interface between you and God. God guides you to be mindful and nonattached to thoughts, words, and actions. And God invites you and encourages you to cleave to all that is holy.

This state of being attached to God is called *devekut. Devekut* is the process of merging with the Divine, going beyond yourself and your self-imposed boundaries. *Devekut* means being intimate with God as sunlight is to the sun. It is being comfortable and cozy with God, like honey on bread. I first heard the phrase "cozy with God" from my teacher Rabbi Zalman Schachter-Shalomi, and it felt so good to me that I put it into practice in my own imaging of God.

Devekut is an intimacy in which all thoughts and ideas are transparent between you and God. It is seeing God through the same eyes that God sees you through. It is synchronizing the rhythm of your heart with the Divine heartbeat of the universe. *Devekut* is your body encoded in the body of God, your soul enveloped by God's soul, and your actions manifesting Divine performance.

Devekut happens anywhere at any time. All it requires is desire and will. Nothing is accomplished without the will to do it. When your will is active in *devekut,* things begin to happen. When a farmer wants to hitch a horse to a wagon, it doesn't happen on its own. The farmer first has to have the desire; then he takes the necessary moves toward the goal. In the same way, you would not turn your head to the left or raise your arm above your head until you had the will to do so. Then, with the desire in place, you turn your head or lift your arm.

Devekut needs no words; neither does it need action. You can cleave to God just by affirming it in your consciousness. The deepest doing is the nondoing before doing anything. That happens when you sit in meditation in a state of *devekut* and sense being in the presence of the all-knowing, all-being, all-holy One. *Devekut* and prayer are closely connected. When you pray with pure intention, you are in *devekut.* When you endeavor to live attached to God in every thought, word, and action, you are living a prayerful life. Prayer is not only a form of recitation;

it is a way of being. Both prayer and *devekut* penetrate beyond the spoken word.

Before we were formed, God created a world full of light. The light separated into tiny sparks and eventually moved into all the forms of life. Within you is a spark of God's light that came from the beginning of creation. The problem is that many people do not remember the spark of light that is within them. If the light is not used, in time it dims and becomes imprisoned behind the *klippot,* or filters, of our lives. Live a prayerful, cozy life with God and you will notice how bright your light can shine and affect in a positive way those you love and the world at large.

When you choose to invite God into your life, you cleave to the holiest aspects of yourself and live a divine, miraculous existence. In the place where you are most open and life affirming, recognize that you and God are one. As you practice *devekut* and cleave to the presence of holiness, move beyond self-awareness and self-consciousness to the momentary stillness and vast emptiness where there is nothing but God. In touching the nothing, you embrace the God in you.

Practice the Meditation on the Flame (page 264)
at least once today.

Travel Lightly and Breathe Fully

And God formed the human out of the dust of the earth
and blew into the human's nostrils a soul of life.

Genesis 2:7

If you try to hold it, you will lose it.

Lao Tzu

A good walker leaves no tracks.

Lao Tzu

Shhh. Pause. Become still. In the calm silence of your heart,
hear the breath of the soul in your body and the breath of the
planet in the universe. Feel it continuously contracting and
expanding. According to kabbalistic cosmology, all creation occurs as a result of contraction and expansion. In the contraction
and expansion, new energy is birthed, new paradigms are
formed, and old ways of being are transformed into new realities. The divine breath, the cosmic womb, the birthing process
that takes place in woman, and the inhalation and exhalation
within your own body are all part of the creative process of
traveling lightly and breathing fully.

The musician breathes consciously before she plays an instrument; the writer breathes consciously before he sets his pen to

paper; the actor breathes consciously before he performs; the painter breathes consciously before she puts the first brush stroke on the canvas. In breathing deeply each one taps into aesthetic inspiration from God and translates it onto an instrument, a written page, a performance, or a painting.

So often in balancing the issues of the heart, the matters of the mind, and the sensuality of the body, your breath is shortened and your life enters the heavy drama of turmoil, indecision, and anxiety. This is because you are forgetting that you are part of a much greater story that holds infinite possibilities beyond the filters of limited perception. Imagine the world as a huge playground. Imagine God creating this enormous playful setting, with colorful displays of enticing experiences, adorned with the appropriate paraphernalia, ready to embark on imaginative excursions. When all was completed, God placed you in this magnificent setting, in the hope that you would play with God and bring to life an otherwise inanimate landscape. God is saying to you, "This world is our playground and I want to play with you! Don't just stand there. Come to life!" You were created to walk lightly, play joyfully, and soar abundantly with the Creator of this universe.

Hold dear to your heart the recognition that thoughts are impermanent and patterns of recognition are forever interchanging. Yet with each inhalation and exhalation, remember: the energy with which you travel lightly and breathe fully is an ever-present element in the story of your life. Infinite energy is carried in the organic, dynamic fluid that flows with each breath you take, and in each contraction and expansion, *zimzum* and *hitpashtut,* of the universe. Whether it is the pulsating energy of your ancestors or your descendants; the oscillating energy of intense *devekut,* or nonattached emptiness; or the rhythmic energy of contraction and expansion, the freedom with which you breathe and the ease with which you live is the energy that is passed from you to the next generation. When all else dissipates in time, the energy you place into the world now lives on as part of your eternal legacy.

When determining the rhythm of your life, leave room for

contraction and expansion. What may fit for today may not suit your needs tomorrow. In the melodies of your heart and the paces of your steps, possibilities are unfolding for an even greater score and grander symphony that is at once both too large and expansive and too small and contracted for the road you are about to travel. In this playground of life, it is not possible to travel one road heavily and leave the rest untouched. For one path or one experience cannot fulfill all your needs for growth and expansion.

Consider the times you have walked through your life heavily and the times you have walked lightly. Notice how moments of heaviness shortened your breath and contracted your energy, while moments of gaiety and lightness expanded your breath and extended your energy. As you walk lightly between the contractions and expansions, you begin recognizing new and renewed areas of joy in aspects of yourself and aspects of universal creation. As you breathe fully with each step you take, you and God derive increased pleasure in the interplay that traverses the worlds within worlds within worlds. With each breath you take, God breathes awakened spirits and universal wonders into you.

Practice the Meditation on the Flame (page 264)
at least once today.

NOBILITY

Your Sovereignty is the source of all the worlds;

And Your dominion is through all generations.

Psalm 145:13

Why is the sea king of a hundred streams?

Because it lies below them.

Therefore it is the king of a hundred streams.

Lao Tzu

*E*NTER THE GATE OF Nobility and access the Nobility within yourself. As you walk through Nobility you arrive at a profound reverence for life and a practical application for birthing and rebirthing possibilities for living. In Nobility you are patient and flexible, accepting change and renewal as part of your daily routine. In Nobility you take all that you have received, experienced, and demonstrated in your life until now and lift it to its highest form in order to serve goodness with dignity and grace. In Nobility you stand with faith on the threshold between what you have accomplished and completed and what you are about to begin.

In the Gate of Nobility you will be given insights that will help you validate the uniqueness of your spirit and uncover the majesty of who you are. You will reaccess your royal lineage and actively restore reverence, nobility, dignity, and goodness to the world. You will learn to expand your reality and grow beyond your past to a future that will be simpler yet vaster than you have known before. You will live with greater harmony and integrity in the spiritual and physical realms of your life simultaneously and feel satisfied, complete, and whole. With confidence in your life's purpose, you will seek to integrate your deepest desires and talents in community with others. You will speak honestly and act reliably with others, while continually reevaluating your life and your service to God and humanity. In the kneading, sculpting, and molding of your life, you will culminate the old and begin the new. As you open to the new, you will learn that letting go is liberating, endings are beginnings, and death is not final.

In the Gate of Nobility you are empowered to become independent while recognizing that you are never alone. In the ability to move beyond yourself, you will recognize that you are one with all there is. You are both an individual and a world, one soul and all souls, one heart and all hearts, one mind and all minds.

As you complete this cycle in the journey through the Ten Gates, you recognize that the bridge between one gate and another is built on the enthusiasm of your own spirit and the accomplishment of your intentions.

Before turning to the first insight in the Gate of Nobility, take some quiet time now and experience the Meditation on Perfection. To benefit from the meditation, read it slowly. Pause between each sentence and experience what you have read. Then spend a moment or two enveloped in the peace that results. Review the Meditation on Perfection after reading and contemplating each of the following insights.

◈ Meditation on Perfection ◈

Pause a moment and sit comfortably in a chair or on the floor. Feel the breath moving into your body as you slowly inhale and slowly exhale. Relax a moment in the delicious calmness of your breath. As you feel yourself becoming quiet and centered, open your eyes and look around at the environment in which you are sitting. Notice the forms, shapes, and colors. Accept everything just as it is and acknowledge the perfection of the universe. Now close your eyes and hear the sounds of your environment. Listen to the cadences and rhythms of all the sounds that you hear, and acknowledge their perfection in the universe. Now look within yourself and sense your inner environment. See, hear, and feel all that is awakening in the world within yourself, and acknowledge the perfection of the universe. In the inner chambers of your imagination, examine the elements of which the universe is composed. See them in their varied compounds and numerous compositions. Feel the wisdom that inhabits their forms and shapes their purpose. Hear the spirits that reside in them and effect their transformations of the universe. Recognize the contents of all that there is below you and above you, and honor the perfection that resides in each of the parts and the divinity that resides in the whole.

Uncover the Majesty of Who You Are

You stand before Me today, all *parts* of you.

Deuteronomy 29:9

Be really whole, and all things will come to you.

Lao Tzu

Today and every day, you stand before God, who unconditionally loves, approves, and accepts you for being just who you are. You are holy. The choices for continuing to live in holiness are eternally available to you. When you stand before God open, vulnerable, aware, and conscious of your commitment to journey the path ahead in the uniqueness of who you are, God supports, assists, and guides you.

The path you choose to journey may or may not be the same as the paths chosen by your parents or grandparents. Whether or not you select to emulate the path of your parents, God encourages you to forge your own vision of holiness. With your entrance into this world came a new light, a new way of being. You are an original, unique person who is in this world in this way for the very first time. Your uniqueness is important to the healing and transformation of the environment, to new ways of seeing, hearing, feeling, and being in life. Every person is a new organism called to fulfill a destiny that contributes his or her uniqueness to a far greater story in a vastly larger world than him- or herself.

You do not need to imitate any other person, not even the rich and the famous. God only wants you to be yourself and to have the strength to act in the uniqueness of who you are. Although you can use lessons from the past to guide you, the steps you are now taking are meant to move you into the future. In one popular story Reb Zusya, who was an introspective Hasidic rabbi, saw a vision of his own death, in which his soul ascended to the heavens and was in the inner chambers of God, reviewing his own life on earth. There he heard God ask him the deepest question of all. God did not ask him why he was not a Moses, but rather, "Why were you not Reb Zusya?" In the simplicity of the question, Reb Zusya understood what his life was all about. His life was for living the uniqueness of who he was.

In *The Teaching of Buddha,* there is a parable of a poverty-stricken woman who inherited a chest. Not knowing that the chest contained gold, the woman continued to live in poverty. One day, another woman who was visiting opened the chest and revealed the gold. How often people bemoan their fate yet do not endeavor to utilize the strength within themselves to make their lives better. Looking around you today, you will probably find it easy to recognize several people who remain locked within an impoverished perception of themselves. Are you one of them?

Sometimes it takes a tragedy for you to see the perfection of who you are. Another Buddhist parable tells of a wrestler who used to wear a precious stone on his head. In the midst of a fight, the wrestler's stone was crushed into his forehead. Thinking he had lost the stone, he went to a surgeon to have his wound dressed. When the doctor began dressing his wound, he found the stone embedded in the flesh of his forehead, covered with blood and dirt. He held up the mirror for the wrestler to see that the precious stone was still there, embedded in the flesh and blood of who he was.

You are born of God and this makes you divine royalty. You come from a family of kings and queens, priests and priestesses. The greatest self-bondage is to forget you are of noble birth and majestic lineage. Remember that you have royal genes and royal power. Remember the majesty of who you are and restore your nobility by actively becoming involved in life. Become a noble being and actively raise the fallen, assemble the fragmented, and advance those who are lagging behind. Become Reb Zusya and manifest your own unique qualities without comparing yourself to another. Open the treasure chest of your soul and uncover the majesty of who you are. Reveal the gold that has lain dormant in a life you have yet to live. Become the fighter and use the gems of your mind to further goodness in the world. Journey to the heavens and see your own life review with the confidence that you are living fully in who you are meant to be. In the Gate of Nobility, God encourages you to complete the sacred tasks for which you were born, with gracious generosity, serene majesty, and sacred nobility.

Practice the Meditation on Perfection (page 294)
at least once today.

Expand Your Reality

This world has no existence on its own. It is through the qualities of our perception that we perceive reality.

Rabbi Nachman of Breslov

The heavy is the root of the light;
The still is the master of unrest.

Lao Tzu

Now that you have journeyed the path of the Tree of Life and are in the tenth gate, of Nobility, how would you define reality? Would you define reality according to your inner world, or your outer environment? Would your definition be based on what others have defined as real, or on what is real for you?

You have learned from the insights of the gates you have journeyed that creation begins as something from nothing and that the possibilities of everything are open to you. With wisdom you have experienced how all things occur simultaneously. With understanding you have witnessed and discerned patterns of recognition with experiences. With unconditional love and compassion this reality, based on your experiences and the recognition of common patterns to these experiences, becomes alive, dynamic, and ever growing.

Real experiences build on and are defined by one another. Patterns of recognition assemble themselves into newer patterns.

When the building blocks of reality become too overwhelming and complex, your foundation weakens, and it is time to go still, detach, and redefine a reality that holds within it sacred order and simplicity. When the Maggid of Metzrich's son, who was evolved in the studies of kabbalah, meditated, his angels would take him to the outer realms of pure emanation. One time when he meditated with his contemporary, Rabbi Schneer Zalman, the Maggid's son was so far out that Rabbi Schneer Zalman was afraid the angels wouldn't bring him back. So he ran into the kitchen and brought back bread and stuffed it into the young man's mouth. This action brought the angel and the young man back. The next morning the Maggid thanked him for what he had done for his son and said, "Do you know what I admire most about you? That you are able to meditate on the highest level of energy, and at the same time go find some bread." Living in the reality of one world does not exclude the possibilities for living in the other worlds at the same time.

There are two basic realities in which you live: the physical world of matter and the spiritual world of energy. In the spiritual realm, matter exists as energy. Energy is beyond time itself. This is the reality the Maggid's son was in when he was deeply immersed in prayer. The world in which he found the bread is the world of physical matter. The physical world is measured by time. In a world measured by time, all things are temporary; nothing is permanent. Events are temporary, possessions are temporary, relationships are temporary, even ideas are temporary. However, the energies that go into the event, possession, relationship, or idea are timeless. It's like the energy you can feel standing in a circus tent long after the people and performers have gone, or like the energy you feel when you think of your first prom or your graduation day, years after the fact. It's also the energy you can feel now while imagining a glorious event happening in your future, like a celebration with loved ones, or an adventurous trip to an exotic place, or the launching of a successful project. The energy that you exert now in the thoughts that you are thinking can be accessed in multiple realities, manifested in numerous locations, and utilized throughout all time.

It is possible to expand your reality to include both the timeless and timely. It is possible to be in harmony in both the spiritual and the physical worlds simultaneously. When Rabbi Shlomo Carlebach composed a new melody, his spirit would soar into the ethers of the universe and grasp a melody lingering in the air. Then Rabbi Shlomo would thank the souls of all times for having placed the melody in his reach. He would often say to us, "Where do you think you get the inspiration for pictures to paint, music to sing, and plays to write? From the ethers of those souls who have placed it in the air for you to grasp! All artists reach into the ethers for their inspiration, even Whitney Houston!"

I was once at a conference when I heard a man named Tom Sawyer speak about how an after-death experience expanded his reality. An important part of his message was that in ultimate reality there is no time. He used prayer as an example. Tom said that prayer recited with pure intention goes beyond time, affecting those who have passed on, those who are here today, and those who are yet to be born. I can understand this in my own experience. Sometimes I feel myself praying for people who are long gone, and I know the energy is reaching them as though they were here now. At other times, when I pray for those who are very present in my life now or those who are yet to be born, I can feel the sensation of the energy of the prayer reaching their spirits.

Thoughts are not meant to be permanent, and patterns of living are always changing, yet the energy behind your thoughts is ever present in the larger story of life. The energy you give to the things that you think, say, and do is available for all time and to all people. Can you imagine what your thoughts, words, and actions of goodness and peace today can do for tomorrow? When you expand your reality, your possibilities are limitless. A soul from yesterday could be healed by the thoughts and intentions you place into the universe today. A child of tomorrow might need to grasp what you thought yesterday. Expand your reality in the world now and you expand the possibilities for the universe of tomorrow.

There is no limit to what is real or to the reality you are creating for yourself right now. It is not in the nature of reality to think that a definition that fits you today will remain sized to your needs in the future. In the nature of reality, life holds more possibilities and unfolds an even greater simplicity, for which today's definitions will be at once too large and cumbersome and too small and contracted.

Take a moment and think of the ways you have defined your reality. As you continue to live in both physical reality and spiritual reality, you notice things begin to happen that coincide with your thoughts. For instance, you think of a friend and he or she calls; or you are in a crowded parking lot when you suddenly find a parking space near where you need to be; or you are troubled by a problem and the solution reveals itself effortlessly. As you define your reality from the perspective of energy and matter, you begin hearing and recognizing how your story intertwines with other stories. A whole new definition of reality unfolds. The reality is new only to you, because you have only just begun opening to it. It has always been part of the Divine patterning of your soul waiting to be activated.

Neither God nor mind nor brain nor life is static. You are in the midst of a dynamic, fluid, ever-changing yet eternal relationship with the universe of your experience. This universe is made up of atoms in perpetual motion, moving in and out of emptiness. Independently and with all other forms of life, you are in a continual exchange and regeneration of atoms. Together with all of creation, both physical and spiritual, animate and inanimate, you share a tremendous treasury of experiences.

How free is your spirit? Does your curiosity lead you to new worlds of experience, or do you confine yourself to the narrow filters of life as it hides itself in the *klippah,* or shell of limitations, you impose on yourself? Do you stand in the light and let the Godsparks in you shine, or do you hide in the shadow? Those who stand in their shadows need only to step aside and experience the fullness of their light. In the words of Abraham Joshua Heschel, "To a large degree, the darkness is due to a failure of experience. Our mind is obscured by the eclipse, not the sun." When you dismantle the *klippah*, you open the door to revelation.

Increase your intelligence by opening your mind to new experiences and discoveries. Grow beyond your limitations and do not be afraid to make mistakes along the way. In the same way an artist uses accidental strokes to enhance the painting and a musician uses impromptu echoes to jazz up the sound, use the stumbling blocks of experience for receiving greater intelligence. Be free to stumble and you will learn new things!

Practice the Meditation on Perfection (page 294)
at least once today.

Dream Bigger Dreams

Where there is no vision, the people will perish.

Proverbs 29:18

The Tao is an empty vessel;

it is used, but never filled.

Lao Tzu

Dreams create worlds. Dreams are dynamic, organic, interactive visions of what is possible. God placed you in this world for a purpose. God is dreaming a dream in you that you are dreaming too. The realization of your dream is essential to the well-being and completion of the universe. Living your dreams creates new worlds for others. Living your dreams is your part in the Divine plan.

Tikkun olam, the transformation of the world, begins with you living the dreams that God is dreaming in you. When you deny your dreams, you deny God's dreams and leave a vacancy in the global vision of holiness. The Baal Shem Tov said that every person has a portion in bringing about an age of enlightenment and in constructing a collective Messiah. When you do your part individually, the global reality moves nearer to completion.

It is never too late to dream and act on your dreams. Even when you are in the autumn and winter of your life, look more to the future than to the past. Do not let health, money, or loss of independence keep you from dreaming. These problems are not excuses for you to give up on your dreams. The very fact that you are still here is an indication that a dream of God lives in you. This dream waits to be brought to life.

Each day is filled with dreams. You have dreams when you are awake and dreams when you are asleep. You have dreams that are narrow and self-aggrandizing and dreams that are wide and all-encompassing. The dreams God is dreaming in you are those visions of holiness that are all-inclusive, personal, and universal. God's dream will transform you, and at the same time it will transform the world. In making your dream come true, you connect with the universal dream. It is like a puzzle whose parts are given in dreams to each man and woman. As new experiences and new people come into your life, you will meet those who will enlarge the puzzle and help complete your dreams. Those who dream bigger dreams live larger lives with fuller meaning and find simpler, more joyful ways to complete the puzzle parts together.

Who are the happiest, richest people you know? Aren't they the people who are living out their visions, regardless of the obstacles and challenges? Aren't they the ones who are dreaming even bigger dreams and contributing their talents and resources to the world? These are the people who are living joyful, enthusiastic lives, regardless of their possessions or lack of possessions. These people possess something more precious than material goods. They possess a spark of God that radiates in all they do. These are the people who follow their bliss and take a caravan of followers along the journey. They are not people who watch the clock or measure time and money. These people are willing to lose themselves in the moment, walk across the boundaries of space, and enter the vast emptiness of new beginnings.

Living your dreams is more than a fantasy. It is the reality of the Divine destined to be lived through you.

How do you know when the dream is real and not a distortion of the ego? You know it is real when it is not filtered through your mind and not colliding with discouraging opinions and negative voices of others. It is real when you can see, touch, taste, hear, and smell it in the depths of your soul. It is real when it has less to do with your security and more to do with the healing transformation of the world. It is real when you start living it and other people join in and support you because they too have the vision.

Ask yourself, "What is the dream I am giving the world?" Then realize it! Live it fully! Make it so real that you can no longer avoid living it. Then you will be doing your part in *tikkun olam,* and others will benefit as a result.

Practice the Meditation on Perfection (page 294)
at least once today.

Walk Your Talk

O God, who will dwell in your tabernacle,

who will live in your holy mountain?

One who walks upright,

practices righteousness and

speaks the truth of the heart.

Psalm 15:1—3

In dwelling, be close to the land.

In meditation, go deep in the heart.

In dealing with others, be gentle and kind.

In speech, be true.

In ruling, be just.

In business, be competent.

In action, watch the timing.

No fight: No blame.

Lao Tzu

Now is the time to pause, completely let go, and renew. If you talk about smelling the roses and taking time off, do it now. If you talk about finishing a project or starting a new one, do it now. If you talk to talk, then keep talking; however, if you talk to do, start doing. There is a time when talk ceases to be essential and turns into chatter. That is the time when what you are saying is no longer connected to what you are doing. And everyone knows that the relevance is not in what you say; it is in what you do.

The mystical path within Judaism stresses your need for wholeness. Within you is the whole universe. You are a microcosm of the macrocosm. When aspects of you function separate from the whole, you become fragmented. When you feel fragmented on the inside, there can be no wholeness on the outside. Your inner world reflects itself in your outside experiences. The feeling of wholeness within all parts of yourself invites congruity into your life. Incongruity within invites isolation and loneliness. The loneliness you may feel at times is for those aspects of yourself that are out of integrity, or incongruent with the other parts of who you are. When you are isolated from yourself, an inner sense of isolation slowly creeps into your relationship with others, with the environment, and eventually with the world. As a result, you think, hear, say, and do through the lenses of isolation. And that doesn't make for a joyous living.

The Jewish mystical tradition stresses the need for individual wholeness before communal integration. When Jacob fled the wrath of his brother, Esau, after he stole the firstborn's blessing, he did not go directly to his mother's uncle. He stayed in the wilderness by himself first. When Moses fled the wrath of the courts, after he killed the Egyptian slave master, he did not go directly to friends or family; he too retreated to the desert for introspection. The journey of the spiritual initiate leads you to peaks and valleys, around stumbling blocks and over self-constructed fences. It beckons you to remember your purpose and destiny, regardless of the rocky path or torrential winds.

When you stand on your own solid ground, others can join you and feel safe, secure, and empowered.

Whether you are at work or at play, in the privacy of your home or in the public marketplace, walking your talk is important to the integrity of who you are and the mission you were born to fulfill. When the king of Moab summoned the prophet-diviner Balaam to curse the Israelites, he sent messengers with all manners of enhancements to convince Balaam to fulfill the task. But Balaam had to be true to himself. God had given him a talent in order to serve God and goodness. In considering the mission, Balaam first went into a meditative state and spoke with God about the appropriateness of cursing the Israelites. The message he received from God was not to perform as the king demanded. Standing on the foundation of his words, he said, "Even if the king gave me a house full of silver and gold, I could not go beyond the word of my God." Even when the king accompanied him to the site where the curse was to occur, Balak said to him, "Listen, God is not a man that God should lie. What God says God does. When God tells me to bless, I must bless." In standing his ground and walking with the integrity of his words, Balaam made peace with himself and with the king of Moab. And what started as a demand for a curse ended up as a blessing for the Israelites, Balaam, and Balak.

Along with the worlds you create for yourself, your thoughts, words, and actions affect the community of people with whom you work and live. People relate to you according to the honesty with which you speak and the reliability with which you act. Discipline yourself to say what you mean and to follow through with what you say. The result of walking your talk is the fulfillment of living your destiny and making a contribution to the quality of life in community with others. The steps you take are an important support for your community.

God will guard your feet as you travel the Divine path. Even though your feet are planted in the soil of the earth, your spirit can soar to the heavens. As you walk your talk, you are living

out your destiny, accessing your divinity, and touching heaven
on earth.

Practice the Meditation on Perfection (page 294)
at least once today.

Return, Redeem, and Redefine

In our daily meditations we pray to the Divine who fills
the worlds and fills our hearts and moves us from rung to
rung until we arrive at where we always have been.

Rabbi Zalman Schachter-Shalomi

Returning is the motion of the Tao.

Yielding is the way of the Tao.

The ten thousand things are born of being.

Being is born of not being.

Lao Tzu

According to the teachings of Rabbi Zalman Schachter-Shalomi,
there are five stages to spiritual progress. Each stage is a rung
on the spiraling ladder of life. The first stage is the Rung of
Love. You step onto this rung energized, enthusiastic, and ready
to begin, regardless of difficulties that lie ahead. Your perspective from this rung is serendipitous and full of expectation. You
are only looking up from here. Being on the Rung of Love is
exciting, especially when you are open to giving and receiving
love. This rung is full of unconditional love, joy, and ecstasy.
However, there are those who jump from ladder to ladder in the
different mystical traditions, so that they can remain in the

passion of the first rung. They enjoy the spiritual high without the discipline to move to the next level. To ascend to the next level you need patience, technical mastery, and spiritual practice.

Second is the Rung of Power. This is the inner, sacred power that comes when you serve goodness, not hierarchical power over something or someone. Spiritual skills such as meditation, prayer, body movement, healthful eating, and selfless service to others is part of the Rung of Power. As you master these skills you feel good with yourself, rather than compete with others who are stepping onto the same rung. At this stage there is developed self-discipline and the commitment to pursue the inner light.

Developing the spiritual skills of inner discipline and external practices brings you to the Rung of Beauty. Here you see, feel, and empower beauty in all the realms and depths of your experiences. This is where your soul and the Divine soul are revealed and dance through your creativity as partners, friends, lovers, parents, and guides. The beauty of your relationship with God gently guides you outside yourself onto the fourth rung, where you share with those who are traveling the spiraling ladder alongside you. This is the Rung of Community. All that you have gained you now put into practice through your service to the community and the world. As you integrate with others, you integrate with God. As you redeem the love, power, and beauty in yourself, you redeem it in others. In the simple, pure integration and interchanges between you and others, you are called onto the fifth rung, for a private audience with the Infinite Source. On this Rung of Union, there is no separation between you and God. This rung is dynamic and ever revolving. You reach it for a moment or second in time and then carry that essence of the union as you return to the other rungs on the spiraling ladder of life.

As you continually turn and return from one spiraling rung to the next, you will discover opportunities for redefining and re-creating your life. You may think that you have reached an apex, yet in the perspective of the spiral, the apex is always turning in on itself. Our real spiritual journey is to turn and return to our Divine nature within.

It is not easy to return, redeem, redefine, and re-create your image of God and life when you are attached to the past. It is easier to regress to old habits, even though they may not work for you. You may be overstressed at work and stop meditating. You may be overwhelmed with personal issues and halt your inner development. You may be tired of being self-responsible and want to climb back into the womb of a mother or the protective embrace of a father. Realize that regression can be a temporary escape from your true destiny. Remember that it is not possible ever to return to what was, for everything is in constant flux, waiting to be redeemed, redefined, and re-created.

A dear friend of mine recently returned from a visit to her family in Europe. She is the mother of a toddler, a college student, and a part-time secretary. Before she left on vacation she kept her spirit up in anticipation of her pilgrimage home. She wanted to return to her childhood environment and be nurtured as she was years ago. She was going home to seek refuge in the sheltering, pampering arms of her parents and grandparents. She felt that if she could just return home, all would be fine. To her dismay, what she found upon her arrival in Europe was that just as she had changed over the years, so too had her family. They were no longer the pampering parents or nurturing grandparents she had remembered. They had redefined their own lives and were no longer the same. What she realized was that the fantasy of what *home* meant to her was no longer in the European village of her childhood. Home is where she is right now. As a result of her pilgrimage home, she is now in the process of returning, redeeming, and redefining her own reality, potential, and possibilities, both physically and spiritually.

As things change, your intentions change and you energize your life with new possibilities for growth. God gives you the energy and insights necessary to propel you upward and onward. God empowers you to work within your own ever-changing image of God and to develop a relationship that you can return to with love, power, and beauty both individually and in community with kindred spirits. You do this by returning, redeeming, redefining, and re-creating your own image of God, and in the process you profoundly recognize and rebirth yourself.

Practice the Meditation on Perfection (page 294)
at least once today.

Welcome New Beginnings

This world is but a hallway to the world to come.

Pirke Avot 4:4

The beginning of the universe

Is the mother of all things.

Knowing the mother, one also knows the sons.

Knowing the sons, yet remaining in touch with the

mother,

Brings freedom from the fear of death.

Lao Tzu

This is called having deep roots and a firm foundation,

The Tao of long life and eternal vision.

Lao Tzu

This world is but a hallway to the world to come. The kabbalists believe that when a person dies, the life force within that person is not completely extinguished. A trace of life force remains, so that he or she can arise in the world to come. The kabbalists, as well as holy men and women of ancient times, were able to facilitate the process of transmigration of souls from one world to the next. Numbers 17:12–13 describes Aaron as lighting the incense and making at-one-ment for the people as he stood between the dead and the living. Sages throughout the ages taught that "lying in the grave" is an idiom for returning the seed of humanness to the womb of re-creation. As one dies, he or she rests in the womb of the mother, earth, who herself rests in the womb of God. The light from the Infinite Source rekindles and renews the soul's ascent and descent as it leaves and reenters the worlds and completes its life purpose.

The kabbalists call this process of transmigration *gilgul,* meaning "wheel." *Gilgul* is the revolutionary wheel of life. Your soul accesses new potential every moment, and new life with each turn of the wheel. Your soul is a sparkling gem on the wheel of the chariot of angels. The wheel takes your soul through lifetimes of experiences. What your soul is experiencing in your body right now, in this world, is only one stop on the wheel. As you fulfill your destiny here, you die to this world, return to the wheel, and reincarnate at the next available turn. Your soul's incarnations continue until you have completed the soul's life purpose here on earth. That time is called the end of days, for you will be beyond time, in the perfection of existence.

Think of the possibilities for your soul's purpose in this lifetime. Notice if there are things that you do or say during the course of this day, such as a meeting with a friend or new acquaintance, that kindles an inner spark of profound satisfaction that seems to bring you closer to your life's purpose. When something feels so perfect, it is meant to be. As you meditate on perfection today, imagine the life purpose of your soul. Imagine the place where your soul came from. Acknowledge the stop it has made on the wheel of life in order to live through you now. Notice how perfect it is that you now have the opportunity to fulfill your soul's mission in this life through conscious living and serving goodness. Become aware of the possibilities for your soul that are inherent in your relationships. The people with whom you travel this lifetime are souls that are attracted to your soul because together there are tasks to perform and missions to accomplish. Another's soul has come into this life to unite with yours, and together you and your acquaintances complete the souls' journey to the next rotation of the wheel of life. Walk in the confidence that you are now fulfilling a soul's purpose in life and effecting a world of difference in a universe of infinite possibilities.

Practice the Meditation on Perfection (page 294)
at least once today.

Know That All Is One

Listen, Israel *(God wrestler)*, God Our God *(God in us)*,
Our God is One *(is at one with God in the universe)*.

Deuteronomy 6:4

The totality of all things goes through one opening; the
roots of all affairs come from one gate.

Huainanzi

All of existence is one life. You were born with a unique goal to
fulfill, which affects humanity and its future. The success of
your mission depends upon your connection to the earth and all
the forms of creation on this planet. Your success depends on
your recognition of the divinity that dwells within all of existence and its integration within you. You are never alone, or
isolated in any task you perform.

You are both an individual and a world. You are never just an
ordinary self, and your life is not just an ordinary life. You are
all souls and all lives. You have the ability to affect an entire
universe by affecting one soul.

You are a soul reincarnating in the hearts of people that
evokes memories and connections. You know when you have
made a soul connection with another person, an object, or a
symbol whose essence touches your soul. You may be standing
in the middle of a new neighborhood and a fragrance coming

from one of the homes evokes a memory of loving, nurturing moments of your past. Or you may be in a crowded arena and the slight expression on a strange face moves you to think of a loved one. Or you may be sitting at a symphony and the chord on the violin strikes a new image in your mind or a new source of accomplishing a difficult task, which you had previously not known. And then there are the chance encounters and the interrelationships of your own family or workforce that bring you to new levels of accomplishment and celebration. These things may not be evident to anyone other than yourself. Yet they profoundly affect the way you think and what you do next.

Focus your awareness today on being at one with all there is. Whether you are engaged in thoughts, words, or actions with yourself or others, recognize that there is no separation. You are the thought, you are the words, you are the actions, and you are all souls. You are one with all that is. Witness the miracles that occur when you rejoin humanity and are no longer separate from anything, anyone, anywhere, at any time.

*Practice the Meditation on Perfection (page 294)
at least once today.*

LivingWaters

I know that this journey through the Ten Gates of the Tree of Life is powerful and life changing. I learned that to keep it to myself and remain in solitude was not the true path of the Tree. To have life is to give life. My intention has been to share this journey with you so that you can share it with others and together we can create a world in which God is accessible and miracles are abundant.

I know it is possible to develop a community and a work environment in which people are in continual spiritual practice with one another. My community is my temple. It is called Temple Adath Or because that means an "assembly of light." Temple Adath Or is a community without walls. Light can neither be confined nor contained within walls. The acronym for Temple Adath Or is TAO, which is the Taoist word for "the way." Tao is the way of oneness. We are a community of people who believe in the oneness and sacredness of all of existence, and we endeavor to live our lives in continuous practice of mystical, spiritual principals based on Torah knowledge and kabbalistic teachings.

Our spiritual lifestyle at Temple Adath Or is evident in the way we work. On any given day you can walk into our office overloaded with work, yet feel an overwhelming sense of pure intention and spiritual focus. When the stress level accelerates to where we are thinking faster than we are breathing, we stop. We pause, let go, and restart on empty. If you were to join in our prayer services you would find a joyous interplay between body movement, silent meditation, ecstatic music and singing, and profound hands-on healing. During the social period following the services many people have remarked on the love and generosity of spirit in our community. We are a family of souls of all ages, economic backgrounds, and religious inclinations who are putting into conscious practice the journey through the Ten Gates of the Tree.

I see my role at Temple Adath Or, along with my husband, as a rabbi, who empowers rather than leads. I empower others to be their own teachers and leaders. And in turn they empower their friends, families, and coworkers. Together we create a community of powerful spirits. There is something beautiful that emerges when you empower others. There is a feeling of security rather than competition; a feeling of love rather than fear; a feeling of growth rather than stagnation; a feeling of being empowered yourself by empowering others.

Sometimes you can empower another through words and language of the heart. Sometimes you can empower another person by showing them the way. Sometimes you can empower another by encouraging them just to *be*. And sometimes you need to create an environment in which all aspects of empowerment come into play and create the foundation for a spiritually miraculous way of living.

I dreamed of a spiritually empowering environment in which every vista, sound, and sensation would capture the imagination, open the heart, and satisfy the soul. I dreamed of a place where you would feel at home, safe, and nurtured in the elegant simplicity of nature; a place where the sights and sounds would echo ancient memories and evoke deepest yearnings within your spirit; a sanctuary for relaxing your mind, stimulating your body, and liberating your soul. This dream is now a reality, and we call it LivingWaters.

LivingWaters is an outgrowth project from our temple community. LivingWaters is a spiritual health spa experience based on ancient kabbalistic teachings and open to people of all faiths and backgrounds. It is staffed by a team of people with a common vision of creating an extraordinary environment for experiencing and empowering spirituality. At LivingWaters people have breakthroughs in their spirits that profoundly transform the way they react to their world. They feel more at peace within themselves, more positive in their relationships, and more confident in their life purpose.

This spiritually healthy environment helps accelerate your growth and encourages you to continue the journey on your own. People who have attended LivingWaters have been inspired to return home to their towns and cities and empower their spiritual growth through empowering others. They are creating rituals with their friends that support an aesthetically beautiful, spirited, conscious way of living. What they have found in the process of sharing this journey is a community of kindred spirits, each one supporting the practice of the other and extending the feeling of family.

I believe that God created each one of us to be who we are and to continue to unfold the magnificence of who we are becoming. As we share our spiritual journey with others, we create new experiences for ourselves and a support system for one another. As we extend our world we extend our image of God and our possibilities for touching the infinite and manifesting miracles. May the journey we have shared in this book become so vital to your life that it spills over into the universe of your experiences and creates new ways for you to be within yourself and in community with others.

We welcome your remarks and inquiries. Let us continue to share our stories and journey of miraculous living.

If you would like to share your experiences while journeying through the Ten Gates of the Tree of Life, please write to me at

LivingWaters

11450 Southwest 16th Street

Davie, Florida 33325

For more information about LivingWaters you may write to the above address or call

(954) 476-7466 or fax (954) 472-6553

Notes

Introduction

page number

21 *One of the first miracles:* Rabbi Zalman Schachter-Shalomi, "Some Gurus Not Inimical to Judaism," in *Zen and Hasidism,* ed. Harold Heifetz (Wheaton, Ill.: Quest Books, Theosophical Publishing House, 1978), 135.

Intention

31 *The Tao that can be told:* Lao Tzu, *Tao Te Ching,* trans. Gia-fu Feng and Jane English (New York: Vintage Books, 1972), 1.

35 *Great fullness:* Ibid., 45.

38 *No one has seen God:* Quoted in Larry Dossey, M.D., *Recovering the Soul* (New York: Bantam Books, 1989), 216.

40 *My God, the soul:* Berachot 60b.

40 *The form of the formless:* Tao Te Ching, 14.

40 *The purpose of your soul:* Zohar 2:94b.

41 *God and the soul:* Zohar 1:46a.

43 *The highest notes:* Tao Te Ching, 41.

44 *As he dismantled:* Aryeh Kaplan, *Innerspace* (New York: Maznaim Publishing Corp., 1990), 140–83.

48 *In seeking Wisdom:* Quoted in Z'ev ben Shimon Halevi, *Kabbalah Tradition of Hidden Knowledge* (New York: Thames & Hudson Inc., 1980), 23.

48 *To talk little:* Tao Te Ching, 23.

49 *As soon as he was cast:* Zohar 1:121a.

page number

52   *You are holy:* Leviticus 19:2.

52   *Thus the sage knows: Tao Te Ching,* 47.

52   *Rabbi Abraham Joshua Heschel:* Abraham Joshua Heschel, *God in Search of Man* (Northvale, New Jersey: Jason Aronson, 1955), 358.

55   *Keep watch over them:* Quoted in *The Book of Leadership and Strategy,* trans. Thomas Cleary (Boston: Shambhala, 1992), 83.

56   *And with your final breath:* For an understanding of the role the Goddess plays in mystical Judaism, see Raphael Patai, *The Hebrew Goddess* (Detroit, Michigan: Wayne State University Press, 1990). [When I use the word Goddess, I am referring to the female aspect of God, God and Goddess are interdependent aspects of the Holy One.]

Wisdom

59   *Look, it cannot be seen:* Lao Tzu, *Tao Te Ching,* trans. Gia-fu Feng and Jane English (New York: Vintage Books, 1972), 14.

63   *. . . it is not the intention:* Quoted in Louis Jacobs, *Jewish Mystical Testimonies* (New York: Schocken Books, 1977), 65–66.

63   *Empty and be full: Tao Te Ching,* 22.

64   *With practice, the journey:* Jacobs, *Jewish Mystical Testimonies,* 65.

67   *When a thought passes:* Quoted in Louis I. Newman, *The Hasidic Anthology* (New York: Bloch Publishing Co., 1944), 255; translation of Esser Orot.

67   *A man's or woman's mind: The Teaching of Buddha* (Tokyo: Bukkyo Dendo Kyokai, 1966), 22.

68   *This is the path of wisdom:* See Aryeh Kaplan, *Gems of Rabbi Nachman* (Jerusalem: Yeshiva Chasidei Breslov, 1980), 50–52.

68   *"Are not My thoughts":* Quoted in Newman, *The Hasidic Anthology,* 255. See Isaiah 55:8, "For my thoughts are not your thoughts and my ways are not your ways."

69   *Thoughts exist in the mind:* Aryeh Kaplan, *Gems of Rabbi Nachman,* 54.

page number

69 *If you perceive space:* Quoted in Chögyam Trungpa, *The Myth of Freedom* (Boston: Shambhala, 1988), 159; "translation of Tilopa's instruction on Mahamudra meditation to his disciple Naropa."

69 *But I am quite sure:* Quoted in Martin Buber, *Tales of the Hasidim, Early Masters* (New York: Schocken Books, 1947), 174.

72 *If the Torah had not been given:* Eruvin 100b.

72 *The ten thousand things:* Tao Te Ching, 42.

73 *You once asked me:* Reproduced with permission of the author, Richard Siegel (1969).

75 *Having striven for mind's nourishment:* Chögyam Trungpa, "Enthronement," in *The Myth of Freedom*, xi.

76 *When "your lips open":* Proverbs 8:6–9.

77 *At the highest level of holiness:* Adin Steinsalz, *Thirteen-Petalled Rose,* trans. Yehuda Hanegbi (New York: Basic Books, 1980), 82.

77 *Let the movements of the body:* Quoted in Trungpa, *The Myth of Freedom*, 160.

78 *He felt as though his I:* See Aryeh Kaplan, *Innerspace* (New York: Maznaim Publishing Corp., 1990), 143.

79 *There he was guided:* Ibid., 144–45.

80 *The Way floats and drifts:* Lao Tzu, *Te-Tao Ching*, trans. Robert G. Hendricks (New York: Ballantine Books, 1989), 86.

Understanding

85 *To walk safely through the maze:* The Teaching of Buddha (Tokyo: Bukkyo Dendo Kyokai, 1966), 238.

87 *Knowledge is the fruit:* See Aryeh Kaplan, *Innerspace* (New York: Maznaim Publishing Corp., 1990), 59.

88 *As you carry the wisdom:* Ibid., 201.

90 *All heavenly lights may appear:* Zohar 2:176a.

90 *Ever desireless:* Lao Tzu, *Tao Te Ching*, trans. Gia-fu Feng and Jane English (New York: Vintage Books, 1972), 1.

94 *If you are without desire:* Quoted in Chögyam Trungpa, *The Myth of Freedom* (Boston: Shambhala, 1988), 162.

page number

97   Q *Who is the Creator?:* Rabbi Bachya ben Joseph ibn Paquda, *Duties of the Heart,* vol. I, trans. Moses Hyamson (Jerusalem: Feldheim Publishers, 1962), 112.

98   *I do not know its name: Tao Te Ching,* 25.

99   *"It is not in heaven":* Deuteronomy 30:11–14.

100 *Knowing others is wisdom: Tao Te Ching,* 33.

103 *. . . and What if isn't a What:* Rabbi Nachman of Breslov, Sippurai Maasiot 13, trans. Rabbi Zalman Schachter-Shalomi.

106 *As one grinds the incense:* Keritot 6b.

106 *Therefore, all things: The Teaching of Buddha,* 100.

109 *Therefore the sage: Tao Te Ching,* 2.

Compassion

113 *Thus, the mind has compassion: The Teaching of Buddha* (Tokyo: Bukkyo Dendo Kyokai, 1966), 416.

117 *When a person is filled:* Meor Eynayim, V'Etchanan, 188.

117 *The sage accumulates nothing:* Lao Tzu, *Te-Tao Ching,* trans. Robert G. Hendricks (New York: Ballantine Books, 1989), 158.

117 *I am good to people:* Lao Tzu, *Tao Te Ching,* trans. Gia-fu Feng and Jane English (New York: Vintage Books, 1972), 49.

118 *Even Job declared:* Job 36:5.

119 *He wrote of himself:* Quoted in Samuel H. Dresner, *Levi Yitzhak of Berditchev* (New York: Hartmore House, 1974), 47–49.

121 *Show me what this:* Martin Buber, *Tales of the Hasidim, Early Masters* (New York: Schocken Books, 1947), 212–13.

121 *. . . return to the simplicity: Tao Te Ching,* 37.

122 *In nonattachment:* See Chögyam Trungpa, *The Myth of Freedom* (Boston: Shambhala, 1988), 7–12.

123 *Making peace with suffering:* See Rabbi David Wolfe-Blank, *The Meta-Siddur* (workbook published by author, 1990), 107.

124 *The Maggid took one good look at him:* Quoted in Buber, *Tales, Early Masters,* 291.

126 *A righteous person:* Noam Elimelech, VaYetze, 65.

126 *. . . do not treat lightly: The Teaching of Buddha,* 414.

page number

127   *What appeared to some:* See Zalman Schachter-Shalomi, *The Dream Assembly* (New York, Amity House, 1988), 109–12.

128   *Faith gives them the wisdom: The Teaching of Buddha,* 356.

131   *The essence of* selfless *service:* Rabbi Bachya ben Joseph ibn Paquda, *Duties of the Heart,* vol. II, trans. Moses Hyamson (Jerusalem: Feldheim Publishers, 1962), 10.

131   *The sage stays behind:* Tao Te Ching, 7.

135   *Rabbi Isaac explains:* Ein Yaakov, Shabbat 1:73.

135   *If a human looks: The Teaching of Buddha,* 414.

139   *The world is always burning:* Ibid., 370.

Strength

143   *When you serve God:* Tzava't ha-Rivash 137.

143   *Now, it's because:* Lao Tzu, *Te-Tao Ching,* trans. Robert G. Hendricks (New York: Ballantine Books, 1989), 160.

148   *It is written that every individual:* Quoted in Aryeh Kaplan, *The Light Beyond* (New York: Moznaim Publishing Corp., 1981), 241–42; translating Sichot HaRan 235.

148   *The one who is attached:* Lao Tzu, *Tao Te Ching,* trans. Gia-fu Feng and Jane English (New York: Vintage Books, 1972), 44.

149   *The opposite of patchwork:* Martin Buber, *The Way of Man* (Wallingford, Pennsylvania: Pendle Hill, 1959, 17–18.

150   *In determining your own guidelines:* Quoted in Edward Hoffman, *The Way of Splendor* (Boulder: Shambhala, 1981), 20–21.

151   *Better stop short: Tao Te Ching,* 9.

153   *The benefits derived:* Zalman Schachter-Shalomi, *The Dream Assembly* (New York: Amity House, 1988), 80–82.

154   *What is valued:* Quoted in *The Book of Leadership and Strategy,* trans. Thomas Cleary (Boston: Shamhala, 1992), 65.

159   *God said: Let one who:* Midrash Tanchuma B, Tzav 6.

159   *If they could rid themselves: The Teaching of Buddha* (Tokyo: Bukkyo Dendo Kyokai, 1966), 414.

159   *The qualities of the animals:* Bahir 109, 123.

160   *The morning he asked his son:* Bereshit Rabbah 55:7.

page number

160   *As soon as Abraham's knife:* Genesis 22:12.

162   *Mastering others requires force:* Tao Te Ching, 33.

165   *I heard from my master:* Quoted in Aryeh Kaplan, *The Light Beyond,* 183; translation of Ben Porath Yosef 45c.

165   *Because the sage always confronts difficulties:* Tao Te Ching, 63.

168   *The Way gives birth to them:* Te-Tao Ching, 20.

Harmony

171   *Welcoming a person:* Zohar 2:23b and Judges 6:24.

171   *Therefore the Sage says:* Lao Tzu, *Tao Te Ching,* trans. Gia-fu Feng and Jane English (New York: Vintage Books, 1972), 57.

176   *The Noble Path: The Teaching of Buddha* (Tokyo: Bukkyo Dendo Kyokai, 1966), 112.

176   *In the wholeness of who you are:* Etz Chayim 39:1.

178   *God created this world:* Zohar 3:20a.

178   *Primal Virtue is deep and far:* Tao Te Ching, 65.

179   *From the Talmud:* See Aryeh Kaplan, *Sefer Yetzirah* (Maine: Samuel Weiser, 1990), 169; see also Hagigah 14a and Moreh Nevuchim 2:6.

179   *All things, even a blade of grass:* Bereshit Rabbah 10:6.

180   *In reality what he fears:* See Louis I. Newman, *The Hasidic Anthology* (New York: Bloch Publishing Co., 1944), 150.

180   *As the prophet Hosea:* Hosea 14:2.

181   *Rather, taste the way: The Teaching of Buddha,* 414.

181   *Then may you know yourself:* Psalm 120:7.

182   *With an open mind:* Tao Te Ching, 16.

184   *She had received prophesies:* Megillah 14a.

188   *Oh my mind!: The Teaching of Buddha,* 304.

190   *Confusion is the midpoint:* See Zalman Schachter-Shalomi, *Gate to the Heart: An Evolving Process* (Philadelphia: Aleph, 1993), 6–8.

192   *In insulting another:* Kiddushin 70a.

192   *If our minds are filled: The Teaching of Buddha,* 246.

194   *Yet when you look:* Nathan Ausubel, ed., *A Treasury of Jewish Folklore* (New York: Crown Publishers, 1948), 60.

page number

194   *So the spirit:* Martin Buber, *Tales of the Hasidim, Early Masters* (New York: Schocken Books, 1947), 271–72.

195   *Everything that would ever be:* Noam Elimelech, VaYechi, 92.

195   *If one is sick of sickness: Tao Te Ching,* 71.

196   *Once again, he stretched himself:* 2 Kings 4:8–37.

197   *Rabbi Nachman stressed:* Aryeh Kaplan, *Gems of Rabbi Nachman* (Jerusalem: Yeshiva Chasidei Breslov, 1980), 89–93.

197   *Love is both an aid:* See Dr. Larry Dossey, *Healing Words* (San Francisco: HarperCollins, 1993).

199   *Whoever prays for others:* Berachot 10b.

199   *This is called the virtue:* Lao Tzu, *Te-Tao Ching,* trans. Robert G. Hendricks (New York: Ballantine Books, 1989), 39.

Success

205   *Success is an attribute:* Quoted in Rabbi Aryeh Kaplan, *A Call to the Infinite* (New York: Moznaim Publishing, 1986), 23; translation of Sefer ha-Ikkarim 4:18.

205   *The Tao of heaven:* Lao Tzu, *Tao Te Ching,* trans. Gia-fu Feng and Jane English (New York: Vintage Books, 1972), 79.

210   *When you want:* Toledath Yaakov Yosef, Kedoshim, 332 (2).

210   *See simplicity in the complicated: Tao Te Ching,* 63.

212   *Rabbi Nachman of Breslov:* Quoted in Zalman Schachter-Shalomi, *Fragments of a Future Scroll* (Philadelphia, Pennsylvania: B'nai Or Press, 1982), 92–93.

214   The human person *models:* Lao Tzu, *Te-Tao Ching,* trans. Robert G. Hendricks (New York: Ballantine Books, 1989), 77.

217   *Do not say:* Sefer Rabbi Israel Baal Shem Tov 162, quoted in *The Baal Shem Tov on Pirke Avot,* trans. Charles Wengrov (Jerusalem: Feldheim, 1974) 50.

217   *A person seeks a path: The Teaching of Buddha* (Tokyo: Bukkyo Dendo Kyokai, 1966), 300.

218   *Their father had died:* Numbers 27:2–7.

220   *Therefore, one who devotes: Te-Tao Ching,* 234.

222   *The envelopments hover:* Likutai MaHaran 21:4–5.

page number

224   *Who is strong?:* Pirke Avot 4:1.

224   *In caring for others and serving heaven:* Tao Te Ching, 59.

227   *In meditation on Torah:* Quoted in Schachter-Shalomi, *Fragments,*
        92.

227   *Empty yourself of everything:* Tao Te Ching, 16.

230   *The great Tao flows eveywhere . . . :* Tao Te Ching, 34.

232   *Even though he already knew:* See Howard Schwartz, *The Captive
        Soul of the Messiah* (New York: Schocken Books, 1983), 93–95.

Glory

239   *Therefore the Sage:* Lao Tzu, *Te-Tao Ching,* trans. Robert G. Hen-
        dricks (New York: Ballantine Books, 1989), 59.

240   *He wasn't sure:* Genesis 32:23–31.

243   *God created the world:* Genesis Rabbah 3:9.

245   *The rabbi said, "You are not yet ready":* See Shlomo Carlebach
        with Susan Yael Mesinai, *Shlomo's Stories* (Northvale, New Jersey:
        Jason Aronson, 1994), 233–34.

246   *Know the strength of man:* Lao Tzu, *Tao Te Ching,* trans. Gia-fu
        Feng and Jane English (New York: Vintage Books, 1972), 28.

249   *The essence of sacred service:* D'rash Tov 42, 46.

249   *Attachment to an ego-personality:* *The Teaching of Buddha* (Tokyo:
        Bukkyo Dendo Kyokai, 1966), 152.

251   *Only then will you be ready:* M'irat Eynayim, Ekev 27.

252   *Stand before it:* Tao Te Ching, 14.

253   *The psalmist proclaims:* Psalm 100:2.

253   *Those who trust in God:* Psalm 5:12.

255   *There is something:* Martin Buber, *The Way of Man* (Wallingford,
        Pennsylvania: Pendle Hill, 1959), 16.

255   *A tree as great as a man's embrace:* Tao Te Ching, 64.

258   *When I weld my spirit:* Quoted in Martin Buber, *Tales of the
        Hasidim, Early Masters* (New York: Schocken Books, 1947), 51.

258   *Whatever words we utter:* *The Teaching of Buddha,* 246.

258   *The rebuker:* See Samuel H. Dresner, *Levi Yitzhak of Berditchev*
        (New York: Hartmore House, 1974), 50.

page number

258   *As for essential talk:* Quoted in Buber, *Tales, Early Masters*, 122.

260   *Therefore their teachings:* Ibid., 73.

Creativity

261   *The Tao of heaven:* Lao Tzu, *Tao Te Ching,* trans. Gia-fu Feng and
       Jane English (New York: Vintage Books, 1972), 77.

265   *The low is the foundation:* Ibid., 39.

267   *You are born of the God:* Exodus 3:14.

270   *If I am not for myself:* Pirke Avot 1:14.

270   *Love the world:* Tao Te Ching, 13.

272   *However, if the ruler:* See Martin Buber, *Tales of the Hasidim, Early
       Masters* (New York: Schocken Books, 1947), 317–18.

272   *Rabbi Nachman calls this:* See Aryeh Kaplan, *Gems of Rabbi Nach-
       man* (Jerusalem: Yeshiva Chasidei Breslov, 1980), 86–87.

274   *Only the Way is good:* Lao Tzu, *Te-Tao Ching,* trans. Robert G.
       Hendricks (New York: Ballantine Books, 1989), 9.

275   *Through sacred sexual practices:* Barbara Walker, *The Women's Ency-
       clopedia of Myths and Secrets* (New York: Harper and Row, 1983),
       550.

277   *Love the world:* Tao Te Ching, 13.

280   *Everyone will find:* Zohar 1:28a.

280   *This recognition:* Joan and Miroslav Borysenko, *The Power of the
       Mind to Heal* (Carson, Calif.: Hay House, 1994), 47.

284   *Truly, great carving is done:* Te-Tao Ching, 80.

284   *The Way's presence in the world:* Ibid., 84.

287   *If you try to hold it:* Tao Te Ching, 29.

287   *A good walker:* Ibid., 27.

Nobility

291   *Why is the sea king:* Lao Tzu, *Tao Te Ching,* trans. Gia-fu Feng
       and Jane English (New York: Vintage Books, 1972), 66.

page number

296 *Be really whole:* Ibid., 22.

299 *This world has no existence:* Likkutei Maharan 219.

299 *The heavy is the root:* Tao Te Ching, 26.

303 *In the words of:* Abraham Joshua Heschel, *A Passion for Truth* (New York: Farrar, Straus, and Giroux, 1973), 19.

304 *The Tao is an empty vessel:* Tao Te Ching, 4.

307 *In dwelling, be close to the land:* Ibid., 8.

309 *Standing on the foundation:* Numbers 22:18.

309 *God will guard your feet:* See 1 Samuel 2:9.

311 *In our daily meditations:* Zalman M. Schachter-Shalomi, *Gate to the Heart: An Evolving Process* (Philadelphia: Aleph, 1993), 8.

311 *Returning is the motion of the Tao:* Tao Te Ching, 40.

312 *You reach it:* Schachter-Shalomi, *Gate to the Heart,* 6–8.

315 *The beginning of the universe:* Tao Te Ching, 59.

315 *This is called having deep roots:* Ibid., 52.

315 *A trace of life force remains:* Bereshit Rabbah 28:3.

316 *Sages throughout the ages:* See Allen Afterman, *Kabbalah and Consciousness* (New York: Sheep Meadow Press, 1992), 36.

316 *That time is called:* Ibid., 35.

318 *Listen, Israel:* The insertions into my translation of the Hebrew words were inspired by my teacher Rabbi Zalman Schachter-Shalomi.

318 *The totality of all things:* Quoted in *The Book of Leadership and Strategy,* trans. Thomas Cleary (Boston: Shambhala, 1992), 82.